ITALY
THE BEAUTIFUL COOKBOOK

AUTHENTIC RECIPES FROM THE REGIONS OF ITALY

STUFFED PIGEONS: (left, recipe page 169), BREAD SALAD WITH TOMATO (top right, recipe page 111) AND TUSCAN RICE (bottom right, recipe page 86).
PHOTOGRAPHED AT BADIA A COLTIBUONO, THE AUTHOR'S RESIDENCE

AUTHENTIC RECIPES FROM THE REGIONS OF ITALY

ITALY
THE BEAUTIFUL
COOKBOOK

RECIPES BY
LORENZA DE' MEDICI

TEXT BY
PATRIZIA PASSIGLI

COLLINS PUBLISHERS

Published in the USA by Collins San Francisco,
1160 Battery Street, San Francisco, CA 94111

Produced by Weldon Owen Inc.
814 Montgomery Street
San Francisco, CA 94133 USA
Phone (415) 291–0100 Fax (415) 291–8841

Weldon Owen Inc.:
President: John Owen
General Manager: Stuart Laurence
Co-Editions Director: Derek Barton
Managing Editor: Beverley Barnes
Editor: Patricia Connell
Translator: Barbara McGilvray
Indexer: Jo Rudd
Production: Mick Bagnato
Co-Editions Production Manager (US):
    Tarji Mickelson
Design and Art Direction: John Bull,
    The Book Design Company
Map and Illustrations: Stan Lamond,
    The Book Design Company
Food Photography: Mike Hallson Photography

Library of Congress
Cataloging-in-Publication Data:

De'Medici, Lorenza.
    Italy, the beautiful cookbook.

    Originally published: Los Angeles:
    Knapp Press, 1988
    Includes index.
    1. Cookery, Italian.   I. Passigli, Patrizia.
    II. Title.
    [TX723.D427   1989]   641.5945   89–15891
    ISBN 0–00–215446–3

97 98 99 00 TOP 12 11 10

Typeset by Authentic Print, Sydney, Australia
Manufactured by Mandarin Offset, Hong Kong
Printed in China

SICILY IS FAMOUS FOR THE VARIETY OF GRAPES IT
PRODUCES AND RAISINS FEATURE PROMINENTLY
IN MANY OF THE LOCAL DISHES
PHOTO: TONY STONE WORLDWIDE

PAGES 2–3: HIGH IN THE DOLOMITES THIS TINY VILLAGE
IS TYPICAL OF THE GERMAN-SPEAKING AREA OF
NORTHERN ITALY
PHOTO: HANS WOLF/THE IMAGE BANK

PAGES 8–9: VENICE, A COSMOPOLITAN CITY OF ARTISTIC
AND INDUSTRIOUS PEOPLE
PHOTO: RAY JOYCE

ENDPAPERS: A RISTORANTE NEAR THE TIBER RIVER, ROME
PHOTO: RAY JOYCE

BEANS WITH BACON (top), CELERY WITH MARROW SAUCE (left) AND BAKED POTATOES AND MUSHROOMS (right, recipes page 198)

Sommario

PHOTO: JOHN G. ROSS/SUSAN GRIGGS AGENCY

ON THE OUTSKIRTS OF ROME IN SPRINGTIME, LOCALS ENJOY A FAVORITE SEASONAL
DELICACY — FRESHLY PICKED YOUNG BROAD BEANS (EATEN AT EASTER WITH STRONG
PECORINO CHEESE) WITH A CARAFE OF A LOCAL DRY WHITE WINE

Introduzione

We know that a country's eating habits are a useful factor in reconstructing its economic and social history. In fact, the presence or absence of certain foods in the national diet constitutes a precise indicator of the level of prosperity and progress that a nation has reached.

But when, where and why have those foods come to be treated and cooked in a certain way rather than any other? How long ago did humans pass from satisfying their hunger as an animal instinct to the pleasure of conscious dining — in other words, to a "culture" of eating? There is an Italian proverb that says, "At the table no one grows old"; perhaps this is why the taste for good food goes a long way back in time, as we know from a host of artistic, literary and scientific evidence.

Let us try to go back to the origins of the great Italian culinary tradition, starting with ancient Rome. To follow its development through the centuries and seek out its roots and motivations means to reaffirm the vitality and relevance of this important "slice" of Italy's historical and cultural heritage. The diet of the ancient Romans was very simple and plain, perfectly in keeping with the people's agricultural way of life. It was based on bread of various kinds — made with milk, with oil, with pepper, or with semolina, for example. In addition to bread, which was often in the form of flat loaves (*focacce*) or oven-dried

biscuits similar to crackers, the Romans ate an abundance of legumes: beans, lentils and lupini beans. Potatoes and green beans were unknown; these did not reach Italy until much later, following the discovery of America. The most common leafy vegetables were various types of cabbage, lettuce, beet and turnips, and the most popular fruits were figs, pears, prunes and grapes.

During the excavation of the Coliseum, the archaeologists who were analyzing the material found among it the pits of olives and plums, some melon seeds, and the remains of blackberries. Apparently spectators at the games used to munch as they watched, to pass the time.

Meat was almost absent from the tables of the poorest households. But it was served often at the tables of the rich, and in a variety of forms: pork, beef, deer, wild donkey, dormouse, kid. The ideal of good eating is made clear in a passage from the *Satire* of Juvenal, a Latin poet of the late first century AD:

"From the countryside at Tivoli we will get a fat kid, the tenderest of the herd. Then there will be mountain asparagus gathered by the farm women after they have finished spinning the wool, and large eggs, still warm. And then bunches of grapes … pears from Segni … apples wonderfully pure of fragrance."

THE PANORAMA ALONG THE LIGURIAN RIVIERA IS CONSTANTLY BREATHTAKING
AND IF YOU CLIMB THE STEEP MOUNTAIN ROADS INLAND, YOU MAY BE
REWARDED WITH VIEWS LIKE THIS ONE OF THE MEDIEVAL BORZONE ABBEY

15

PREVIOUS PAGES: THE MEDIEVAL TOWN OF RIOMAGGIORE, ON THE RUGGED
COASTAL STRIP OF LIGURIA, IS NORTH- WEST OF LA SPEZIA
PHOTO: AUSTRALIAN PICTURE LIBRARY

The only beverage drunk by our Roman forebears was wine, flavored with leaves of roses, violets and citron, with cinnamon and cloves. The favorite condiment was *garum*, a liquid obtained from various kinds of decomposing fish, which was used for eggs, meat, and fruit tarts.

The first century AD saw the beginning of the era of "culinary cosmopolitanism" in Rome. On the one hand, the process of Romanization that followed Rome's conquests carried Latin customs and usages beyond her borders, while on the other, the traditional Roman lifestyle was refreshed with changes brought from the East after the conquest of Greece. Into the kitchens came artichokes from Africa, cherries from Asia Minor, pistachio nuts from Syria, peacocks from Samos and dates from Egypt. Gastronomy reached a peak of sophistication bordering on the dissolute, as we see with the famous supper of Trimalchio described by Petronius in his *Satyricon* (first century AD):

"First of all we were offered a pig with a crown of sausages … and homemade bran bread…. The next dish was a cold cake with hot honey, over which Spanish wine had been poured…. After that we found before us a portion of bear meat…. And lastly we were offered soft cheese, fruit mustard, a snail for each person, some tripe, a dish of liver, some smothered eggs, turnips, mustard…. Then a bowl of olives in vinegar was passed around…. When the prosciutto arrived, we surrendered…."

BUSINESS IS LESS THAN BRISK FOR THIS MODERN *GELATAIO*, HIS VAN DECORATED WITH FANTA AND COCA COLA CANS

SURROUNDED BY THE FRAGRANT OLIVE TREES AND VEGETABLE CROPS THAT PROVIDE ITS LIVELIHOOD, A FAMILY ENJOYS A MEAL OF *RIGATONI* AND WHITE WINE

And how were these dinners organized? The diners would be stretched out on couches around the tables, there were no tablecloths, and one ate with one's hands and took home the leftovers at the end of the meal. There were three stages to the banquet: first a kind of appetizer course consisting of light foods, wine and honey; then the meal itself with the main dishes; and finally a dessert consisting of dried and spicy foods. They would begin at five in the afternoon and go on late into the night.

The art of cooking with all its refinements was part of the "good government" of family and home that was a fundamental principle of the Roman social system. And so at the time of the Empire a number of works were dedicated to gastronomy as a science. They were guidebooks to the good life, with recipes and advice about health and about the maintenance of house and garden. A book written in Nero's time, *De Re Rustica*, by Lucius Junius Columella, not only gives instructions for rearing domestic animals, growing cereals and keeping a garden; it also teaches us how to make vinegar, fruit mustard, olives in brine, wine, salt pork, jams and meat pies. But the oldest cookbook, in the strict sense of the term, is *De Re Coquinaria* by Celius Apicius, a collection of recipes probably compiled in 230 AD. Alongside traditional recipes from Roman kitchens, such as marinated fish and barley porridge, we find highly sophisticated prescriptions — unquestionably for gourmets — for things like roast of swan, parrot or ostrich, and dormouse cooked in honey. This recipe for baked kid would not, barring the antique ingredients, be out of place in a book of recipes today:

"Clean and bone the kid, remove the internal organs … and wash them. Into a mortar put some pepper, ligusticum, root of laserwort, two fruits of the bay tree, a little pyrethrum, and two or three brains. Chop this mixture finely, soak it in garum sauce and salt it. Then pour over it sixteen measures of milk and two spoonfuls of honey. Use this mixture to fill the intestines, and wind them in a spiral around the kid … then put the kid into a baking dish … with sauce, oil and wine. When it is half cooked, finely chop some pepper and ligusticum, sprinkle some of the cooking liquid over them and add cooked must. Stir all these ingredients and pour the mixture into the baking dish. When it has finished cooking, arrange it, reduce it with starch, and serve."

This kind of cooking, needless to say, was destined for the tables of the wealthy, while the diet of the common people, right up to the time of the Late Empire, continued to consist of more or less the same basic elements that it always had: porridge of spelt or barley, cheese, olives, marinated fish — but no meat. Lettuce was widely used, and the Roman soldiers even used to sow lettuce seeds around their encampments. This was the simple way of eating, which the early Christians set in contrast to the baroque culinary excesses of the decline of the Empire. They upheld the moral values of frugality and simplicity. It was written in the Psalm, "The Lord will see to thy nourishment"; and in the gospel, "Be not too concerned for your life and what ye shall eat." And so gradually and inevitably, with the spread of Christianity, greed came to be considered one of the deadly sins with which man could stain himself.

The strictness and severity of the early Christians' customs, the barbarian invasions that followed the fall of the Western Empire, and most of all a serious economic crisis finally swept away the culinary excesses of the Roman table. From the fifth century on, food customs derived from the barbarian culture began to creep into the Italian cuisine. One example is the modern steak tartare, which is simply an echo of the raw meat the barbarians used to hang beneath their saddles to ripen during their endless marches on horseback. At the end of the journey, they would eat it seasoned with local herbs.

Not until the time of Charlemagne was there a return to a grand cuisine. There are records of parties and banquets at the Court of Aix-la-Chapelle overflowing with roast meats, pies with a variety of rich fillings, and sumptuous cakes. And even within the walls of prosperous convents and monasteries there was no shortage of game, vegetables and sweetmeats.

It was in the passionate Middle Ages that an international cuisine began to take shape, belying the popular image of a period of decadence and a general return to the savage state. This European cuisine was based on the almost standardized

THE PRAGLIA MONASTERY IN THE EUGANEAN HILLS OF THE VENETIAN REGION, WITH ITS FINE EXAMPLE OF AN ITALIAN GARDEN, WAS FOUNDED IN THE ELEVENTH CENTURY

recipe books used in the kitchens of the courts and the aristocracy: for the first time local and national boundaries were overcome, at least in the kitchen. Foods were always flavored with spices; saffron, cinnamon, pepper, nutmeg, cloves and ginger were used to season soups, meats and breads, clearly indicating the influence of a different gastronomic tradition. The great Arab culture was in fact spreading across Europe, especially in the areas of science and philosophy. Treatises on medicine, astronomy and mathematics, lists of plants and animals, and herbals were translated into Latin and circulated widely. And in some of them, culinary matters were discussed — for example, in the *Liber de Ferculis et Condimentis* and the *Tacuinum Sanitatis*. The latter gives the following instructions for the making of *tagliatelle*: "The housewife shall work the dough on the table with strong hands, and the young girls from time to time with delicate fingers shall remove the *tagliatelle* spread out to dry"; and for thrush: "At the beginning of winter choose birds that have been nourished on juniper berries and myrtle berries." For fish, the advice is that, "fish from the sea are superior to freshwater fish; those from fresh water are to be selected from the rocky bottom, small and thin skinned; as for their preparation, roasting over coals or on a grill is better than boiling, and boiling is better than frying."

We are now about to enter that wonderful period, the Renaissance, when Italy as mistress of civilization and culture was also to lead the rest of the world in the art of cooking. Two late-fourteenth-century manuscripts, the *Libro della Cocina* (*Book of the Kitchen*) and the *Libro per cuoco* (*Book for the cook*), may be seen as the two earliest fundamental works of modern gastronomy. In both these books of recipes, one compiled by an anonymous Tuscan author and the other by an anonymous Venetian, the basic difference between northern Italian cooking and the cuisine of the south and the center is clearly defined: in the first, lard or pork fat is used — in other words animal fat — and in the second, olive oil. Both books were probably intended for use by cooks in the homes of the nobility, where the favorite pastime was the banquet — a gathering together at the table for the enjoyment of the company and some excellent food. The guests would tell each other of their gastronomic exploits with great enthusiasm, relating where and how they had sampled some wonderful delicacy. It had become fashionable to be a gourmet, and members of the wealthy merchant society would amuse themselves not only by eating, but by talking about it. The pleasures of the palate also found considerable space in the literature of the time, where they were celebrated and exalted in verse and prose, beginning with Boccaccio's *Decameron*, from which we quote a famous example taken from the tale of Calandrino and the heliotrope. Maso gives this description of the imaginary Bengodi, the land of milk and honey:

"And there was a mountain made of grated Parmesan cheese, and on it there were people who did nothing else but make macaroni and ravioli, and cook it in broth made from capons, and then they threw it down, and he who caught the most ate the most."

In the second half of the fifteenth century the classical phase of the art of cooking reached its peak via two complementary developments — one technical and practical, the other theoretical.

The first produced the *Libro de Arte Coquinaria* (*Book of Culinary Art*) by Maestro Martino, and the second the *De Honesta Voluptate et Valetudine* by Bartolomeo Platina. Martino was from Como, and was cook to the patriarch of Aquileia in Rome; it appears that in the kitchen he was without equal. He had the distinction of being able to translate his extraordinary practical skills into a series of prescriptions which, far from being disconnected and informal, were actually structured into a treatise. Platina, on the other hand, was a learned scholar, who tried by means of a series of rules of good cooking and good health to encourage the spread of a lifestyle marked by a stern morality.

During the sixteenth century, the precise duties of kitchen staff were defined, and a highly specialized professional emerged in the person of the *trinciante* or carver, a kind of surgeon to whom table etiquette entrusted the delicate task of cutting up the food on each diner's plate. His immediate superior was the steward, who was really the head of the kitchen and serving staff, with responsibility for all household provisions and for the complex task of making up dinner lists according to the likes and dislikes of those invited, and lists for feast days and special ceremonies.

Both these positions were much coveted in the courts of the Italian Renaissance, and often they were occupied by gentlemen of esteem, like Cristoforo da Messisburgo who served at the Court of Ferrara and earned the title of Count Palatine. He wrote a book called *Banchetti Compositioni di Vivande, et Aparecchio Generale* (*Banquets, Composition of Meals, and General Equipment*), published in 1549, "in which it is taught how to make every kind of dish according to the occasion, whether meat or fish, and how to organize banquets, set tables, furnish palaces and decorate rooms for every great Prince...." Likewise, the Florentine Domenico Romoli, nicknamed Panunto ("oiled bread"), who wrote a similar work called *Dell'ufficio dello Scalco, dei condimenti di tutte le vivande, le stagioni che si convengono a tutti gli animali, uccelli et pesci* (*Of the office of Steward, of seasonings for all dishes, the seasons most suitable for all animals, birds and fish*), published in 1560.

But the most famous cook and author of the century was without doubt Bartolomeo Scappi, "secret cook to Pope Pius V," to whom the Pope granted printing rights for the publication of a vast treatise (900 pages) entitled *Opera ... divisa in sei libri* (*Work ... divided into six volumes*) of which

THE UNIQUE CHARM OF VENICE — LOOKING ACROSS THE CANALE DE SAN MARCO TO SAN GIORGIO
MAGGIORE, WITH GONDOLAS BOBBING GENTLY ON THE TWILIGHT WATERS

"the second deals with various dishes made with meat, both of quadrupeds and of birds. In the third we read of the condition and seasons of fish. The fourth gives lists of courses for presentation at the table, both meat dishes and others...." This was published in 1570. It is to Scappi that we owe the exact description (supported by twenty-seven beautiful engravings) of the "places assigned" to the preparation of foods, or in other words the various areas that made up the kitchen. Next to a room with cooking rings, fireplace, sinks and kneading troughs, where the cooking and actual making up of meals took place, there was "a room" that had to be "spacious, light and airy," "where one can knead dough and work with sauces and flavors." This too was equipped with ovens, cooking rings, sideboards and other items in constant use. Then there was a small open courtyard "where one may work in every kind of weather, plucking birds, skinning animals ... scraping fish and cutting up herbs," with a bench, sink, vats, and a grinding wheel for sharpening knives. There was also a "small room which must be in a cool location" for "keeping oils, lard, pork fat, butter and all kinds of foods," and finally another room "quite large, and a good distance away ... for storing kitchen utensils, coal, baskets, cheese molds and other items that are used for carrying."

It was also at the sixteenth-century courts that the foundations of modern tablesetting were laid. Up to that time, a "setting" had consisted of a flat plate or wooden tablet like a chopping board, on which the diner would place his food before carrying it to his mouth with his hands. (It was only late in the seventeenth century that the use of the fingers for eating dishes with sauces and gravies began to be regarded as bad-mannered.) It was generally expected, however, that each guest would bring his or her own glass (usually a metal goblet), a rudimentary spoon, and a knife with a pointed blade that was used for cutting and skewering the food as well as for self-defense.

When Catherine de' Medici married the King of France she introduced the French court to the idea of using a fork — which up to that time had been an exclusively Italian custom (or rather, to be precise, Florentine). But until the following century it remained no more than a fashion, a curiosity reserved for those few who had learned to manipulate it gracefully. To convey some small idea of the way people generally behaved at the table (where they attacked and devoured the food, rather than eating it), we give a few precepts from *Il Galateo* (*The Book of Etiquette*) by Giovanni della Casa, which was an attempt to teach manners to the nobility in the second half of the sixteenth century. "Nor would I advise you to

PHOTO: DAMM/ZEFA

AN AMALFI FISHERMAN MENDS HIS NETS IN THE QUIET OF THE LATE AFTERNOON

invite others to drink from that glass of wine to which you have put your lips and from which you have drunk … Much less must you offer a pear or other fruit which you have bitten into … And the well-mannered man must take care not to get his fingers greasy so that his napkin becomes stained, for it is nauseating to see." They were as yet very difficult rules to follow for guests at the magnificent tables of the Late Renaissance who, "in the manner of pigs with their snouts all dangling in the slops, never lifted their faces," who would dirty "their hands almost to the elbow," and "also very often" wipe their sweat and blow their noses with their napkins, and rinse their mouths and spit out the wine in public.

But let us get back to the kitchen. From the end of the sixteenth century, unknown fruits, plants and animals, as well as vast amounts and countless varieties of spices, began to flow in from the New World. Firstly there were corn (the first seeds of which were brought to Europe by Christopher Columbus) and potatoes. Then followed beans, tomatoes, turkey, cane sugar, coffee, chocolate and so on.

So recipes were enriched with new ingredients, and at the same time the techniques of cooking were refined and became highly complex, in an effort to make the most of previously unknown tastes and flavors. Meat in particular was cooked in several stages — first boiled, then roasted and finally reheated in gravies and sauces made with hot or sweet spices that were appropriately minced or chopped.

So ended the gastronomic Renaissance, with tables of sumptuous splendor and richness that seemed to want to satisfy taste, touch, sight and smell all at the same time.

In the seventeenth century, Italian cuisine gradually lost its supremacy in Europe, edged out by the French *haute cuisine*. The only cookery book worthy of note in this twilight period was *l'Arte di Ben Cucinare* (*The Art of Cooking Well*) by Bartolomeo Stefani, head chef at the court of the Gonzaga. Endowed with a very pleasing and harmonious writing style, Stefani may be considered the last exponent of the Renaissance tradition and the first modern Italian gastronome. In his book we read for the first time about "ordinary food," that is to say the everyday meals that silently accompanied the formal eating of grand dinners. As a good cook and home economist, Stefani suggested recipes with ingredients and quantities to suit the financial capabilities of a middle-class family.

Here, for example, is the recipe for a sauce to go with meat:

"Take a pound of jasmine flowers, pound them in a mortar with half an ounce of cinnamon, two Neapolitan *mostaccioli** soaked in a pound of rose vinegar, and two ounces of sugar, putting the said mixture on to boil in a small glazed stone jar with the lid on.... This sauce will be useful for baked livers, lamb chops and other things."

The budget was given, in Mantuan *lire*, for a family of eight, and underneath the total of 6 *lire* 19, Stefani noted that "these things may be bought everywhere, showing the truth of the proverb that things are the same all the world over."

The year 1715 saw the death in France of the Sun King, the splendor of whose rays had already penetrated the kitchens of Italy. The fashion of eating "in the French manner" was popular in the palaces of the nobility: for a dish to be properly appreciated, it had to be "finished in Paris." Even the terminology used in recipe books of the time closely followed the usage on the other side of the Alps, so that alongside a *timballo di maccheroni alla napoletana* we find *entrées* of kid's head, and next to the *tordi alla fiorentina* a *coli* of capon.

In 1797 a sort of encyclopedia of gastronomy in several volumes was published in Rome under the title *L'Apicio Moderno ossia l'arte di apprestare ogni sorta di vivanda* (*The art of preparing every kind of food*). Its author, Francesco Leonardi, "cook to Her Majesty Catherine II, Empress of all the Russias," may legitimately be called the first Italian expert on international cooking. There are recipes from Poland, Turkey, Spain, England, France and China alongside those from every region in Italy. Also worthy of note is the author's attempt to trace a basic history of cookery from the time of the Romans to his own era.

By this time Europe was on the threshold of great political and social upheavals. The fundamental principles of the French Revolution and the victories achieved by the Industrial Revolution began to be felt all over Europe, and in cooking as well as in most other areas. The concept of

*hard biscuits containing candied fruit.

nation, the formation of national states, the rise and consolidation of a strong new middle class, and finally the migration from agricultural areas into the urban and industrial centers heralded new approaches to cooking and eating. It could be said that the way we eat today goes back directly to the food traditions that were established during the course of the nineteenth century. The French method of serving, for example, as adopted during the Renaissance, with all the dishes presented on the table at the same time, gave way to the so-called "Russian" serving style with one course following another.

As national unification proceeded in Italy, traditions and usages of a local and regional nature began to spread beyond their natural narrow confines to mingle and integrate with one another. Unlike France, Italy had never had an academy or official school of cuisine to lay down laws and principles in culinary matters. And so a kind of gastronomic eclecticism emerged, made up of many parts, which was to become the basis of modern Italian gastronomy.

For instance, it was thanks to Garibaldi, one of

A RESTAURANT IN ONE OF THE NARROW BACK STREETS OF ROME. THE INVITING DISPLAY OF FRESH PRODUCE IS AN INDICATION OF THE DELIGHTS WITHIN

THIS COURTYARD IN VIA MONSERRATO WITH ITS SMALL SQUARE PAVING BLOCKS IS TYPICAL OF THE ENTRANCES TO MANY OF THE OLD BUILDINGS IN THE HISTORIC CENTER OF ROME

the architects of a united and independent Italy, that the tomato (production of which had been exclusively confined to the south) came into national use. The soldiers of Garibaldi's Thousand returned home from the southern expedition telling of an unforgettable dish they had eaten: pasta with tomato sauce!

As well as the tomato, the potato was reinstated in the nineteenth century after hundreds of years of neglect. The authorities actually encouraged its use with a publicity campaign, publishing poems, elegies, pamphlets and scientific papers on the beneficial effects of this "American" vegetable. In 1801 Vincenzo Corrado, author of a popular recipe book called *Il Cuoco Galante* (*The Gallant Cook*), added to the fifth edition a "Treatise on Potatoes" that dealt with the many culinary uses of the tuber, which had been brought in from America. The recipe for gnocchi in particular is worth quoting, since gnocchi were destined to become a classic of Italian cooking:

"After the potatoes have been baked in the oven, the best portion of their flesh is pounded with one-quarter the amount of hard-cooked yolks of egg, the same quantity of veal fat, and the same of ricotta. These are blended together and then bound with a few beaten eggs, flavored with spices and divided into small morsels the length and breadth of half a finger, which, after they have been coated in flour, are put into boiling water on the fire, and when they have boiled for a short time, they are served in a dish with grated cheese and meat sauce added."

The invention of a machine for making spaghetti and macaroni, and hence the introduction of commercially produced pasta, also goes back to the first decade of the nineteenth century. Then in the 1840s the distinguishing characteristics and bouquets of the major Italian wines were established, and Parmesan cheese took on its definitive form and flavor.

Thus the nineteenth century was a time of decisive importance in the history of Italian cuisine, as we can see from the innumerable recipe books published in that period. We shall limit ourselves here to quoting one, the *Trattato di Cucina, Pasticceria moderna, Credenza e relativa Confettuaria* (*Treatise on Cooking, Modern Cake-making, Tasting of Foods and related Confections*) written by Giovanni Vialardi, who was assistant head chef to Carlo Alberto and Vittorio Emanuele of Savoy. Published in 1854 and containing two thousand recipes meticulously compiled, it may be considered the major cookery book of the post-*Risorgimento* period. Its stated intent was to teach "an economical, simple, elegant and middle-class method" of preparing "stocks, soups, sauces and gravies; fried foods, children's dishes; compound dishes, cold plates, poultry, meats, fish, cakes and pastries of various kinds ... preservation of foods...."

SIENA, ONE OF THE MOST EXCITING OF THE TUSCAN MEDIEVAL HILL TOWNS, IS A MYSTICAL AND PASSIONATE ART CENTER. DOMINATING THE SKYLINE IS THE TORRE DEL MANGIA OF THE MAGNIFICENT PALAZZO PUBLICO WITH ITS MANY FAMOUS FRESCOES AND PAINTINGS

WINE AND OLIVE OIL ARE TWO ESSENTIAL INGREDIENTS IN ITALIAN COOKING, AND
THE SIGHT OF NEAT ROWS OF VINES GROWING ALONGSIDE OLIVE TREES
IS NOT UNCOMMON

VOTIVE OFFERINGS TO PATRON SAINTS OR TO THE
VIRGIN MARY ARE AN AGE-OLD TRADITION IN ITALY. THE DECORATIVE
SHELLS AND STONE ANCHOR IN THIS CORNER SHRINE ARE IN KEEPING WITH
THE CHARACTER OF THE TINY SEASIDE VILLAGE OF CAMOGLI, NEAR PORTOFINO

The day of the costly and complicated "court cuisine" was finally over, and a new gastronomic culture was developing, in perfect accord with the middle-class lifestyle that was by this time triumphant all over Europe.

In order to understand the reasons for this new culinary philosophy, it is necessary to digress briefly into the area of the so-called popular cuisine. What were the ordinary common people eating while all those sumptuous feasts were being set out in the palaces of the nobility?

By and large the diet of the lower classes had not undergone any notable changes. For two thousand years it was based essentially on large quantities of cereals (buckwheat, millet, spelt and, after 1600, corn), together with seasonal fruit and vegetables, fish and game. Domestically produced meat (pork, goat, mutton, chicken) was very scarce and was reserved for the Sunday meal, which was by tradition richer than the weekday fare. The staple diet was soup made with cereals and vegetables and served with black bread, and, from the seventeenth century on, polenta made from corn.

The largely static nature of the so-called "poor cuisine," the fact that for centuries it remained unchanged, was a direct consequence of the equally unchanging state of general poverty. A hungry man will seek to feed himself, and only then, when he feels satisfied and well nourished, will he begin to choose what he will eat. So, to satisfy one's hunger was the lot of those who were not born into the aristocracy or clergy. In 1555 an established professional artist, Jacopo Carucci (known as Pontormo), noted in his diary: "On the second day of February, on Saturday evening and Friday I ate a cabbage and both those evenings I had for supper 16 ounces of bread." Things were a little better on 30 March: "I ate 10 ounces of bread and two eggs and a salad of borage." Even in 1880, for the wooden puppet Pinocchio, hero of the great Italian children's story, gastronomic appeal was represented by "a large piece of bread" accompanied by "a fine plate of cauliflower dressed with oil and vinegar" and for dessert "a fine sweetmeat filled with nectar."

The diet of farm laborers in northern Italy around the same time consisted almost solely of polenta, we are told by Villari in his *Lettere Meridionali* (*Letters from the South*), published in Turin in 1885. In the evening, "though not always," "onions and inedible cheese" were added, and once a week "bread and soup." D. Orano, in his *Come vive il popolo di Roma* (*How the people of Rome live*) of 1912, related that at that time, just prior to the First World War, the basis of daily nourishment for "hundreds and hundreds of ordinary families" in Rome was "a soup consisting of water, lard, herbs and preserves and pasta."

Despite the incessant repetition of the same ingredients, however, the soups, *focaccia*, freshly caught ocean fish, eggs, and the chicken reserved for Sundays and feast days all took on a new taste in each area. Local variations such as climate, the type of vegetables grown, or the wildflowers of the locality, and subjective variables depending on the individual cook, such as proportions of ingredients and other little personal "secrets" — not to mention the good and bad humors governing each day — had a noticeable effect on flavors and their infinite nuances.

So we can see that between noble cuisine and poor cuisine the same kind of relationship held as there is between the official and literary language of a country and its many dialect variations — they coexisted and developed parallel to each other, with frequent interchange and reciprocities.

Then from 1891, beginning with the first edition of Pellegrino Artusi's *La Scienza in Cucina e L'Arte di Mangiar Bene* (*Science in the Kitchen and the Art of Eating Well*), a new national culinary model began to emerge in Italy, bringing together the two cultures of ceremonial dining and the family table.

This deservedly famous cookbook teaches us, in the name of common sense, good taste and the sovereign rule of balance, not only how to eat deliciously, but also how to live wisely with our own bodies, regulating ourselves "to maintain a healthy balance" by becoming accustomed from childhood "to eat of everything" and not become slaves to our stomachs. Here is cooking as science, and also as culture: the old Italian regional recipes, reviewed, corrected and clarified by Mr Artusi, constitute a true wealth of culinary information and ideas which must be studied if today we are to speak again of a civilization of the table.

DAWN BREAKS THROUGH THE APPENNINE HILLS OF EMILIA. THIS SERENE LANDSCAPE AT BEDONIA IS IN THE PARMA AREA, HOME OF THE WORLD-FAMOUS HAM AND PARMESAN CHEESE

Il Nord-Ovest

PHOTO: GRAZIA NERI

Il Nord-Ovest

The northwestern regions include Lombardy, Piedmont, Val d'Aosta, and Liguria. On the whole, the land is rich, life is prosperous, and food is to be enjoyed as one of its pleasures. Liguria is possibly the exception — a narrow strip of rugged land wedged between the Alps and the sea, but as compensation it has beautiful seaside resorts and boasts some of the most wonderful vegetables and herbs. Val d'Aosta is another favorite tourist region, famous for its soups and game, castles and mountain scenery. The generous cuisines of Lombardy and Piedmont are dominated by rice (risotto originated in Lombardy), butter and cheese, with the addition of the delicious white truffles of Piedmont.

For Ligurians there are two traditional topics of conversation: taxes and eating. The reason is that for many centuries Liguria has been a very unproductive area, far more barren than other regions of Italy. Wedged between the sea and the mountains, it is a narrow strip of rugged country where only a certain type of agriculture is profitable (or in fact possible), and that is fruit and vegetable growing. Instead of vast stretches of grain-growing and pastureland, there are thousands upon thousands of kitchen gardens and terraced hillsides where the famous Ligurian vegetables are grown.

The diet here has always been frugal and basically vegetarian — what the Italians call *di magro*. But, while the ingredients may be thrifty, the preparation is anything but simple. The modesty of the basic elements is transformed and enriched by lengthy preparation and cooking in many different stages.

In addition, there are two ingredients on which Ligurian cuisine can always rely: fish from the

IN PIEDMONT, THE TENTH-CENTURY BENEDICTINE ABBEY, SAGRA DI SAN MICHELE LOOKS ACROSS THE PLAINS OF THE RIVER PO TO THE SNOWY PEAKS OF THE ALPS.

PREVIOUS PAGES: PORTOFINO ON THE ITALIAN RIVIERA
PHOTO: GUIDO ALBERTO ROSSI/THE IMAGE BANK

Gulf of Genoa, and the herbs that grow all over the hills. These two components, together with prime produce from the local vegetable gardens, make up the culinary heritage of the region. One of the herbs, basil, is the basic ingredient of *pesto*, which is the trademark sauce of Liguria. It is used in the making of minestrone, and is served with *lasagne* and *trenette* (a kind of flattened spaghetti). The name *pesto* comes from *pestare*, to pound, and the sauce is made by pounding basil, garlic, oil, Sardinian pecorino cheese, marjoram and parsley together in a mortar and diluting the mixture with olive oil. The other characteristic sauce of this region is walnut sauce, made by mixing garlic, basil and grated cheese with walnuts and pine nuts. It is generally used for *ravioli di magro*, ravioli filled with wild herbs and ricotta cheese. Ricotta is the main ingredient in another famous Ligurian classic, the *torta pasqualina* or Easter pie, which also includes eggs, cooked beet greens and puff pastry.

This series of links between the various gastronomic specialties shows how nothing is left to chance in Ligurian cooking; everything is governed by the firm principle of using only local produce and resources.

This "protectionist" line of thinking in culinary matters is also valid for fish, which is only considered good if it comes from the gulf. It may be fried, made into soup, or stewed; the only exception to this tradition is *stoccafisso*, salt cod, originally imported by the fishermen who used to venture into northern European seas. It has been adopted in Liguria for the traditional Friday dish — dressed up, of course, with the local produce in the form of onions, garlic, carrots, celery, parsley, mushrooms, tomatoes and pine nuts.

Visitors to Val d'Aosta usually go there to admire the spectacular scenery: Monte Bianco, Monte Rosa, the Gran Paradiso, the castles, forests, belltowers and mountain hamlets. One would imagine that the inhabitants of these majestic, austere-looking places had a lifestyle to match, and that simplicity and temperance reigned unchallenged at the table as well. But a visit to one of the castles, or to a *malga* (the characteristic farmhouse of the area), shows, by how much space is dedicated to the kitchen, the importance that was given to food and to everything connected with its preparation. There is a late-fifteenth-century fresco in the castle at Issogne depicting scenes from the daily life of that time; its most conspicuous features are a large table set for a banquet, the baker's, butcher's and grocer's shops, and a fruit and vegetable market. You can see foods that today, five centuries later, are still part of the local diet — butter, cheese, sausages, roast game, buckwheat bread and meat. So the cuisine of this small region is conservative, welcoming very few innovations from other regions. At the same time it is refined and elaborate, as befits an area whose per capita

A MOUNTAIN FARMHOUSE NESTLES IN THE VELVETY GREEN PASTURE LAND OF THE VAL CANNOBINA IN PIEDMONT. SUCH ALPINE SCENERY IS TYPICAL OF THE APPROACH TO THE SWISS BORDER

PHOTO: MICHAEL BOYS/SUSAN GRIGGS AGENCY

THE PROPRIETORS OF THIS TINY WATERFRONT TRATTORIA IN LA SPEZIA PREPARE FOR THE DAY AHEAD WHEN TABLES WILL BUZZ WITH THE CHATTER OF
PATRONS WHO COME TO ENJOY PASTA WITH PESTO SAUCE, OR SOME OF THE MANY LIGURIAN FISH AND SEAFOOD SPECIALTIES

income is the highest in Italy and which has always been linked with France, through its history, culture and geographical position.

Soups form the basis of the diet in this region, and they nearly all have a common ingredient: meat broth — the real thing, made with beef, chicken or veal plus vegetables and herbs. This makes them especially flavorful and invigorating, perfectly suited to the cold winter climate. One example is *seupa*, which consists of layers of black bread, butter and *fontina* (one of the excellent local cheeses), steeped in broth and baked in the oven. Another is *valpeulleunenze*, which is distinguished from the classic soups by the addition of layers of boiled cabbage leaves and a few spoonfuls of gravy from a roast of beef.

A first course worthy of great occasions is *polenta concia*, a rich and ancient dish that has not changed over the centuries and which the mountain people, aristocrat and peasant alike, used to eat on Sundays. It consists of layers of polenta, fontina and melted butter, baked and served sprinkled with truffles.

Meat, too, has a prominent place on the Val d'Aostan table — beef and veal in particular, for cattle breeding is one of this region's economic resources. Classic dishes include the *carbonnade* (cubed beef dredged in flour, browned in butter and cooked in red wine) and the *cotoletta valdostana*, a veal chop stuffed with prosciutto, fontina

and white truffles, coated in breadcrumbs and fried in butter. In the hunting season the cuisine is even richer, with chamois, hare, partridge, dormouse and marmot served braised, roasted, *in salmi* (marinated in wine), with peppers, or stewed in Barolo wine.

As you sit down to dine in Val d'Aosta, you may find yourself being offered a strange wooden cup with a lid, somewhat baroque in design. This is the *grolla* (the name is derived from the Holy Grail, the chalice used by Christ at the Last Supper), which is usually filled with wine and enthroned amid the diners. Tradition requires that everyone partake of it, so it is passed from hand to hand like a peace pipe; refusing to drink is out of the question.

A true Milanese will tell you there are few of his kind left — and indeed, most of the people who live in or around Milan are not of Milanese origin. This is because rapid and continuous industrial progress has necessitated bringing in labor, in the beginning from neighboring areas and later from all over Italy. Milan and the area around it have become a compound metropolis, a mosaic of different traditions mixing and fusing into a new collective identity.

For this reason, the Lombards are particularly attached to their local dialect and their culinary traditions — to their own small, ancient world, which is to be protected and preserved. Living in

ONE OF THE MANY SPLENDID BAROQUE ROOMS IN THE ROYAL PALACE AT GENOA

is born the subtle *sapore lombardo,* "the flavor of Lombardy." Unobtrusive, yet rich, it is the dominant characteristic of this regional cuisine.

Brief mention must be made of the local cheeses, given their well-deserved international repute. We begin with gorgonzola, first produced in the town of the same name back in the eighth century; it is a strong cheese, made from full-cream milk and marbled with greenish streaks of mold. Then comes mascarpone, which is pure cream; *quartirolo,* a fuller-flavored cheese that is lower in fat; numerous varieties of *robiola;* a soft, buttery cheese called *crescenza;* and *stracchino,* which derives its name from *stanchino* ("a little tired"): it was once believed that the flavor and consistency of cheeses depended on the cows being milked while they were tired after grazing. Finally, there is *lodigiano,* a light and nourishing cheese that is served grated over all kinds of first courses: pumpkin *tortelli,* the buckwheat *pizzoccheri* of Valtellina, the handmade *ravioli* known as *casonsei,* and *zuppa pavese* (a dish of toasted bread, egg and broth that was invented by a farm woman to satisfy the hunger of Francesco I when he was a prisoner of the Spaniards.)

We must also say a few words about meat. In Lombardy there is a kind of mystique surrounding the one type of meat that is eaten more often than any other (though it is little used in other regions). It is the so-called "pink" meat: milk-fed veal. Here this delicately flavored meat is a status symbol, cooked in hundreds of different ways. The most famous, of course, is *cotoletta alla milanese,* veal coated in egg and breadcrumbs and fried in butter, which has become an international dish. Other traditional favorites, apart from veal, are tripe, *osso buco, cassoela* (a mixture of different kinds of pork cooked with vegetables and herbs) and *bollito.*

And to end with a flourish, we have the *torta del Paradiso,* Paradise cake, made with butter, eggs, flour and sugar and flavored with lemon rind. It is a practical cake which, as any Italian would tell you, is to be expected because it originated in Pavia. It goes equally well with breakfast, lunch, afternoon tea or as dessert with dinner, and is enjoyed by adults and children alike.

"On the evening of the battle of Marengo, it being impossible in the turmoil of that day to find the kitchen wagons, the cook improvised for the First Consul and the generals a dish, using stolen chickens, which... was called Chicken Marengo; and it is said that from that day on the cook always found favor with Napoleon...." So wrote Artusi, and historians by and large agree with this version of the story — except that credit for the recipe should go not to the future French Emperor's cook, but rather to an anonymous Piedmontese peasant woman who simply cooked the chicken as she had learned to do from her mother, as was the local custom, with a small amount of butter and oil, nutmeg, wine, flour and parsley. The tale serves to illustrate the Piedmontese tradi-

a region that alone produces nearly 60 percent of the nation's income means living a constant contradiction between progress and conservatism, between ancient customs and new social mechanisms. From a gastronomic viewpoint Lombardy offers great variety because of the range and quality of its food products. There is nothing monochromatic about this cuisine: its many shades of taste and ingredients come from sources ranging from the Alps to the fertile plains of the Po, and from Lake Garda to Ticino.

Of special excellence are the first courses made with rice, which has been the traditional cereal of Lombardy since the fifteenth century — although it originally came from the East and was introduced into Europe by the Arabs. We have *riso alla certosina,* a favorite dish of monks in days gone by; rice served with frogs captured in the paddy fields; rice with mushrooms; rice cooked in milk; rice with beans and several varieties of cabbage... and *risotto alla milanese,* otherwise known as "the gold of Milan" because of the golden yellow of the saffron, a flavoring extracted from the crocus flower.

The forefathers of the Lombards were already aware of the virtues of rice — that it is easy to digest, a cure-all for the stomach and medicinal for sufferers of high blood pressure — but in the local kitchens it always has the company of white onions. If the onion is sliced very thinly — not chopped — and softened in butter, it disintegrates, generously giving up its flavor and melting into the rice. Out of this traditional association, which recurs in risottos, soups and minestrones,

PHOTO: GRAZIA NERI

A CLUSTER OF SNOW-COVERED *RACARDS,* BARNS OF LARCH LOGS USED BY
FARMERS FOR STORING HAY, NESTLES IN THE VILLAGE OF VALTOURNANCHE,
VAL D'AOSTA

PHOTO: MORTON BEEBE/THE IMAGE BANK

MOUNTAIN HOMES ON THE TERRACED HILLSIDES HIGH ABOVE THE
BEAUTIFUL LAGO MAGGIORE, IN ITALY'S LAKE DISTRICT

tion of creating masterpieces of imagination and refinement, using nothing more than the most common ingredients.

Why are the Piedmontese epicurean by nature? Because they concern themselves with the pleasures of the table and the full enjoyment of eating. The most obvious illustration of this is the recipe for *bollito*, one of the traditional dishes of the region. It is substantial and rich, designed to satisfy body and spirit, to fill both the heart and stomach. Its secret lies in the number of different meats it combines — turkey, beef, pork, veal, chicken and goose; and in the variety of vegetables — cabbage, potatoes, onions and lentils; in the quality of the sauces — mustard, green sauce, pickles, must (grape juice) sauce; and in the preparation time, which is at least four hours.

The search for happiness through food is demonstrated by listing the ingredients in some Piedmontese dishes. What could be richer than a *fonduta*? It is a thick cream, made by mixing cheese with butter, eggs and milk, which is served simmering, sprinkled with paper-thin slices of white truffle.

Speaking of truffles, once we have established that they constitute one of the undisputed plea-

sures of life, we realize it is no coincidence that they grow in Piedmont. They were a favorite of Messalina and the Emperor Claudius in ancient Rome, of Madame Pompadour in Paris, and of Marilyn Monroe in the United States. The gastronomic philosopher Brillat-Savarin maintained that these "diamonds of the kitchen" made "women more tender and men more amiable."

There is no doubt that the joys of Piedmontese cooking belong to winter, or at least autumn. This is evident from the ingredients, the preparation times and Piedmontese dining habits: the people enjoy being at home, sitting in the warmth with friends before a piping hot meal, while outside it is freezing. The cuisine of this region is poorer in summer, and borrows dishes from other regions. The gastronomic year here finishes in spring, with asparagus, which is produced by the ton and dispatched all over Italy. And what a wonderful finish: asparagus tips in vinegar, asparagus soup, asparagus croquettes, fricassee of asparagus, asparagus with melted butter and cheese, *ad infinitum*. In autumn the cycle begins again with the first delicacy on the calendar: a salad of *ovoli*, the brilliant orange oval mushrooms of Piedmont. *Buon appetito*!

LAGO D'ORTA IS ONE OF THE SMALLEST ITALIAN LAKES. IT HARBORS THE TINY ISLAND OF SAN GIULIO, WHICH IS COVERED IN TERRACES, TREES AND FLOWER GARDENS

PHOTO: AUSTRALIAN PICTURE LIBRARY

Gli Antipasti

PHOTO: AMEDEO VERGANI/THE IMAGE BANK

OLIVE OIL IS, AND ALWAYS HAS BEEN, AN ESSENTIAL PART OF ITALIAN COOKING, WITH THE OLIVE HARVEST A TIME FOR FAMILY AND FRIENDS TO SHARE FOOD AND LAUGHTER

Gli Antipasti

BLACK, GREEN, BROWN, PLUMP AND JUICY OLIVES, SOME SPICED WITH GARLIC AND HERBS, SHARE TUBS WITH OTHER *ANTIPASTO* INGREDIENTS

Antipasto: the Latin prefix *anti-* gives the word an almost solemn ring. The meaning is clear: an *antipasto* comes before the meal (*il pasto*), and its function is to prepare the stomach for the courses to follow by stimulating the production of gastric juices. So the *antipasto* is to be merely tasted, savored slowly in minimal amounts rather than devoured. Otherwise it takes the place of the meal, becoming an epilogue instead of a prologue.

What are Italian *antipasti* like? While there are many different kinds, they follow one general rule, which is that hot ones are served before a reasonably light meal, cold ones before a substantial meal. Both hot and cold are commonly served at cocktail parties and receptions. Also, they must have a certain harmony with the rest of the menu — they should bear some relation to the dishes that follow.

The visual element of *antipasti* dishes is important, so that the appetite is stimulated in the imagination even before it is stimulated by the taste. A skillful blending of colors and garnishes is all part of the exercise: preparing a plate of *antipasti* is like playing with a puzzle.

Another factor to be considered is that *antipasti* are often made up of raw vegetables; to keep them from darkening once they have been cut,

PHOTO: GEORGE WRIGHT

PREVIOUS PAGES: A MOUTH-WATERING AND COLORFUL DISPLAY OF VARIOUS *SOTTACETI* (VEGETABLES PRESERVED IN VINEGAR)
PHOTO: PAT LACROIX/THE IMAGE BANK

one must use a very sharp stainless steel knife and keep the vegetables covered until they are served.

Most of the recipes here have one indispensable ingredient in common: extra virgin olive oil. Just as olive trees have been a constant feature of the Italian landscape for thousands of years, so olive oil has always played a leading role in Italian cooking — at least in three-quarters of the peninsula. There is an old saying that wine lifts the spirits and oil lifts the taste, which confirms the dominant role of olive oil in the kitchens of peasant and aristocrat alike. The Roman *bruschetta*, the Piedmontese *carpaccio*, seafood salads, the Tuscan raw vegetable dip *pinzimonio* — none of these would be the same without the unmistakable taste of extra virgin olive oil.

Although they are drawn from many different areas, most of these recipes have decidely "poor" origins, as the ingredients clearly show: eggplants, salads, anchovies, pizza, *focaccia*. The only one

boasting more noble origins is the Russian salad (which the Russians call French!), a cosmopolitan dish the quality of which depends on the consistency of the mayonnaise and the selection of vegetables. The mayonnaise must be made by hand with very fresh eggs and ... olive oil.

Pâté of guinea fowl, on the other hand, has French roots, as have all the so-called *terrine* that came into Piedmont across the Alps and spread gradually all over the country. Purely Italian, but certainly in the "rich" class, is the salad of *ovoli* and truffles, an *antipasto* worthy of the most important of dinners. The only one of these recipes that requires any elaborate preparation, in comparison to the simplicity of the others, is the eggplant with mozzarella, which needs to be cooked in two stages. This dish was originally created as a complete one-course meal for the tables of Sicilian peasant farmers; it contained a perfect balance of vitamins, proteins and fats in the form of vegetables, cheese and olive oil.

A TEMPTING ARRAY OF TRADITIONAL *ANTIPASTO* INGREDIENTS

EGGPLANT WITH MOZZARELLA

Campania

MELANZANE ALLA MOZZARELLA
Eggplant with Mozzarella

Eggplant is one of the most popular vegetables in the cooking of Campania. It is fried, grilled, sautéed in slices with a little oil, or used to add flavor to pizzas and spaghetti. Best for cooking are the very dark purple, long eggplants, which have few seeds. They must be firm to the touch and have a shiny skin, which indicate freshness.

12 slices eggplant (aubergine), cut ⅜ in (1 cm) thick
salt
12 tomato slices
12 fresh basil leaves
12 thin slices mozzarella
¼ cup (2 fl oz/60 ml) extra virgin olive oil
freshly ground pepper

Lightly sprinkle the eggplant slices with salt on both sides. Place them between two plates and top with a weight. Let eggplant drain for about an hour.

Salt the tomato slices and let them drain for 1 hour.

Pat the eggplant slices dry. Cook them on a hot grill for a few minutes on each side or until tender. Arrange them on a plate and place a tomato slice, a mozzarella slice and a basil leaf on each. Drizzle with oil, season with salt and pepper and serve.

SERVES 6

Piemonte

PATERINI DI FARAONA
Pâté of Guinea Fowl

Chicken liver, ham or pigeon are also used to make these little pâtés, which can be set in the center of a plate and surrounded by a ring of chopped aspic or a decoration of parsley leaves. Small pâtés in many variations are one of the most important Piemontese antipasti.

½ (2 lb/1 kg) guinea fowl, pheasant or squab
5 oz (155 g) butter
6 juniper berries
2 bay leaves
salt and freshly ground pepper
¼ cup (2 fl oz/60 ml) brandy
1 cup (8 fl oz/250 ml) meat broth (stock)
¼ cup (2 fl oz) cold water
2 teaspoons unflavored gelatin

Clean the guinea fowl and cut it up. Melt 2 tablespoons (40 g) butter in an ovenproof skillet with the juniper berries, bay leaves and a pinch each of salt and pepper over moderate heat. Add the guinea fowl and brown on all sides. Warm the brandy, pour it over the meat and flame it, shaking skillet until flames subside. Transfer the skillet to a preheated 350°F (180°C) oven and bake for 1½ hours.

Remove the meat from the bones and chop it coarsely. Place in a food processor with the cooking juices and the remaining butter and puree. Bring broth to boil. Sprinkle gelatin over the cold water and let soften for 5 minutes. Add to broth and stir until gelatin is dissolved.

Rinse out 6 individual molds with cold water. Pour enough of the broth into each to just cover the bottom. Refrigerate until set, about 1 hour.

Fill the molds with the guinea fowl mixture and pour another thin film of aspic on top. Return to the refrigerator for several hours. Pour remaining aspic into a 9 x 5-in (23 x 13-cm) loaf pan and refrigerate until firm.

Unmold the pâtés onto a serving plate. Chop the remaining aspic into small cubes and pile around pâtés as a garnish.

SERVES 6

Umbria

CROSTINI ALLE OLIVE
Fried Bread with Olives

Umbrian olives are black and rather small. They are full of flavor and can be sliced very thinly, mixed with olive oil and kept for long periods in glass jars. The resulting olive paste, diluted with more oil, makes an excellent sauce for spaghetti, and can be given an extra nuance with a pinch of fennel seeds or a little grated orange rind.

10 oz (315 g) fresh *porcini* mushrooms, champignons or button mushrooms
¼ cup (2 fl oz/60 ml) extra virgin olive oil
1 garlic clove, peeled
salt and freshly ground pepper
6 slices firm, coarse-textured bread
½ cup (2 oz/60 g) black olives, pitted

Trim, wash and slice the mushrooms. Heat half the oil in a skillet over high heat. Add mushrooms and garlic and fry for 5 minutes or until just tender. Add salt and pepper and remove the garlic.

Toast the bread slices in a 350°F (180°C) oven until golden. Combine olives and remaining oil in a food processor and puree. Spread on the slices of toast, cover with the mushrooms and serve.

SERVES 6

PÂTÉ OF GUINEA FOWL (right) AND FRIED BREAD WITH OLIVES (left)

SALAD OF *OVOLI* AND TRUFFLES

Piemonte

INSALATA DI OVOLI E TARTUFI

Salad of Ovoli and Truffles

Ovoli (spectacular scarlet and orange mushrooms) are now fairly rare and hence highly prized, and white truffles are tubers that grow mainly in the Alba area between October and January. Dogs with a particularly keen sense of smell are specially trained to find the truffles. They grow beneath the roots of chestnut trees, always in the same places — which the truffle gatherers never reveal to anyone else. The Piedmontese white truffle has a wonderfully distinctive scent that is much sought after. It is served sliced over pasta, rice, eggs or polenta.

Ovoli have an orangey-red cap, and are used for this recipe before the cap opens, when they have an oval form — hence the name.

1 truffle (1 oz/30 g)
6 *ovoli* mushrooms or champignons
½ white inner celery stalk
1 oz (30 g) Parmesan cheese
salt
juice of ½ lemon
6 tablespoons extra virgin olive oil
freshly ground pepper

Brush the truffle and wipe the mushrooms with a cloth to rid them of dirt, but do not wash them. Slice them very thinly and place in a salad bowl. Cut the celery into very fine julienne strips, eliminating any coarse strings, and scatter over the mushrooms and truffle. Using a vegetable peeler, shave the Parmesan very thinly over the top of the other ingredients.

In a small bowl dissolve a pinch of salt with the lemon juice. Whisk in the oil with a fork and pour the dressing over the salad. Season with pepper and serve at once.

SERVES 6

Toscana

CROSTINI DI FEGATINI
Chicken Liver Croutons

Chicken liver croutons are a classical component of Tuscan anti-pasto dishes and usually accompany prosciutto, salami and finocchiona (a sausage strongly flavored with fennel seeds). In recent years the croutons have also become popular garnished with chopped tomato and flavored with basil and extra virgin olive oil.

1–2 *porcini* mushrooms or champignons
extra virgin olive oil
4 large chicken livers
6 fresh sage leaves
2 garlic cloves, chopped
freshly ground pepper
½ cup (4 fl oz/125 ml) *vin santo**
salt
1 anchovy fillet

1 heaping tablespoon capers, drained
1 egg yolk
milk, if needed
12 slices firm, coarse-textured bread

Soak the mushrooms in hot water and cover for at least 10 minutes. Drain well.

Heat 2 tablespoons olive oil in a heavy-bottomed skillet over medium-high heat. Add the chicken livers, sage, garlic, mushrooms and some pepper and cook, stirring constantly, for about 10 minutes or until the livers have lost their red color. Add the *vin santo* and cook until evaporated. Season with salt to taste.

Add the anchovy fillet and capers. Transfer mixture to food processor and puree. Blend in the egg yolk.

Lightly coat the slices of bread on both sides with olive oil and toast in a preheated 375°F (190°C) oven until golden brown. Allow to cool. Spread the mixture on the croutons and serve immediately.

**Vin santo is a Tuscan dessert wine. Substitute a dessert wine or sweet Marsala.*

SERVES 6

CHICKEN LIVER CROUTONS

ANCHOVIES WITH LEMON

HAM AND MELON

Liguria

ACCIUGHE AL LIMONE

Anchovies with Lemon

Anchovies are a common Mediterranean fish, inexpensive and tasty. They are usually preserved in salt or oil. If fresh anchovies are unavailable, shrimp (cooked prawns) or langoustines (cooked scampi or crayfish) may be substituted.

1 lb (500 g) fresh anchovies
juice of 6 lemons
salt and freshly ground pepper
¼ cup (2 fl oz/60 ml) extra virgin olive oil
1 tablespoon chopped parsley
grated rind of ½ lemon

Remove the heads from the anchovies, open them and remove the bones. Wash and dry the fillets and lay them on a serving plate. Pour lemon juice over them, add salt and pepper and refrigerate for at least 2 hours.

Just before serving, drain off the juices. Pour the oil over the fillets and sprinkle with the parsley and lemon rind.

SERVES 6

Emilia-Romagna

PROSCIUTTO E MELONE

Ham and Melon

This is certainly one of the best-known Italian summer hors d'oeuvres. The ham produced in San Daniele, in the Friuli region, is considered to be the best, but the most famous without doubt is that of Parma.

In Tuscany the ham is saltier; sometimes it is made from wild boar, in which case it is very lean and full of flavor. This prosciutto (uncooked ham) can also be served with figs or kiwi fruit.

1 large ripe cantaloupe (rockmelon) or honeydew melon
freshly ground pepper
12 slices prosciutto

Peel the melon and cut into slivers, removing seeds and fibers. Arrange the slivers radiating out from the center of a serving plate. Sprinkle with pepper.

Lightly curl the slices of ham in the center of the plate. Chill well and serve.

SERVES 6

Campania

PIZZELLE
Little Pizzas

These little pizzas are often served as part of family meals in Neapolitan homes. They are traditionally topped with tomato and Parmesan cheese, but are also very good with ricotta, or with endive sautéed in oil and garlic. A similar dish is served in Emilia-Romagna, where it is called gnocchi fritti *or "fried gnocchi."*

1 cup bread flour or all purpose (plain) flour
¼ teaspoon dry yeast
5 tablespoons lukewarm water
1 lb (500 g) ripe tomatoes, peeled and coarsely chopped
salt
1 tablespoon sugar
4 garlic cloves
1 red chili pepper
3 tablespoons extra virgin olive oil
3 cups (24 fl/750 ml) oil for deep frying
6 fresh basil leaves

▪▪ Place the flour in a large bowl. Dissolve the yeast in 1 tablespoon lukewarm water and add to flour. Gradually add the remaining water to the flour, mixing until a firm, elastic dough forms. Knead for a few minutes. Form into a ball and let rise in a warm place for about 2 hours.

▪▪ Place tomatoes in a saucepan with a little salt and the sugar. Cook over medium heat until they are softened and the liquid has evaporated.

▪▪ Chop the garlic with the chili pepper. Sauté them in the olive oil until garlic is lightly colored. Stir into the tomato sauce and keep hot.

▪▪ Roll the dough into a log 1 in (2.5 cm) thick. Cut into 1-inch (2.5-cm) pieces. Roll out each piece on a floured work surface.

▪▪ Heat the oil in a cast iron skillet and fry the pizzas, turning once, until each is puffy and light brown.

▪▪ Drain pizzas on paper towels and transfer to a serving platter. Add the basil to the tomato sauce. Serve sauce with the pizzas. Garnish with basil sprig.

SERVES 4

47

RICE CROQUETTES

Lazio

SUPPLÌ DI RISO
Rice Croquettes

One of the favorite antipasto dishes in Latium. The croquettes are also typical of Sicily, where they are known as arancini di riso *(rice oranges). They may be round or oval in shape, and are excellent for picnics and parties. Try stuffing them with a cube of ham or* provolone *cheese, or with chicken livers that have been sautéed in butter and chopped.*

2 tablespoons butter
1⅔ cups (10 oz/315 g) Arborio rice
3 generous cups (26 fl oz/800 ml) broth (stock)
6 tablespoons freshly grated Parmesan cheese
salt and freshly ground pepper
1 egg yolk, beaten
6 oz (185 g) mozzarella cheese, cut into small dice
1 egg, beaten
1½ cups fine dry breadcrumbs
oil for deep frying

Melt the butter in a saucepan. Add rice and brown for a few minutes over high heat.

Meanwhile, bring stock to boil in another saucepan. Add it to the rice a little at a time over medium-low heat; at the end of 15 minutes' cooking time the rice should be very dry. Add the Parmesan, adjust seasoning with salt and pepper and turn rice out onto a board to cool.

When the rice is cold, thoroughly mix in the egg yolk. Form into balls the size of an egg. Push a hole into the center of each, put in a cube of mozzarella and close the rice mixture over it. Roll each ball in beaten egg and coat with the breadcrumbs.

Heat the oil in a deep fryer until just before smoking. Fry the croquettes until golden brown. Drain well on paper towels. Serve hot, warm or at room temperature.

SERVES 6

Piemonte

PEPERONI ALLE ACCIUGHE
Peppers with Anchovies

This is one of the classic antipasto dishes of Piedmont. The peppers that grow around Asti are highly prized for their plumpness and sweet taste. They are also eaten raw, cut into strips and dipped in bagna cauda, *a hot, garlic-flavored anchovy dip.*

4 anchovy fillets preserved in salt
3 bell peppers (capsicums), a combination of yellow (or green) and red
1 tablespoon finely chopped fresh oregano
1 garlic clove, very thinly sliced
1 tablespoon capers, drained and finely chopped
salt
¼ cup (2 fl oz/60 ml) extra virgin olive oil

Wash anchovy fillets under running water for several minutes to rid them of their salt. Bone them and cut into small pieces. Wash, dry and halve the peppers; remove ribs and seeds. Bake in a preheated 400°F (200°C) oven for 20 minutes. Remove from oven and let cool. Cut into strips.

Place peppers on a serving dish and sprinkle with oregano, garlic, capers and anchovies. Season with salt to taste. Drizzle with oil.

Let stand for 2 hours to blend flavors before serving.

SERVES 12

Piemonte

CARPACCIO ALLA PARMIGIANA
Parmesan Carpaccio

Carpaccio, *the famous dish launched by Arrigo Cipriani at Harry's Bar in Venice, has in reality always been the main component of the delicious Piedmontese antipasto assortment. Traditionally, these wafer-thin slices of raw meat are garnished with flakes of Parmesan cheese, finely sliced white truffle, olive oil, lemon juice and salt.*

1 egg, hard-cooked (hard-boiled)
2 oz (60 g) Parmesan cheese (in one piece)
½ celery stalk, including leaves
8 oz (250 g) rump roast (steak), sliced paper thin
2 tablespoons fresh lemon juice
salt and freshly ground pepper
¼ cup (2 fl oz/60 ml) extra virgin olive oil
1 tablespoon very fine julienne strips of lemon peel

Sieve the hard-cooked egg. Shave very thin slices from the Parmesan cheese.

Mince the celery and celery leaves separately.

Lay the meat slices on a serving plate and sprinkle with lemon juice, salt, pepper and oil.

Cover meat with cheese, minced celery and leaves, lemon peel and sieved egg. Serve immediately.

SERVES 6

PARMESAN *CARPACCIO* (left) AND PEPPERS WITH ANCHOVIES (right)

SEAFOOD SALAD

Lazio

INSALATA DI MARE
Seafood Salad

Every region bordering the sea has its fish salad. In Liguria, the Veneto and Tuscany, the fish is simply dressed with extra virgin olive oil, chopped parsley and lemon juice; in the south, vegetables preserved in vinegar with olives and capers are included in the mixture.

7 oz (220 g) small cuttlefish or squid
7 oz (220 g) medium-size shrimp or green (uncooked)
   prawns, shelled
2 lb (1 kg) mussels
2 lb (1 kg) clams
1 yellow or red bell pepper (capsicum)
½ cup (2 oz/60 g) black olives, pitted
1 tablespoon capers, drained
salt
juice of 1 lemon
⅓ cup (3 fl oz/100 ml) extra virgin olive oil
freshly ground pepper
1 tablespoon chopped parsley
1 tablespoon chopped chives

Remove head and beak from the squid and clean out insides. Wash under cold running water and rub off spotted outer skin. Cut the tentacles of the squid in small pieces and the body into small dice. Cook in boiling water with the shrimp for a few minutes or until shrimp turn pink in color. Drain.

Clean the mussels and clams and steam them in a large covered stockpot over moderate heat for several minutes to open them. Discard any that do not open. Remove the mussels and clams from their shells. Cut the pepper in half and remove the seeds and stem. Bake in a preheated 400°F (200°C) oven for 20 minutes. Remove the skin and cut the flesh into thin strips.

Mix all the fish together in a salad bowl. Add the olives, capers and pepper strips. To make dressing, dissolve salt in lemon juice and whisk thoroughly into the oil. Pour dressing over salad and toss. Adjust seasoning with salt and pepper. Sprinkle with parsley and chopped chives, if desired.

SERVES 6

Marche

OLIVE FRITTE
Fried Olives

These are a specialty of the city of Ancona. They may be stuffed in various ways — with leftover roast chicken mixed with cooked ham or prosciutto, with beef or pork, with chicken livers, or with anchovies preserved in oil. They can also be served as an accompaniment to meat dishes.

3 oz (90 g) pork
2 oz (60 g) sliced *pancetta* or rindless bacon
salt and freshly ground pepper
1 cup (8 fl oz/250 ml) dry white wine
¼ cup coarsely torn fresh bread (without crust)
1 egg yolk
2 tablespoons freshly grated Parmesan cheese
pinch of freshly grated nutmeg
24 giant green olives, drained
1 egg
½ cup all purpose (plain) flour
1 cup fine dry breadcrumbs
4 cups (1 qt/1 l) oil for deep frying

Cut the pork into small pieces. Sauté the bacon in a skillet until it begins to color. Add the pork and a little salt and pepper and cook until golden. Add the wine, lower the heat and simmer gently for about 1 hour, adding a little water if necessary to keep the mixture moist.

Drain off the liquid and chop the meats very finely. Soak the fresh bread in water and squeeze dry. Add bread to the meat with the egg yolk, Parmesan and nutmeg. Pit the olives with an olive pitter and fill them with the prepared mixture, using a pastry bag fitted with a small round tip. Beat the whole egg with a pinch of salt in a deep dish. Roll the olives in flour, then in the egg, and then in dry breadcrumbs. Heat the oil in a deep skillet and fry the olives in it until golden. Drain on paper towels and serve very hot.

SERVES 6

FRIED OLIVES

CARROTS WITH HORSERADISH

Trentino-Alto Adige

CAROTE AL RAFANO
Carrots with Horseradish

Horseradish grows easily and can quickly take over in the garden. It can be picked in any season, but for a stronger flavor, the roots are best picked in winter. They must be scrubbed under running water and put into water acidulated with lemon juice before they are grated.

1 lb (500 g) carrots
1 lemon
¼ cup (2 fl oz/60 ml) cream
¼ cup (2 fl oz/60 ml) yogurt
6 tablespoons grated horseradish
salt and freshly ground pepper

Wash and peel the carrots. Place in a bowl of water with a few ice cubes and juice of 1 lemon. Refrigerate for a couple of hours. Dry the carrots and cut them into strips using a vegetable peeler. Blend the cream and yogurt; add the horseradish with salt and pepper to taste.

Put this mixture in a bowl, arrange the carrots around it and serve. Garnish with fresh herbs, radishes and chopped parsley, if desired.

SERVES 12

Toscana

SCHIACCIATA AL ROSMARINO
Flat Bread with Rosemary

Tuscan schiacciata, *a flat pizza-type bread, is usually only sprinkled with oil and coarse salt, but it can also be flavored with rosemary or sage. It is similar to the Ligurian* focaccia, *which has thinly sliced onions or olives scattered on it.*

½ oz (15 g) fresh yeast or 1 envelope (¼ oz/7 g) dry yeast
½ cup (4 fl oz/125 ml) tepid water
4 cups bread flour or all purpose (plain) flour
3 tablespoons extra virgin olive oil
leaves of 1 large fresh rosemary sprig
coarse salt

Dissolve the yeast in tepid water and let stand for 10 minutes. Heap the flour on a board and make a well in the center. Pour the dissolved yeast into this and add sufficient water to make a soft dough. Knead the dough until very smooth and elastic, at least 10 minutes. Form it into a ball. Sprinkle the inside of a large bowl with flour. Place dough in bowl and cover with a clean cloth. Let stand in a warm place until doubled in volume.

Knead the dough again briefly. Roll out on a lightly floured baking sheet into a circle about ⅜ in (1 cm) thick. Let rise again for 30 minutes. Brush the top with oil and sprinkle with rosemary and coarse salt. Bake in a preheated 450°F (230°C) oven until golden brown. Let cool slightly before serving.

SERVES 6

Lazio

BRUSCHETTA
Garlic Toast

In Rome it is called bruschetta, *in Tuscany* fett'unta *(literally "oiled slice"): the important thing is that this should be made with bread that has excellent taste and texture, and with a good-quality extra virgin olive oil.* Bruschetta *can also be served with slices of tomato and a few fresh basil leaves. Sometimes the tomato is rubbed into the bread with the garlic.*

6 slices coarse-textured bread, cut ⅜ in (1 cm) thick
3 garlic cloves, halved
6 tablespoons extra virgin olive oil
salt and freshly ground pepper

Toast the bread slices, and while still hot rub each well with the cut side of a garlic clove. Drizzle a tablespoon of olive oil over each slice. Add a little salt and plenty of pepper. Serve immediately.

SERVES 6

FLAT BREAD WITH ROSEMARY (top) AND GARLIC TOAST (bottom)

VEGETABLE DIP

RUSSIAN SALAD

Toscana

VERDURE IN PINZIMONIO
Vegetable Dip

Tuscan cooking is based above all on the region's famous extra virgin olive oil. The most highly prized oil is produced in the hills of the Chianti area. When it is newly pressed, in December, its taste is slightly sharp, and this is the best time for dipping fresh vegetables into it. To produce the best-quality oil, the olives must be not quite ripe; they are cold-pressed using a grindstone.

1 fennel bulb
2 carrots, cut into lengthwise strips, or 6 baby carrots
1 celery heart
1–2 raw baby globe artichokes
1 head *radicchio**
1 Belgian endive (chicory) or curly endive
½ cup (4 fl oz/125 ml) extra virgin olive oil
pinch each of salt and freshly ground pepper

Scrape and trim the vegetables as necessary and wash them well. Separate the *radicchio* and endive into leaves.

Dry the vegetables and place them in a bowl in the center of the table. Divide the oil among 6 small bowls, add salt and pepper and place a bowl on a plate before each diner. Dip one leaf or cut vegetable at a time into the bowl of oil before eating.

*Radicchio and endive can be replaced with two other varieties of lettuce if desired.

SERVES 6

Lombardia

INSALATA ALLA RUSSA
Russian Salad

This is called Russian salad because it is made up of many ingredients more or less casually thrown together. In Italy a very untidy room is referred to as "a real Russia"! This dish is usually among the items offered as an antipasto *in restaurants.*

2 medium-size boiling potatoes
1 cup (4 oz/125 g) shelled peas
1 cup (4 oz/125 g) green beans, trimmed
2 carrots, peeled
1 beet (beetroot)
1 egg
1 egg yolk
½ cup (4 fl oz/125 ml) extra virgin olive oil
juice of 1 lemon
¼ cup (2 fl oz/60 ml) milk
salt and freshly ground pepper

Boil potatoes in their skins. Drain and peel them and allow to cool slightly.

Boil the peas, beans and carrots until just tender; boil the beet separately. Cut the potatoes, beans, carrots and beet into small cubes. For mayonnaise, blend the egg and yolk in a blender or food processor. With machine running, add oil in a slow, continuous stream. Blend in lemon juice and then milk. Season to taste with salt and pepper.

Mix the vegetables with enough mayonnaise to dress them to taste. Pile the salad on a plate to serve. Remaining mayonnaise can be kept refrigerated and used at another time.

SERVES 6

Piemonte

UOVA SODE RIPIENE
Stuffed Eggs

This is an elegant antipasto with many possible variations: the hard-cooked yolk may be mixed with mayonnaise and capers, herbs and butter, mayonnaise and shrimp (prawns), ham and butter, or anchovies and parsley. The eggs can be made ahead and kept in the refrigerator, covered with plastic wrap, for a few hours.

6 large eggs
3½ oz (100 g) canned tuna, drained
2 tablespoons finely chopped parsley
salt and freshly ground pepper

STUFFED EGGS

6 anchovy fillets, halved lengthwise
12 black olives

Place the eggs in a saucepan of cold water, bring to boil and cook for 8 minutes. Drain and place in a bowl of cold water to cool. Shell eggs and cut in half lengthwise.

Carefully scoop out the yolks. Combine them in a food processor with the tuna, parsley, salt and pepper to taste, and puree. Refill the egg halves with this mixture, molding with a wet teaspoon, or pipe with a wide fluted nozzle in a pastry bag. Wrap an anchovy piece around each olive, place on top of eggs and serve on fresh vine leaves, if desired.

SERVES 6

Lombardia

INSALATA DI PETTI DI POLLO
Chicken Salad with Walnuts

This famous old recipe from Mantua once stipulated breast of capon rather than chicken breast, because it is more tender. In many regions of Italy capons are bred solely for the traditional Christmas dinner and are served boiled with green sauce or mostarda di Cremona, which is a fruit relish consisting of candied fruit preserved in a spicy mustard syrup.

1 carrot, chopped
1 green celery stalk, chopped
a handful of parsley (½ cup loosely packed)
1 bay leaf
2½ cups (1 pint/500 ml) water
salt
1 whole chicken breast, about 8 oz (250 g)
2 tablespoons raisins
1 inner white celery stalk, cut into fine julienne strips
1 tablespoon fresh lemon juice
3 tablespoons extra virgin olive oil
1 small lettuce, divided into leaves
8 walnuts, shelled and chopped

Combine the carrot, green celery, parsley, bay leaf and water in a saucepan. Add salt to taste. Bring to boil and simmer, partially covered, for about 30 minutes.

Add the chicken breast and poach just until firm and cooked through. Drain, cool, then skin and cut into julienne strips.

Soak raisins in lukewarm water for 30 minutes; drain. Mix celery strips, chicken and drained raisins.

Whisk the lemon juice, oil and a pinch of salt. Arrange the lettuce in 6 small bowls or on a serving plate. Spoon the chicken salad into each lettuce leaf. Drizzle with the oil and lemon dressing. Decorate with walnuts or parsley and serve.

SERVES 6

CHICKEN SALAD WITH WALNUTS

II Nord-Est

PHOTO: AUSTRALIAN PICTURE LIBRARY

Il Nord-Est

The three regions that make up northeastern Italy have all been considerably influenced by other cultures. The Veneto, which contains the magical city of Venice, is a cosmopolitan area of artistic and industrious people with refined tastes. Friuli-Venezia Giulia was actually part of Austria until World War I and, as such, retains Austro-Hungarian legacies, such as goulash, in its cooking. Similarly, Trentino-Alto Adige, a mountainous area characterized by clean air and heavy, filling food, was originally part of Bavaria.

Venetian cuisine may be seen as a combination of local cuisines, with variations on a theme expressed according to the geography of the area: lake, plain, hill, coast or mountain. But they all have a common matrix, which is the Venetian tradition. The city of Venice — marine republic, center of financial power, city-state of merchants and navigators for seven hundred years — has always been the reference point for the inland area, and culinary matters are no exception. It was to Venice that the agricultural products of the very fertile surrounding plains flowed, and from there that the abundant goods imported from the Orient, mythical land of spices, herbs and exotic fruits, were distributed inland. First among them was rice, which, having first arrived in Spain and then spread throughout Europe, found its ideal habitat right here, in the Veneto, and gradually became one of the unifying elements of the local culinary traditions.

Rice was used to prepare a first course that was served to the Doge on St Mark's Day — feast day of Venice's patron saint, *San Marco*. The dish's dialect name is *risi e bisi*, which in standard Italian is *riso e piselli*, rice and peas. The numerous risottos of the Veneto can ultimately be traced to this

MAGNIFICENT BUILDINGS, COOLING SEA BREEZES, TRANSLUCENT LIGHT AND WONDROUS FOOD COMBINE TO ENTICE TOURISTS TO VENICE

PREVIOUS PAGES: HIGH IN THE MAJESTIC *DOLOMITI* OF THE NORTHERN VENETO REGION TOWER MT. SORAPISS AND MT. ANTELAO

PHOTO: INTERNATIONAL PHOTOGRAPHIC LIBRARY

dish, their sometimes extraordinarily imaginative pairings of ingredients testifying to the almost unlimited creativity of the local cooks. We find rice with fish — black rice with cuttlefish ink, seafood risotto, risotto with mussels, crab, scampi, clams — and classic risottos of rustic origin using pumpkin, parsley, asparagus, chicken giblets, pigeon, frogs, beans... all linked by a common destiny, which is to be cooked to just the right consistency, neither too solid nor too liquid but *all'onda* — as the Venetians say, "like a wave" — perhaps because of the importance of the sea in the history of the Venetian region.

The other food that found its ideal growing conditions in this region, after being imported from America, is corn. It is used to make polenta, a thick mixture of cornmeal, water and salt, which is still often cooked on an open wood fire as it has been for centuries. Cut into oblong or diamond shapes, it is the most nutritious accompaniment to game in the mountain areas; to cod, liver and pork in the lowlands; and to every variety of salt- and freshwater fish found on Venetian tables.

Also worthy of particular mention is the *radicchio rosso* of Treviso. This is one of the most popular and best known of salad vegetables, with its origins in the Veneto. There are many ways of serving it, perhaps the most characteristic being crisply grilled. Its flavor is slightly bitter, yet delicate and refined — like that of Venetian cooking in general.

A VENETIAN BUSKER WITH A PIANO ACCORDIAN — A FAMILIAR SIGHT IN THE CITY'S SQUARES AND TAVERNS

BRIGHTLY-PAINTED HOUSES AND FISHING BOATS CHARACTERIZE THE QUAINT VENETIAN VILLAGE OF BURANO, ALSO FAMOUS FOR ITS EXQUISITE LACE

A FARMING AREA IN VAL GARDENA, FRIULI, WITH ITS FAIRYTALE SETTING
OF SNOW-SPRINKLED MOUNTAINS AND WOODED VALLEYS

EATING OUT IN VENICE IS FUN! YOU ARRIVE BY BOAT OR GONDOLA AND
HAVE A CHANCE TO CONTEMPLATE THE HOUSE SPECIALTIES ALONG THE WAY

Although administratively this is a single region, from the gastronomic point of view it is
definitely two. In Friuli, cooking is essentially
homely, with obvious Venetian peasant origins,
whereas Venezia Giulia has a cosmopolitan
cuisine with pronounced Austrian, Hungarian
and Slavic influences.

Beans (Carnia beans in particular are famous),
polenta (both yellow and white), pork and dairy
products are the basic foods of the Friulan table,
enriched along the coast by the addition of fish,
either fried or in *brodetto*, the local fish soup. Yet
masterpieces are created from these age-old, simple ingredients.

The first of these is San Daniele prosciutto,
world renowned since medieval times. Its sweet,
succulent flavor is due to the fact that the pigs
graze freely in the fields and woods, and are not
confined to restricted spaces. Alongside the prosciutto we find *musett*, a kind of pork sausage, and
broàde, a vegetable dish made from turnips
ripened in the residue of grapes after wine-
making, then cut into strips and cooked with
onions and pork fat. *Jota* is a bean soup with
cabbage and pork fat, flavored with cumin and
bay leaves; *cialsons* are ravioli made from pasta
rolled out as thinly as possible by hand and filled
with ricotta, raisins, breadcrumbs, parsley and
nutmeg. But the peak of simplicity and exquisite

taste is reached with the local *frittata*, known as a *settemplice*, which is made from eggs alone (with no milk added) and seven different finely chopped herbs; it is cooked in a saucepan rather than the usual omelet pan so that the center remains soft. Then there is the *frico* (or *fricco*), consisting of thinly sliced apples and cheese that are fried as a kind of flat cake or *tortino* and seasoned with salt and pepper.

In the cuisine of Trieste and Giulia, on the other hand, we find echoes of central Europe. A bowl of steaming goulash soup (beef, onions, tomatoes, potatoes and paprika); a plate of hot cooked ham with a sauce of *cren*, or horseradish, grated into sour cream; a soup of garlic, spinach and flour — these dishes conjure up images of a legendary past, of Austrian archdukes and *Belle Epoque* adventurers and decadent intellectuals.

Also very strong in this area is the tradition of cooking with fish. Fish are plentiful and very popular, and come to the table in the form of simple soups and crab soups. Cod with raisins and pine nuts, and many shellfish dishes, complete this traditionally aristocratic cuisine.

The fact that this is a border region with a multi-ethnic population means that its sophisticated cuisine draws on the best of its various traditions. The south Tyroleans, for example, have taken from the cuisine of Trentino a minestrone made with potatoes and beans, while the *Trentini* have adopted the *canederli* and goulash of the local German-speaking inhabitants. Together these groups have assimilated Austro-Hungarian and Venetian traditions simultaneously. Because it is a mountainous region with a decidedly harsh climate, the overall diet is hearty and laden with calories. Moreover, because Trentino-Alto Adige went through a splendid late-Renaissance period with the great Bishop Princes, there is nothing of

PHOTO: DAVID BROWNELL/THE IMAGE BANK

A CHURCH AT ROVERETO, TRENTINO, PRECARIOUSLY PERCHED IN THE TINY MOUNTAIN CREVICE

the primitive or rustic in its cuisine. On the contrary, it could be seen as having inherited what is truly an art of cooking.

Every ingredient undergoes lengthy treatment, and each dish is prepared with patient care. This is a cuisine of ancient traditions and long cooking times, jealously preserved and handed down from generation to generation. In an account of 1673 we read that Trentino "produces everything that is necessary for human sustenance …cattle … pigs …courtyard animals"; that "great is the return from dairy products"; that "the wines are all good, generous and worthy of esteem"; that game abounds, "alpine hen, quail, turtledove, thrush, razorbill, forest peacock, hare, deer, chamois," not to mention fish — "tench, barbel, trout, shad, etc. etc."; that the fruit is exquisite, particularly bilberries and apples.

The description could have been written today. Meat, particularly game and pork, is still the mainstay of the local diet, alternating with freshwater fish — trout above all. And the raw material still goes through successive stages of preparation, to be transformed into an end product of extreme refinement. It is worth mentioning *speck*, the characteristic smoked meat of this area; it is boned and halved ham, pickled in brine with herbs and spices and then salted and sprinkled with black pepper before being smoked and hung for at least eight months. Patience and perseverance are required for the cooking of roebuck, for *canederli*, for the local thick soups and, last but not least, for the sweets that are the gastronomic pride of this region: pastries filled with fresh and dried fruits, cakes swimming in cream, fritters and tarts. And even the "national" vegetable, sauerkraut, which is flavored with juniper berries, stewed in pork fat and served piping hot as an accompaniment to meat, requires considerable perseverance on the part of the cook.

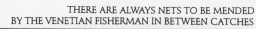

THERE ARE ALWAYS NETS TO BE MENDED BY THE VENETIAN FISHERMAN IN BETWEEN CATCHES

PHOTO: FULVIO ROITER/THE IMAGE BANK

AN HISTORIC REGATTA IN VENICE, WITH GAILY-DECORATED GONDOLAS AND SUMMER CROWDS GATHERING ON THE GRAND CANAL

I Primi

PHOTO: ALAN BLAIR

A STALL AT THE SATURDAY MORNING MARKET IN CEFALÙ, SICILY

I Primi

MAKING SPAGHETTI ON THE *CHITARRA* (see recipe page 104)

Pasta is undeniably *the* great factor in the Italian diet, quite apart from the folklore generally surrounding it. People mention the word with a knowing wink and a sly look, conjuring up visions of the stereotypical glutton — always male — with a napkin tucked into his collar and fork poised to attack a huge plate of spaghetti and sauce. Leaving aside the banality of this "local color," it is nonetheless true that pasta is something quite serious and important. Firstly, it is an extraordinary invention that has become a trademark of Italian culture, and secondly it is a food that has remained constant through the centuries and has gained worldwide approval. And today, thanks to knowledge of calories and superfluous fats, pasta has returned like a triumphant queen to our tables. As well as tasting delicious, it is considered to be a key food in the new anticholesterol diet.

But let us take a step back into the past. Pasta, as the name clearly indicates*, is a "paste" made from flour (wheat, buckwheat, etc.), water and salt. With eggs added, it becomes "Sunday pasta." The first pasta-making machines were invented just over a hundred years ago; before that it was made by hand, mainly in the kitchens of southern

The Italian word pasta *also means pastry or dough.*

PHOTO: MARKA MILANO

Italian homes. The flour was heaped on the table in the shape of a small mountain (or rather, volcano), worked long and energetically, rolled out with a rolling pin, left to rest, and finally cut. This skill belonged to the female members of the family, and was passed from mother to daughter. Its spread throughout the world was due not only to those early Italian women but also to the cooks in Italian courts of the late sixteenth century, who began to export this gastronomical wonder abroad. It is said that when Catherine de' Medici became the bride of the King of France, she took with her not only the rudiments of good table manners, but also the recipe for a famous pasta pie, *Maccheroni alla Medici*, which included among its ingredients thrushes, truffles and a sauce of mushrooms. There is also a story that Queen Victoria was a glutton for pasta; because she needed to watch her weight, however, the royal cooks invented a light soup for her consisting of chicken bouillon and the Italian soup pasta known as *pastina*.

Today, very few people know how to make by hand those very fine sheets of pasta, soft and strong like a piece of silk. This ancient knowledge is almost lost. Italian *bucatini, maccheroni, tagliatelle, lasagne, rigatoni, fusilli, orecchiette, vermicelli, farfalle, torciglioni* and spaghetti, produced by the 240 pasta factories throughout the country, travel the world with a turnover of 1650 billion *lire* annually. But even this huge industry retains a certain respect for quality, as befits a product boasting such illustrious antecedents.

After spaghetti, Italians love rice, particularly those who live in the northern regions. It is more

PHOTO: ANGELO GIAMICCOLO/GRAZIA NERI

A SELECTION OF BREADS FRESH FROM THE OVEN, ABRUZZI

AN ARRAY OF FRESHLY MADE PASTA IN THE KITCHEN OF THE EL TOULÀ RESTAURANT IN ROME

PHOTO: JOHN G. ROSS/ROBERT HARDING PICTURE LIBRARY

dominant at today's tables than many other forms of pasta. Rice was brought to Spain from the East by the Arabs some time before the eleventh century; from there the Aragonese brought it to the south of Italy. Then it began a long march towards more suitable growing areas, moving north from Campania into Tuscany, and then on to Piedmont, Lombardy and the Veneto, where it met with resounding success: the Venetians' "national dish" of rice and peas was even served at ceremonial banquets in the dining halls of the Doge. Rice became firmly established in the north during the seventeenth century, while in the south macaroni and spaghetti were dominant.

What is the predominant characteristic of rice? It is an energy-giving food, light and very nutritious. There are various types, known as common, semifine, fine and superfine according to the length of the grain, which varies from 5.4 mm to 6.4 mm. The common variety is preferred for soups; the semifine for *antipasto* dishes, buttered rice, *supplì* and molded rice dishes; and the fine or superfine for *risotto* and side dishes. In contrast to pasta, which claims the limelight, rice is an excellent supporting cast member. It accompanies any kind of main course splendidly, and welcomes all kinds of seasonings. We might borrow from wine terminology and say that rice is generous.

What are the oldest kinds of first course, with their origins lost in antiquity? Without doubt those based on bread, such as *canederli*, bread soups like *acquacotta, ribollita,* and *pappa al pomodoro; panzanella, pancotto, passatelli* … and the fourteenth-century *panunto* and *panlavato.* Gnocchi were also made with leftover bread, as one seventeenth-century cook wrote:

"there are others who grate a loaf of bread, add flour and water to give it body, and then when they have formed little pieces of this mixture they press them against the *grattaccia* with their finger … and call them *strozzapreti* or *maccheroni;* we call them gnocchi. These, after they have been cooked in boiling water, are put into a bowl and butter and cheese are mixed in; they are better still if they are cooked in milk. Then for fast days, garlic sauce can be poured over them, or walnuts or almonds…."

These were ingenious ways of using bread, a food that had been known since the Bronze Age — a sacred food full of symbolic meanings. It was a crime or a mortal sin to waste bread or throw it away.

The success of these dishes depends largely on the quality of the bread, which nowadays, at least in major cities, no longer has the consistency it once had. As a result, when it is soaked, instead of having a crumbly texture it becomes a glutinous mass that is unsuitable for the bread-based soups mentioned above. But with patience and perseverance it is still possible, particularly in country areas, to find "real" bread — in other words, quality.

MAKING MOLDS FOR GORGONZOLA CHEESE

PHOTO: FABBRI EDITORI MILANO

CAPPELLETTI (bottom), *TORTELLONI* (top) and
CANNELLONI SHELLS READY FOR FILLING (right)

69

MUSSEL SOUP

Friuli-Venezia Giulia

IOTA
Vegetable Soup of Trieste

Iota is a soup of white beans, cabbage and bacon fat which shows the Austrian influence. It is a typical dish of Trieste, and for special occasions it is sometimes enriched with pieces of pork. Very simple and tasty, iota is a classic dish in the homes of the poor, as polenta once was in the Veneto.

10 oz/315 g dried white beans
3 oz/90 g bacon fat or salt pork, chopped
2 bay leaves
8 cups (2 qt/2 l) water
¼ cup (2 fl oz/60 ml) extra virgin olive oil
2 garlic cloves, crushed
1 tablespoon all purpose (plain) flour
1 lb (500 g) cabbage, chopped
⅔ cup (3 oz/90 g) cornmeal
salt and freshly ground pepper

⚹ Soak the beans in cold water to cover for 12 hours. Drain and place in a saucepan with bacon fat and bay leaves. Add the water and simmer for 1 hour.
⚹ Heat oil in a deep skillet. Add garlic and flour and fry until golden. Add the cabbage and cook over very low heat for 5 minutes. Add this mixture to beans and cook for 5 minutes. Sprinkle in cornmeal and mix well.
⚹ Season with salt and pepper and simmer for 45 minutes. Pour the soup into plates and serve.

SERVES 6–8

Liguria

ZUPPA DI COZZE
Mussel Soup

The true specialty of Ligurian cooking is fish, always absolutely fresh and very simply cooked in its own broth with a little oil. For a short time in spring, tiny baby fish called gianchetti *(fry) are to be found. These are cooked in soup, boiled and eaten with oil and lemon, or mixed with egg and fried as fritters.*

4 lb (2 kg) mussels
2 tablespoons extra virgin olive oil
2 garlic cloves, chopped
3 tablespoons chopped parsley
juice of ½ lemon
½ cup (4 fl oz/125 ml) dry white wine
1 cup (8 fl oz/250 ml) water
salt and pepper
6 slices firm, coarse-textured bread

⚹ Scrub and wash the mussels. Place in a large covered stockpot over moderate heat just until they open; discard any that do not open. Strain mussel liquid.
⚹ Heat oil in a saucepan over low heat. Add garlic and cook until fragrant. Stir in parsley, lemon juice, mussel liquid, wine, mussels and water and cook for 5 minutes. Season with salt and pepper.
⚹ Meanwhile, toast bread in the oven until golden. Place a slice in each soup bowl. Pour soup over and serve.

SERVES 6

Trentino-Alto Adige

MINESTRA D'ORZO
Barley Soup

In the Trentino region barley often replaces beans in soup. It can be cooked with vegetables such as cabbage or peas and is particularly good if a ham bone, boiled pork rind or small pork ribs are added to the stock and removed at the end of cooking.

1 cup (7 oz/220 g) pearl barley
2 tablespoons (1½ oz/40 g) butter
3 oz (90 g) *pancetta* or rindless bacon, chopped
½ onion, chopped
1 celery stalk, chopped
1 shallot, chopped
8 cups (2 qt/2 l) broth (stock)
1 tablespoon chopped parsley

⚹ Soak the barley in cold water to cover for 12 hours. Drain. Melt butter in a large skillet and sauté the bacon, onion, celery and shallot until onion is translucent. Pour in the broth and bring to boil. Add the barley and cook until tender, about 1 hour. Pour the soup into a tureen, sprinkle with parsley and serve.

SERVES 6

VEGETABLE SOUP OF TRIESTE (top) AND BARLEY SOUP (bottom)

TOMATO AND BREAD SOUP

TWICE-COOKED SOUP

Toscana

PAPPA AL POMODORO
Tomato and Bread Soup

The Tuscans do not like to throw bread away. When it is stale they use it in a number of delicious hot and cold dishes, such as this famous "tomato pap," a very tasty thick soup that is simple to make — but the bread and oil must be of the best quality.

1 cup (8 fl oz/250 ml) extra virgin olive oil
3 garlic cloves
½ cup fresh sage leaves
8 oz (250 g) stale, firm, coarse-textured bread
salt and freshly ground pepper
8 cups (2 qt/2 l) light meat broth (stock)
2 lb (1 kg) peeled tomatoes

Heat the oil in a saucepan over moderate heat. Add the garlic and sage leaves and cook until the garlic begins to color.

Meanwhile, slice the bread very thinly. Add the slices to the oil and brown well on both sides, stirring with a wooden spoon. Season with salt and pepper. Bring the broth to boil in a large saucepan.

Put the tomatoes through a food mill directly into the bread mixture or finely chop and cook for a few minutes over high heat, stirring. Pour in the boiling broth, reduce the heat and simmer, covered, for 40 minutes. Taste and add salt if necessary.

Pour the soup into a tureen and serve.

SERVES 6

Toscana

RIBOLLITA
Twice-Cooked Soup

Ribollita literally means "reboiled." This soup is usually made in plentiful quantities and the next day is boiled again for a few minutes, so that it ends up very thick. A little additional oil is drizzled in before serving. Black cabbage has long, very dark leaves. In its absence, Savoy cabbage may be substituted.

1¼ lb (600 g) fresh haricot beans, shelled (or dried haricot beans, soaked overnight)
½ cup (4 fl oz/125 ml) extra virgin olive oil
½ onion, finely chopped
1 carrot, finely chopped
1 celery stalk, finely chopped
2 garlic cloves, finely chopped
3 oz (90 g) *pancetta* or rindless bacon
1 lb (500 g) black or Savoy cabbage, chopped
10 cups (2½ qt/2.5 l) broth (stock)
1 tablespoon fresh thyme
12 thin slices of firm, coarse-textured bread
salt and freshly ground pepper

Simmer the beans in water just to cover over very low heat for 1½ hours. Put a little more than half of them through a sieve, or puree in a food processor.

Heat 2 tablespoons oil in a large saucepan over moderate heat. Add the onion, carrot, celery, garlic and *pancetta* and cook for a few minutes. Add the cabbage and cook, stirring, for a minute or two. Add the broth and thyme and bring to boil, then simmer, covered, over very low heat for 2 hours.

Add the bean puree and the whole beans and simmer, uncovered, for another 10 minutes. Pour the soup over the bread slices in a flameproof casserole and set aside, covered, in a cool place.

The next day, bring the soup to boil and simmer for 2 minutes. Pour into soup bowls. Add the rest of the oil, and salt and pepper to taste. Serve hot.

SERVES 6

Marche

ZUPPA DI CIPOLLE
Onion Soup

The people of the Marches are accustomed to eating very rich dishes. These are often based on homemade pasta, or on soups made with chickpeas or dried beans and flavored with pork rind, ham bones, guanciale (bacon made from pig's cheek) or cured ham.

ONION SOUP (left) AND FENNEL SOUP (right)

7 oz (220 g) chickpeas
2 lb (1 kg) onions, sliced
1 celery stalk, chopped
a handful of fresh basil leaves, chopped
2 oz (60 g) unsmoked bacon
¼ cup (2 fl oz/60 ml) extra virgin olive oil
2 small pork ribs
10 oz (315 g) ripe tomatoes, put through a food mill
8 cups (2 qt/2 l) water
salt and freshly ground pepper
6 slices firm, coarse-textured bread
additional chopped fresh basil for garnish

Soak the chickpeas in water to cover for 12 hours; drain. Fry the onion, celery and basil gently with the bacon and oil in a large saucepan until the onion is translucent.

Add the pork ribs, tomato puree, water and chickpeas and simmer for 2 hours. Remove the pork ribs and season the soup with salt and pepper.

Toast the bread slices in the oven and place in the bottom of a soup tureen. Pour the soup over them, sprinkle with chopped basil and serve.

SERVES 6

Sardegna

MINESTRA CON I FINOCCHI
Fennel Soup

Sardinia is predominantly shepherding country. In its high, bleak mountains many local products are used in cooking, particularly wild greens and herbs. This soup is traditionally made with the small wild fennel that grows in abundance everywhere, but cultivated fennel can very well be used as a substitute.

4 fennel bulbs
1 tablespoon extra virgin olive oil
6 cups (1½ qt/1.5 l) broth (stock)
salt and freshly ground pepper
1 tablespoon chopped parsley

Clean the fennel bulbs and discard the stalks and tough outer layers. Slice the bulbs thinly, then chop finely. Place in a saucepan with the oil and cook over low heat for 10 minutes. Pour in the broth, season with salt and pepper, and bring to simmer.

Simmer for 30 minutes then pour the soup into a tureen, sprinkle with chopped parsley and serve.

SERVES 6

CHICKPEA SOUP

"COOKED WATER" SOUP

Lazio

MINESTRA DI CECI

Chickpea Soup

Dried legumes such as chickpeas, beans and lentils are often the basis of tasty soups, either thick or thin, particularly in winter when fresh vegetables are more difficult to come by.

In soups, short pasta is used; it may be thick or thin, but it always has a hole in the middle.

10 oz (310 g) dried chickpeas
8 cups (2 qt/2 l) broth (stock)
1 fresh rosemary sprig
6 tablespoons extra virgin olive oil
2 garlic cloves, chopped
1 can (8 oz/250 g) peeled tomatoes
1 cup (4 oz/125 g) *cannolicchi* pasta
salt and freshly ground pepper

Wash the chickpeas well and soak them in cold water to cover for 12 hours. Drain chickpeas and place in a saucepan with the broth and rosemary. Bring slowly to boil, then simmer for 2 hours.

Put half the chickpeas through a sieve with their cooking liquid or puree in a food processor. Heat the oil in a saucepan over moderate heat. Add the garlic and fry gently until the garlic colors. Add the tomatoes and cook for about 10 minutes to blend the flavors. Add the whole and pureed chickpeas with broth and bring to boil, then immediately add the pasta and cook until *al dente*. Taste for salt and pepper and serve immediately. Garnish with rosemary.

SERVES 6

Toscana

ACQUACOTTA

"Cooked Water" Soup

This is a soup from the hunting area around Grosseto. The region is famous for its Festival of the Wild Boar and for its "cowboys" — cowherds on horseback who are actually said to have defeated Buffalo Bill in a rodeo.

¼ cup (2 fl oz/60 ml) extra virgin olive oil
1 lb (500 g) onions, sliced
2 celery stalks, finely chopped
2 carrots, finely chopped

1 lb (500 g) plum (egg) tomatoes
12 very thin slices of firm, coarse-textured bread
6 cups (1½ qt/1.5 l) water
3 eggs
salt and freshly ground pepper

Heat the oil in a large saucepan and sauté the onions over moderate heat until translucent. Add celery and carrots. Put tomatoes through a food mill held directly over the saucepan. Simmer the mixture over low heat for about 30 minutes.

Meanwhile, toast the slices of bread in a 375°F (190°C) oven. Place them on the bottom of a soup tureen. Add the water to the tomato mixture and simmer for 5 minutes.

Beat the eggs in a bowl, add salt and pepper and pour over the bread slices. Add the soup and let stand for 5 minutes to allow the bread to absorb the flavors. Serve hot sprinkled with chopped parsley, if desired.

SERVES 6

Lombardia

ZUPPA PAVESE

Pavia Soup

Pavia is a small but very old city to the south of Milan, and this soup is its specialty. The type of broth used is very important to the success of the dish: it must be clear broth made from fairly lean meat or from chicken, which can then be used to make a salad.

3 tablespoons (2 oz/60 g) butter
6 slices firm, coarse-textured bread
6 cups (1½ qt/1.5 l) meat or chicken broth (stock)
salt
6 eggs
freshly ground pepper
6 tablespoons freshly grated Parmesan cheese

Melt the butter in a saucepan and fry the bread slices on both sides until golden brown. Divide among 6 soup bowls. Place bowls in an oven which has been preheated to 350°F (180°C) and turned off.

Meanwhile, bring broth to boil, adding salt if necessary. Break an egg onto each slice of bread, pour the boiling broth over it and add pepper to taste. Sprinkle with Parmesan. Garnish with chopped parsley and a little grated nutmeg if desired and serve.

SERVES 6

LETTUCE IN BROTH

Liguria

LATTUGHE IN BRODO
Lettuce in Broth

Stuffed vegetables are a source of pride in the cooking of Liguria. Zucchini (courgettes), artichokes, tomatoes, leaves of salad greens, zucchini flowers, potatoes and mushroom caps are filled with a wide variety of tasty stuffings, always with an abundance of herbs. Porcini (boletus) mushrooms, dried at home by the country women who gather them during the autumn, are often used in the fillings.

6 small-leaf lettuces
1 oz (30 g) dried *porcini* mushrooms or champignons
2 tablespoons fresh marjoram leaves
2 garlic cloves
1 cup coarse stale breadcrumbs, soaked in milk and
    squeezed dry
2 eggs
¼ cup (1 oz/30 g) freshly grated Parmesan cheese
salt and freshly ground pepper
1 egg white, beaten
6 tablespoons extra virgin olive oil
6 cups (1½ qt/1.5 l) light meat broth (stock)
6 slices firm, coarse-textured bread

☙ Remove the outside leaves of the lettuces and extract the hearts, leaving heads intact. Soak the mushrooms in lukewarm water to cover for 30 minutes. Drain the mushrooms and chop together with 2 lettuce hearts, the marjoram, garlic and breadcrumbs. Mix in 2 eggs, Parmesan, salt and pepper.
☙ Bring a saucepan of water to boil, drop in the lettuces and blanch for a few seconds. Drain and open them carefully. Fill with the prepared stuffing and reclose them, brushing them with the beaten egg white to hold them together so that the filling cannot come out.
☙ Pour 1 tablespoon oil and ¼ cup (4 fl oz/60 ml) broth into a saucepan, add the lettuces and cook, covered, for a few minutes over low heat, turning occasionally.
☙ Bring the rest of the broth to boil.
☙ Brush the slices of bread with the remaining oil and toast in a preheated 350°F (180°C) oven, until golden brown. Place one slice in the bottom of each soup bowl, top with lettuce, pour the boiling broth over and serve.

SERVES 6

Abruzzi and Molise

ZUPPA DI SCAROLA
Escarole Soup

Abruzzi is a mountainous area particularly rich in certain vegetables such as cardoons and fennel, salad greens like endive and chicory, and wild herbs such as dandelion and nettles, which are gathered in the fields during the spring and made into tasty soups.

8 cups (2 qt/2 l) chicken broth (stock)
1 carrot, diced
1 celery stalk, diced
1 onion, sliced
2 oz (60 g) pork fat, finely chopped
¼ cup (2 fl oz/60 ml) extra virgin olive oil
4 garlic cloves, finely chopped
1 lb (500 g) escarole (curly endive), shredded
salt and freshly ground pepper
3 eggs, well beaten
1 tablespoon chopped parsley
¾ cup (3 oz/90 g) grated pecorino or Parmesan cheese

☙ Bring the broth to boil. Add the carrot, celery and onion and simmer over low heat for 1 hour.
☙ Combine the pork fat, oil and garlic in a saucepan and fry gently until the garlic begins to color. Add the escarole and cook for 10 minutes, stirring frequently. Add salt and pepper. Transfer escarole mixture to the pot of broth and simmer for 10 minutes. Remove from heat, stir in the eggs and mix well. Serve sprinkled with parsley and grated cheese.

SERVES 6

ESCAROLE SOUP (top) AND MUSHROOM SOUP (bottom)

SWEET AND SOUR CREAM SOUP SERVED WITH *GRISSINI* (BREADSTICKS)

Liguria

MINESTRA AI FUNGHI
Mushroom Soup

In the woods of Liguria in autumn it is easy to find porcini *(boletus) or* ovoli *mushrooms, both of which are used in many Ligurian dishes. If* porcini *mushrooms are unavailable, cultivated white mushrooms or champignons may be substituted. Instead of parsley you can use marjoram or thyme, which give a stronger flavor.*

The taglierini *may be made at home or bought ready-made. They are very thin strips of egg pasta like fine* tagliatelle, *and are used mostly in broth.*

7 oz (220 g) *porcini* or *ovoli* mushrooms or champignons
6 cups (1½ qt/1.5 l) chicken broth (stock)
7 oz (220 g) dried *taglierini* (fine noodles)
2 tablespoons chopped parsley
salt and freshly ground pepper

Clean the mushrooms with a cloth to rid them of dirt, but do not wash them. Cut into julienne strips.
Bring broth to boil and add mushrooms. As soon as it returns to boil, add noodles and cook just until pasta is *al dente*. Sprinkle with parsley, add salt and pepper, and serve.

SERVES 6

Toscana

GINESTRATA
Sweet and Sour Cream Soup

This is a delicate soup typical of the Chianti area. Like all the sweet and sour dishes found in Italian cooking, it is a very old recipe. The soup has a creamy consistency and is served in small quantities, because it is very filling.

pinch of ground cinnamon
pinch of grated nutmeg
1 tablespoon sugar
6 egg yolks
pinch of salt
6 cups (1½ qt/1.5 l) chicken broth (stock)
½ cup (4 fl oz/125 ml) *vin santo* or sweet white wine
3 tablespoons (2 oz/60 g) butter

Mix together the cinnamon, nutmeg and sugar. Beat the eggs in a saucepan. Add the salt, broth and *vin santo*. Stir in the butter; continue stirring over moderate heat until the soup thickens. *Do not boil* or eggs will curdle.
Pour soup into cups, sprinkle with the spice mixture and serve.

SERVES 6

VEGETABLE SOUP WITH RICE (left) AND BLACK RISOTTO (recipe page 83)

Lombardia

MINESTRONE DI RISO
Vegetable Soup with Rice

In Lombardy a thick minestrone with rice is most often eaten in summer, served cold. The rice is only minimally cooked, as it continues to cook when poured into the soup bowls. If the soup is to be served hot, the rice is cooked for 16 minutes and the minestrone is then served immediately.

1 cup (6 oz/185 g) dried *borlotti* (red) beans
2 oz (60 g) *pancetta* or rindless bacon, finely chopped
1 medium-size onion, finely chopped
2 tablespoons (1½ oz/40 g) butter
2 celery stalks, diced
2 medium-size carrots, diced
2 zucchini (courgettes), diced
2 medium-size boiling potatoes, diced
salt and freshly ground pepper
4 large ripe tomatoes, peeled and chopped
1 tablespoon tomato paste (puree)
8 cups (2 qt/2 l) meat broth (stock)
1 cup green beans, cut into short lengths
½ cup (3 oz/90 g) Arborio (short grain) rice
2 tablespoons chopped parsley
6 tablespoons freshly grated Parmesan cheese

🍲 Soak *borlotti* beans overnight in cold water to cover; drain. Combine bacon, onion and butter in a large saucepan and cook over medium heat until golden, stirring frequently.
🍲 Add the celery, carrots, zucchini, red beans and potatoes, season with salt and pepper and cook, stirring, for 5 minutes. Add tomatoes, tomato paste, broth and green beans and bring to boil. Lower heat and simmer, covered, for 2 hours.
🍲 Add rice and cook uncovered over high heat for 5 minutes.
🍲 Pour soup into bowls and stir 1 tablespoon Parmesan into each. Cool completely before serving.

SERVES 6

Toscana

CACIUCCO ALLA LIVORNESE
Livorno Fish Stew

Livorno, or Leghorn, is a city by the sea, famous for its beautiful seventeenth-century port, its naval academy, and its fish soup called caciucco, *of which crustaceans and mollusks are essential ingredients.*

½ cup (4 fl oz/125 ml) extra virgin olive oil
1 medium-size onion, finely chopped
1 medium-size carrot, finely chopped
1 celery stalk, finely chopped
½ cup parsley leaves, chopped
a small piece of hot red chili pepper, minced
1 small lobster, in shell
1 lb (500 g) large shrimp (king prawns), in shell
1 medium cuttlefish or squid, cleaned and sliced into rings
10 oz (315 g) octopus, cut into small pieces
1 cup (8 fl oz/250 ml) dry white wine
½ cup (4 fl oz/125 ml) hot water
10 oz (300 g) plum (egg) tomatoes, put through a food mill
salt
1 lb (500 g) fresh mussels
1 lb (500 g) fresh clams
2 red mullet or small red snapper, filleted and cut into
   pieces
1¼ lb (625 g) fillets of white-fleshed fish (scorpionfish or
   bream), cut into pieces
10 oz (315 g) dogfish or shark, cut into pieces
8 thin slices of firm, coarse-textured bread
2 garlic cloves, halved and crushed

🍲 Heat the oil in a large saucepan over moderate heat. Add the onion, carrot, celery, parsley and chili pepper and cook until onion begins to color. Add the lobster, shrimp, squid and octopus and mix well. Cook gently for 10 minutes. Pour in the wine and hot water.
🍲 Remove the lobster and shrimp, add the tomatoes and simmer for 10 minutes. Season with salt. Remove all the seafood and set aside.
🍲 Steam the mussels and clams in another large saucepan of water over moderate heat just until open. Strain the cooking liquid and add it to the soup. Add all the remaining fish and simmer until opaque. Return the reserved seafood to the stew.
🍲 Meanwhile, toast the bread slices and rub with the garlic. Place in the bottom of a soup tureen. Pour in the fish stew and serve very hot.

SERVES 8

RICE WITH PEAS

RISI E BISI
Rice with Peas

This is a fairly liquid rice dish, with the grains well separated. It has the consistency of a thick soup, not of a risotto.

3 tablespoons (2 oz/60 g) butter
½ onion, chopped
2 oz (60 g) *pancetta* or rindless bacon, chopped
4 cups (1 qt/1 l) meat broth (stock)
10 oz (315 g) shelled peas
1⅔ cups (10 oz/315 g) Arborio rice
salt and freshly ground pepper
½ cup (2 oz/60 g) freshly grated Parmesan cheese
1 tablespoon chopped parsley

Melt the butter in a large skillet. Add onion and *pancetta* and cook until onion is translucent.

Meanwhile, bring the broth to boil in a saucepan. Add the peas and rice to the bacon mixture and pour half the broth over. Gradually add almost all of the boiling broth and cook for 15 minutes.

Season with salt and pepper, stir in the Parmesan and enough additional broth so that the mixture is fairly liquid. Sprinkle with parsley and let rice rest for a couple of minutes away from the heat before serving.

SERVES 6

RISOTTO AI FINOCCHI
Rice with Fennel

In this region rice is served in a thousand ways, in combination with every imaginable vegetable and with meat, fish, shellfish and sausages. It was once grown in the Po Delta and in the area around Verona.

3 fennel bulbs, thinly sliced
6 oz (185 g) butter
salt
1 small onion, chopped
2 cups (13 oz/410 g) Arborio rice
½ cup (4 fl oz/125 ml) dry white wine
4 cups (1 qt/1 l) chicken broth (stock)
1 cup (4 oz/125 g) freshly grated Parmesan cheese
7 sprigs fennel greens, chopped
freshly ground pepper

Place fennel in a saucepan with 1 tablespoon butter. Add salt, cover and cook for about 30 minutes over very low heat. Add another tablespoon butter.

Sauté the onion in the remaining butter until translucent. Add the rice and stir for a couple of minutes over low heat.

Add half the wine and cook over high heat, stirring constantly and adding the rest of the wine and the broth. The rice should always be covered by a "veil" of broth.

After 14 minutes, remove rice from heat and add the Parmesan, sliced fennel, chopped fennel greens, salt and pepper. Cover and let rest for 2 minutes before serving.

SERVES 6

RICE WITH FENNEL

Veneto

RISOTTO NERO
Black Risotto

This rice dish has become a classic worldwide, both for its unusual black color and for its very delicate taste. Cuttlefish ink is now also used to color pasta.

10 oz (315 g) cuttlefish or whole squid
½ onion, chopped
1 garlic clove, chopped
3 tablespoons extra virgin olive oil
salt and freshly ground pepper
2 cups (13 oz/410 g) Arborio rice
4 cups (1 qt/1 l) boiling fish broth (stock)
3 tablespoons (2 oz/60 g) butter
1 tablespoon chopped parsley

❧ Clean the cuttlefish by removing eyes, beak and transparent quill. Remove and reserve ink sac. Place cuttlefish in a bowl of cold water and soak for 30 minutes. Peel off as much skin as possible, cut the cuttlefish into strips and wash in plenty of cold water.
❧ Sauté onion and garlic in the oil until translucent. Add the cuttlefish and cook over moderate heat until golden, stirring from time to time. Add salt and pepper, reduce heat, cover and cook for 30 minutes.
❧ Add the rice and stir briefly over high heat to blend flavors. Pour in several ladlefuls of boiling broth, the ink from the cuttlefish sac, and then little by little the rest of the boiling broth. Reduce heat to low and cook for about 15 minutes, stirring constantly.
❧ Stir in the butter and parsley, remove from heat and let rice rest for a couple of minutes, covered. Stir once more and serve.

SERVES 4–6 *Photograph page 80*

Lazio

POMODORI RIPIENI DI RISO
Rice-stuffed Tomatoes

Tomatoes filled with rice are one of the most popular summer dishes in Rome. They may be eaten hot, but they are often also served cold. The important thing is to use tomatoes that are very ripe and not watery, and to use lots of herbs to flavor them. In winter they may be flavored with plenty of dried oregano.

6 good-sized ripe tomatoes
½ cup (3 oz/90 g) Arborio rice
1 tablespoon chopped fresh oregano
1 tablespoon chopped fresh marjoram
1 tablespoon chopped fresh mint
1 tablespoon chopped parsley
¼ cup (2 fl oz/60 ml) extra virgin olive oil
salt and freshly ground pepper

❧ Cut a slice from the top of each tomato to make a cap. Carefully hollow out the tomato and sieve the flesh into a bowl. Add the rice, herbs, 3 tablespoons oil, salt and pepper and let stand for about 30 minutes to blend the flavors.
❧ Meanwhile, sprinkle the insides of the tomatoes with salt and turn them upside down to drain out their moisture.
❧ Preheat oven to 350°F (180°C). Drain the rice, reserving

RICE-STUFFED TOMATOES

the tomato liquid. Fill the tomatoes with the rice and pour a little tomato puree on top of each. Replace the caps on the tomatoes and arrange in a baking dish that has been brushed with the remaining oil. Bake for 1 hour or until the rice is tender and dry, gradually adding the reserved tomato liquid as it is absorbed.

SERVES 6

Lombardia

RISO AL BURRO E SALVIA
Rice with Butter and Sage Leaves

This is a very simple way of serving rice; it is also suitable for tagliatelle or ravioli. The best rice to use is the large-grained Arborio, which is grown in Lombardy and Piedmont, particularly in the area around Vercelli.

3 cups (1¼ lb/625 g) Arborio rice
6 tablespoons freshly grated Parmesan cheese
5 oz (155 g) butter
18 fresh sage leaves
salt

❧ Bring about 3 quarts (3 liters) salted water to boil in a large saucepan. Add rice and boil over high heat for 16 minutes. Drain the rice, turn it onto a serving dish and sprinkle with cheese.
❧ When rice is almost ready, heat butter with sage leaves in a skillet until butter turns chestnut brown. Pour over the rice and serve.

SERVES 6

RICE WITH BUTTER AND SAGE LEAVES

Lombardia

RISOTTO AL SALTO
Crisp Rice Cake

When Milanese cooks have some risotto left over, they sauté it in a thin layer until it is golden and very crisp. Sautéed rice is the specialty generally served at the Savini or the Biffi Restaurant after an opera performance at La Scala.

3 oz (90 g) butter
3 tablespoons (2 oz/60 g) beef marrow
½ onion, chopped
1⅔ cups (10 oz/315 g) Arborio rice
½ cup (4 fl oz/125 ml) dry white wine
¼ teaspoon saffron
about 4 cups (1 qt/1 l) broth (stock)
salt and freshly ground pepper
6 tablespoons freshly grated Parmesan cheese

Melt 3 tablespoons of the butter with the marrow in a large skillet. Add onion and sauté until brown. Add rice and cook for a few minutes to let it absorb flavor. Pour in the wine and cook until evaporated.

Dissolve saffron in a tablespoon of broth and add to rice; add remaining broth a little at a time. Season with salt and pepper to taste. Cook for 15 minutes, stirring constantly with a wooden spoon; at the end of this time the rice should be fairly dry.

Spread rice on a board and let stand until completely cooled. Melt half the remaining butter in a nonstick skillet. Cover the bottom of the skillet with a layer of rice ¼ in (0.5 cm) thick, pressing down lightly. Brown over low heat for 20 minutes.

Turn rice cake out onto a flat saucepan lid for a moment. Add remaining butter to the skillet. Slide rice back into the pan and brown the other side, shaking skillet from time to time to prevent sticking.

Place rice cake on a serving plate and sprinkle with Parmesan. Serve at once.

SERVES 4

CRISP RICE CAKE

Lombardia

RISOTTO ALLO ZAFFERANO
Saffron Rice

The best-flavored saffron is produced in the Abruzzi near the town of l'Aquila; in Sardinia; and in Kashmir. The most highly prized is in thread form — the intact pistils of the crocus from which saffron is harvested — but it is more commonly found powdered.

Rice with saffron is also known as risotto alla milanese *because it is a traditional specialty of Milan.*

3 oz (90 g) unsalted butter
½ cup (4 oz/125 g) beef marrow
1 small onion, finely chopped
2 cups (13 oz/410 g) Arborio rice
½ cup (4 fl oz/125 ml) dry white wine
6 cups (1½ qt/1.5 l) meat broth (stock), boiling
¼ teaspoon saffron
1 cup (4 oz/125 g) freshly grated Parmesan cheese
salt and freshly ground pepper

Melt half the butter and the marrow in a deep skillet over moderate heat. Add onion and sauté until translucent.

Add rice and stir for 2 minutes. Pour in wine and cook until it evaporates. Add boiling broth ½ cup at a time, stirring constantly until each addition is absorbed before adding the next. The rice should always be covered by a "veil" of broth.

Add saffron, dissolved in a little broth. When rice is cooked to porridge consistency — after about 15 minutes — add Parmesan cheese, remaining butter, and salt and pepper to taste.

Cover and let risotto rest for a few minutes before serving.

SERVES 6

Friuli-Venezia Giulia

POLENTA E SALSICCIA
Polenta and Sausages

Polenta, which in this region is finely ground, is the basis of many dishes. It is toasted under the broiler (grill), served in slices with mountain cheese, or eaten with stewed pork, salami slices or oven-baked sausages.

6 cups (1½ qt/1.5 l) water
salt
2⅔ cups (13 oz/410 g) fine cornmeal
1½ lb (750 g) Italian sausages
3 tablespoons (2 oz/60 g) butter
1 tablespoon red wine vinegar

Bring water to boil in a large saucepan with a generous pinch of salt. Sprinkle in cornmeal, stirring constantly with a wooden spoon. Cook for 40 minutes, stirring frequently.

Prick the sausages with a fork. Melt butter in a cast iron skillet. Add sausages and fry slowly for 10 minutes, turning from time to time. When they are cooked, drizzle vinegar over them and let it evaporate.

Spoon polenta onto a serving plate. Top with sausages and spoon melted sausage fat over it. Serve at once.

SERVES 6

SAFFRON RICE (top left) AND POLENTA AND SAUSAGES (bottom)

Toscana

RISO ALLA TOSCANA
Tuscan Rice

Tuscany is one of the richest vegetable growing areas of Italy. For this reason, vegetables are featured in many dishes both as part of the ingredients and as garnishes.

3 cups (1¼ lb/625 g) Arborio rice
1 lb (500 g) zucchini, chopped
½ lb (50 g) zucchini flowers, pistils removed
4 oz (125 g) butter, melted
2 tablespoons chopped parsley

Cook the rice in plenty of boiling salted water until *al dente*; drain.

Meanwhile, sauté zucchini and half the flowers in 2 oz butter over high heat for 2 minutes. Add to rice with the remaining butter and the parsley.

Place the rice in a mold just large enough to hold it. Press down lightly, then turn out onto a serving plate and garnish with the remaining flowers.

SERVES 6   *Photograph page 4*

POLENTA PIE

Val d'Aosta

POLENTA CONCIA
Polenta with Cheese

Polenta is made with cornmeal, which in Piedmont and Lombardy is ground rather coarsely and in the Veneto more finely. It is found in all the regions of northern Italy and was once the staple dish of the poor.

When cooked it may be turned into a bowl rinsed with cold water and unmolded onto a plate. Leftovers are cut into slices and may be fried in oil or butter until crisp.

6⅓ cups (1⅔ qt/1.6 l) water
salt
2⅔ cups (14 oz/440 g) coarse cornmeal
7 oz (220 g) fontina or Gruyère cheese, thinly sliced
5 oz (155 g) butter

Bring water to boil, add salt and sprinkle in cornmeal, stirring constantly. Cook over low heat for 40 minutes; polenta is cooked when it begins to leave the sides of the saucepan. Add cheese and cook, stirring constantly, for 5 minutes.

Heat the butter until it turns chestnut brown.

Turn the polenta out onto a serving dish, pour the butter over it and serve.

SERVES 6

Veneto

POLENTA E LATTE
Polenta and Milk

One of the simplest, tastiest and most nourishing ways of eating polenta is with milk. This is one of the first foods given to babies as soon as they have been weaned. If sugar is sprinkled on the polenta, it can become an excellent dessert.

6 cups (1½ qt/1.5 l) water
pinch of salt
3¼ cups (13 oz/410 g) cornmeal
4 cups (1 qt/1 l) milk, room temperature

Bring the water to boil with salt in a large saucepan. Gradually sprinkle in cornmeal and cook until thick, about 40 minutes, stirring frequently. The polenta is cooked when it comes away easily from the sides of the saucepan.

Spoon the polenta into bowls, pour the milk over it and serve at once.

SERVES 6

Veneto

POLENTA PASTICCIATA
Polenta Pie

Corn was apparently shipped to Venice following the return of local merchants from America, and it at once became very popular.

POLENTA WITH CHEESE

BUCKWHEAT POLENTA (top) AND POLENTA AND MILK (bottom)

In the form of polenta it makes the accompaniment for fegato alla veneziana, *the famous dish of liver and onions; for the small birds the Italians use in their cooking; and for eel — all very popular foods in this region.*

6 cups (1½ qt/1.5 l) water
salt
3¼ cups (13 oz/410 g) cornmeal
¼ cup (2 fl oz/60 ml) extra virgin olive oil
½ onion, chopped
1 celery stalk, chopped
1 carrot, chopped
2 to 3 fresh sage leaves, chopped
1 teaspoon chopped fresh rosemary
10 oz (315 g) lean beef
1 can (1 lb/500 g) peeled tomatoes
freshly ground pepper
5½ oz (165 g) butter
6 tablespoons all purpose (plain) flour
4 cups (1 qt/1 l) milk
pinch of grated nutmeg
1 cup (4 oz/125 g) freshly grated Parmesan cheese

Bring the water to boil with salt in a large saucepan. Gradually stir in the cornmeal, and cook until thick, about 40 minutes, stirring frequently. The polenta is cooked when it comes away easily from the sides of the saucepan. Spread polenta ⅜ in (1 cm) thick on a wet board or table. Smooth the surface and let cool.

Heat oil in a large, deep skillet. Add onion, celery, carrot, sage and rosemary and fry gently until onion is translucent. Add the beef and brown well over moderate heat for about 20 minutes. Remove from heat, chop meat finely and return to heat. Add the tomatoes and salt and pepper, cover and cook slowly for 30 minutes.

Preheat oven to 350°F (180°C). Use the rim of a glass to cut the polenta into circles. Arrange a layer of polenta in a buttered 9-in (23-cm) baking dish.

Melt 4 oz (125 g) of the butter in a saucepan over low heat. Stir in flour; cook, stirring, for 2 minutes. Whisk in milk and cook, whisking constantly, until sauce boils and thickens. Season with salt, pepper and nutmeg. Spoon half the sauce over polenta circles. Spread with half the tomato sauce and dot with half the remaining butter. Repeat layers with the remaining ingredients.

Sprinkle with Parmesan and bake until bubbly, about 20 minutes. Let pie rest 5 minutes, then serve.

SERVES 6

Trentino-Alto Adige

POLENTA DI GRANO SARACENO

Buckwheat Polenta

Buckwheat polenta makes a nourishing substitute for cornmeal polenta. It is best made in winter, when the cabbages have been through frost and are tastier and much more tender. Turnip slices may be used instead of cabbage.

7 oz (220 g) *pancetta* or rindless bacon, diced
6 cups (1½ qt/1.5 l) water
salt
3¼ cups (13 oz/410 g) buckwheat flour
1 lb (500 g) cabbage
3 oz (90 g) butter
7 oz (220 g) fontina or Gruyère cheese, thinly sliced

Fry the bacon in a dry cast iron frying pan until crisp.

Bring the water to boil with salt. Sprinkle the flour over the surface of the water, stirring constantly. Continue cooking until polenta begins to come away from the sides of the saucepan. Meanwhile, boil the cabbage in another saucepan until tender. Drain and shred it. Add the bacon, butter, cheese and cabbage to the polenta and continue stirring for a couple of minutes. Serve hot.

SERVES 6

Liguria

TORTA DI VERDURA
Vegetable Tart

Liguria is famous for its vegetables and for the many wild herbs that are used in its stuffings, sauces and soups. The oil used is almost always extra virgin olive oil, which is produced in particular in the area around Imperia.

2 cups (8 oz/250 g) all purpose (plain) flour
½ cup (4 fl oz/125 ml) extra virgin olive oil
3 eggs
salt
a handful (¼ cup) dried *porcini* mushrooms or champignons
1 onion, chopped
6 anchovy fillets in oil
1 lb (500 g) beet greens or spinach leaves, shredded
2 tablespoons chopped fresh marjoram
2 tablespoons water
freshly ground pepper
3 oz (90 g) ricotta

Heap flour in a mound on a board and make a well in the center. Add ¼ cup (2 fl oz/60 ml) oil, 1 egg and a pinch of salt to the well, then work in enough water to make a soft dough. Knead until smooth and elastic. Cover with a cloth and let rest.

Soak mushrooms in lukewarm water for about 30 minutes; drain and chop coarsely.

Heat remaining oil in a saucepan and sauté onion over low heat until translucent. Add anchovies, beet greens, marjoram, drained mushrooms and 2 tablespoons water. Season with salt and pepper, cover and simmer for 10 minutes.

Remove from heat. Beat remaining 2 eggs with ricotta, add to saucepan and mix well. Let filling cool.

Roll out dough and use it to line a buttered 10-in (25-cm) tart pan. Spread with prepared filling. Bake the tart in a preheated 350°F (180°C) oven for about 40 minutes. Serve hot.

SERVES 4–6

VEGETABLE TART

Campania

PIZZA MARGHERITA
Traditional Pizza

Pizza dough forms a base for a great variety of toppings, from the simplest — such as garlic and oregano — to seafood, different cheeses or vegetables. The margherita *is perhaps the most traditional version.*

1 oz (30 g) fresh yeast or 1 envelope dry yeast
4 cups (1 lb/500 g) all purpose (plain) flour
1 lb (500 g) plum (egg) tomatoes, peeled and cut into thin
    wedges
10 oz (315 g) mozzarella, sliced
1 tablespoon chopped fresh oregano or 1½ teaspoons dried
    oregano
¼ cup (2 fl oz/60 ml) extra virgin olive oil

Dissolve the yeast in ½ cup (4 fl oz/125 ml) warm water. Heap the flour in a mound on a board, make a well in the center and pour in the dissolved yeast. Add enough extra water to form a soft dough. Knead until smooth and elastic. Cover with a towel and let rise in a large bowl until doubled in volume.

TRADITIONAL PIZZA

6 cups (1½ qt/1.5 l) milk
salt
3 scant cups (13 oz/410 g) fine semolina
3 eggs
freshly ground pepper
¾ cup (3 oz/90 g) freshly grated Parmesan cheese
¼ cup (2 fl oz/60 ml) extra virgin olive oil
1 can (1 lb/500 g) peeled plum (egg) tomatoes, drained
10 oz (315 g) mozzarella, thinly sliced
2 tablespoons fine dry breadcrumbs
1 tablespoon chopped fresh oregano or 2 teaspoons dried
  oregano

⁂ Bring the milk to boil with a little salt. Sprinkle the semolina over the surface, stirring all the time, and cook for 20 minutes. Let cool to lukewarm. Beat the eggs with a little salt and pepper. Add to semolina with the grated cheese and mix well.

⁂ Coat a large round pizza tray with some of the oil. Turn the semolina mixture into it and cover with the drained tomatoes. Arrange the mozzarella slices on top and dust with breadcrumbs and oregano. Sprinkle with the remaining oil.

⁂ Preheat oven to 400°F (200°C). Bake pizza for 20 minutes. Transfer it to a napkin-lined plate and serve. Garnish with parsley if desired.

SERVES 6–8

TOMATO PIZZA

⁂ Press and stretch dough out in a circle ⅜ in (1 cm) thick on a floured board with the fingertips; do not use a rolling pin.

⁂ Flour a baking sheet and place the dough onto it. Cover the pizza base with the mozzarella slices, top with tomato, sprinkle with oregano and drizzle the oil over. Bake in a 450°F (230°C) oven until the crust is lightly browned. Serve hot.

SERVES 4–6

Emilia-Romagna

GNOCCATA AL POMODORO

Tomato Pizza

This Romagna version of Neapolitan pizza has become very popular. It is a modern dish made possible by the fact that mozzarella, which is only produced in the South, is now distributed all over Italy.

Parma is now a major producer of the plum (egg) tomatoes that are canned and sold all over the world.

POTATO PIE

VEGETABLE PIE

Puglia

TORTA TARANTINA
Potato Pie

In this potato pie, which resembles pizza, mozzarella cheese and anchovies are used for added flavor. It is very similar to the potato "gâteau" (gattò di patate) prepared in middle-class Neapolitan kitchens; this, however, is filled with mozzarella and ham.

2 lb (1 kg) baking potatoes
1 can (1 lb/500 g) peeled tomatoes, chopped
salt
¼ cup (2 fl oz/60 ml) extra virgin olive oil
freshly ground pepper
10 oz (315 g) mozzarella, sliced
8 anchovy fillets in oil, chopped
1 teaspoon dried oregano

Boil the potatoes in their skins in salted water until tender. Place the tomatoes in a colander and sprinkle heavily with salt. Allow to drain for 10 to 15 minutes to rid them of as much moisture as possible.

Peel the potatoes and force through a sieve. Mix in half the oil and salt and pepper to taste.

Oil a round pizza tray and spread the potato mixture over it. Arrange the mozzarella slices on the potato layer and scatter the anchovies on top.

Preheat oven to 400°F (200°C). Arrange the tomato over the potatoes, sprinkle with the oregano and drizzle the rest of the oil over. Bake for 20 minutes. Serve hot sprinkled with chopped parsley if desired.

SERVES 4–6

Emilia-Romagna

ERBAZZONE
Vegetable Pie

In Emilia-Romagna pasta is often replaced by pies made with vegetable fillings, or by a very thin, soft type of flat bread called piadina, *which is filled with slices of prosciutto, ricotta or spinach sautéed with garlic. These pies are excellent for picnics.*

2½ cups (10 oz/315 g) all purpose (plain) flour
3 tablespoons (2 oz/60 g) lard or margarine
2 lb (1 kg) beet greens or spinach leaves
1 large onion, finely chopped
7 oz (220 g) *pancetta* or rindless bacon, finely chopped
¾ cup (3 oz/90 g) freshly grated Parmesan cheese
3 oz (90 g) prosciutto, chopped

Heap the flour on a board and make a well in the center. Add the lard and enough lukewarm water to make a soft dough. Knead until smooth and elastic. Wrap in a sheet of plastic and let dough rest in a cool place until you are ready to use it.

Boil the beet in a large pot of salted water until wilted. Drain and squeeze dry; chop coarsely.

Fry onion and *pancetta* together gently until the onion is golden. Add the beet greens and cook, stirring, for a few minutes. Remove from heat, add the cheese and mix well.

Roll out ⅔ of the pastry to line a buttered 9-in (23-cm) pie dish. Add filling and cover with the prosciutto.

Roll the remaining pastry into a circle and use it to cover the pie, crimping the edges. Prick with a fork to allow steam to escape.

Preheat oven to 350°F (180°C). Bake the pie until golden brown, about 40 minutes. Let cool briefly before serving. Garnish with parsley.

SERVES 4–6

Umbria

SPAGHETTI ALLA PASTA DI OLIVE
Spaghetti with Olive Paste

Produced in Umbria and Liguria and sold in jars, olive paste is mostly used to spread on bread croutons, but it is also delicious as a dressing for pasta or to add flavor to meat or fish.

3 garlic cloves, chopped
½ cup (4 fl oz/125 ml) extra virgin olive oil
3 oz (90 g) black olives, pitted and minced
2 anchovies
salt and freshly ground pepper
1¼ lb (600 g) spaghetti
1 small black truffle, thinly sliced, optional

SPAGHETTI WITH OLIVE PASTE (left) AND SPAGHETTI WITH CLAM SAUCE

Fry the garlic gently in a small saucepan with half the oil. Pound the olives to a paste in a mortar with the anchovies and the rest of the oil, or grind in a blender or food processor. Season with salt and pepper.

Bring a large saucepan of salted water to boil, add spaghetti and cook until *al dente*. Drain and toss with the olive paste. Scatter truffle slices on top.

SERVES 6

Campania

SPAGHETTI ALLE VONGOLE
Spaghetti with Clam Sauce

This sauce may be prepared with or without tomatoes. If tomatoes are used, 1 lb (500 g) are added to the oil and garlic and left to reduce for 1 hour. The opened clams are added to the sauce with the reduced clam liquid for the last five minutes of cooking.

4 lb (2 kg) clams in the shell or 18 oz (560 g) canned baby
　　clams in water, drained and liquid reserved
freshly ground pepper
½ cup (4 fl oz/125 ml) extra virgin olive oil
6 garlic cloves, chopped

salt
13 oz (410 g) spaghetti
¼ cup chopped parsley

Scrub the clams well and rinse them. Place in a large skillet over moderate heat until all the shells have opened; discard any unopened clams. Lift clams from the pan with a slotted spoon, set aside and keep warm.

Strain the liquid left in the pan and return it to the heat. Add pepper and cook the liquid over fairly high heat until reduced to ¼ cup (2 fl oz/60 ml).

Pour the oil into a small skillet, add the garlic and fry gently until golden. At the same time, bring a large saucepan of salted water to boil, add spaghetti and cook until *al dente*.

Drain the spaghetti and place in a serving bowl. Toss with the oil, garlic and clam cooking liquid. Scatter the clams on top, sprinkle with chopped parsley and serve.

SERVES 6

TAGLIATELLE WITH PROSCIUTTO

Emilia-Romagna

TAGLIATELLE AL PROSCIUTTO
Tagliatelle with Prosciutto

Tagliatelle is traditionally served with a meat sauce prepared in the same way as the one used to fill the cannelloni *on page 108, but they are also often eaten with a simple cream and ham sauce, or with cream and mushrooms. The flavor of meat sauces also varies, because each cook puts her own imagination into the making of them.*

2½ cups (10 oz/315 g) all purpose (plain) flour
3 eggs
7 oz (220 g) cooked ham, coarsely chopped
1 cup (8 fl oz/250 ml) cream
3 oz (90 g) butter
pinch of grated nutmeg
¾ cup (3 oz/90 g) freshly grated Parmesan cheese
salt and freshly ground pepper

Heap the flour on a board and make a well in the center. Add the eggs and work into a soft, smooth dough. Let rest, covered, while preparing sauce.

Combine the ham, cream, butter, nutmeg and half the Parmesan in a saucepan and heat through. Season with salt and pepper.

Roll dough out into a thin sheet and cut into *tagliatelle* ⅜ in (1 cm) wide. Bring a large pot of salted water to boil and cook the *tagliatelle* in it until *al dente*. Drain. Serve topped with the ham sauce and the remaining Parmesan cheese.

SERVES 6

Friuli-Venezia Giulia

GNOCCHI DI PRUGNE
Prune Gnocchi

This dish, Austrian in origin, is especially popular among the families of Trieste. Austrian influence is still very evident in the Venezia Giulia region, particularly in the big families which at one time were often connected by birth to the Austro-Hungarian Empire.

12 dried prunes
2 lb (1 kg) baking potatoes
2½ cups (10 oz/315 g) all purpose (plain) flour
1 egg
salt
3 oz (90 g) butter
½ cup (2 oz/60 g) fresh breadcrumbs
pinch of ground cloves

Soak the prunes in lukewarm water to cover for 1 hour. Drain prunes, pit them and cut into small pieces. Set aside.

Boil the potatoes in their skins until tender. Drain and peel them. Force through a sieve and mix with ⅔ of the flour, the egg and a pinch of salt.

Knead the potato mixture well with floured hands. Form it into oval gnocchi about 1 in (2.5 cm) long. Insert a piece of prune into each and close the mixture over it. Arrange the gnocchi in rows on a floured board.

Bring a large saucepan of salted water to boil. Cook the gnocchi a few at a time, lifting them out with a slotted spoon as they rise to the surface. Arrange on a serving dish.

Heat half the butter in a skillet. Fry the breadcrumbs with the cloves until they begin to color. Brown the remaining butter in a small skillet. Drizzle over the gnocchi, scatter with breadcrumbs and serve.

SERVES 4–6

Emilia-Romagna

MALFATTI DI RICOTTA
Ricotta Gnocchi

These gnocchi are called malfatti *("badly made") because they are shaped by hand and therefore are irregular in appearance. They may be prepared ahead and covered with bechamel sauce that has been flavored with a few sliced* porcini *(boletus) mushrooms, then baked until heated through.*

2 cups chopped cooked spinach (made from
    2 lb/1 kg fresh spinach)
2 cups (8 oz/250 g) freshly grated Parmesan cheese
½ cup (2 oz/60 g) all purpose (plain) flour
1 cup (8 oz/250 g) ricotta cheese
2 eggs
pinch of grated nutmeg
salt and freshly ground pepper
3 oz (90 g) butter, melted

In a large mixing bowl, combine the spinach with ½ cup of the Parmesan cheese, ¼ cup flour, ricotta, eggs, nutmeg and salt and pepper to taste. Mix well.

With the help of a spoon, shape the spinach mixture into ovals about the size of a walnut and roll each one in the remaining flour.

Bring a pot of lightly salted water to boil and cook the gnocchi a few at a time until they float to the surface. Drain in a colander and arrange on the serving dish. Pour the melted butter over the gnocchi, sprinkle with the remaining Parmesan and serve.

SERVES 4–6

PRUNE *GNOCCHI* (top) AND RICOTTA *GNOCCHI* (bottom)

ROMAN-STYLE *GNOCCHI*

Lazio

GNOCCHI ALLA ROMANA
Roman-style Gnocchi

Gnocchi alla romana is another famous dish prepared in every family kitchen in Rome. Its popularity has spread, and it has now become part of the local fare in many other regions of Italy as well. The gnocchi must be golden on the outside and served with plenty of butter.

6 cups (1½ qt/1.5 l) milk
3 scant cups (13 oz/410 g) semolina
3 egg yolks
3 oz (90 g) butter
¾ cup (3 oz/90 g) freshly grated Parmesan cheese

Bring the milk to boil in a large saucepan. Add the semolina all at once, stirring rapidly so that no lumps form. Cook over low heat for about 20 minutes or until the mixture comes away easily from the sides of the pan. Remove from heat and let cool a little. Add the egg yolks one at a time, then half the butter and half the Parmesan.

Turn the semolina out onto a board wet with cold water and spread it into a circle about ¼ in (.5 cm) thick. Smooth the surface with a spatula dipped in cold water and let cool completely. Cut the semolina into 2-in (5-cm) circles, using a glass.

Preheat oven to 400°F (200°C). Butter a large baking dish and arrange the gnocchi in it in a single layer, slightly overlapping. Melt the remaining butter and pour it over the gnocchi; sprinkle with the remaining Parmesan. Bake until golden, about 40 minutes. Serve hot.

SERVES 6

PENNE CON I BROCCOLI
Pasta with Broccoli

In summer, when broccoli (normally an autumn vegetable) is not available, this dish can be made with swiss chard or beet greens. Housewives in Italy prefer to buy only vegetables that are in season, thinking, quite rightly, that they have more flavor.

¼ cup (1 oz/30 g) raisins
½ cup (4 fl oz/125 ml) extra virgin olive oil
½ onion, chopped
1 can (1 lb/500 g) peeled tomatoes, sieved
salt and freshly ground pepper
2 lb (1 kg) broccoli
13 oz (410 g) *penne* (straight pasta tubes), cooked *al dente*
6 anchovy fillets in oil, mashed
2 garlic cloves, chopped
¼ cup (1½ oz/45 g) pine nuts
6 tablespoons grated pecorino cheese

Soak the raisins in lukewarm water to cover until needed. Heat half the oil in a skillet over moderate heat. Add the onion and sauté until translucent. Add the tomatoes, season with salt and pepper, cover and cook for about 1 hour to reduce the sauce.

Meanwhile, separate the broccoli into florets and stems. Peel and slice the stems. Drop into a saucepan of boiling salted water with *penne* and cook until *al dente*.

Fry the anchovy fillets gently with the garlic in oil until garlic is fragrant. Add to the tomato sauce. Mix in the drained raisins, pine nuts and broccoli florets and cook sauce over low heat for 5 minutes, stirring frequently.

Pour sauce over the cooked pasta and mix well. Sprinkle with the grated cheese. Serve at once.

SERVES 6

PASTA WITH BROCCOLI

WIDE RIBBON NOODLES WITH HARE SAUCE

Toscana

PAPPARDELLE ALLA LEPRE
Wide Ribbon Noodles with Hare Sauce

The Tuscans are great hunters, and in autumn they love to eat game — hare, pheasant, even wild boar. They serve it roasted and stewed, and make marvelous game sauces for pasta or rice.

1¼ lb (600 g) hare or rabbit meat
1 cup (8 fl oz/250 ml) dry red wine
2 fresh rosemary sprigs
salt
½ cup (4 fl oz/125 ml) extra virgin olive oil
1 small onion, chopped
1 garlic clove, chopped
1 celery stalk, chopped
2 bay leaves
1 tablespoon juniper berries
freshly ground pepper
1 tablespoon tomato paste (puree)
1¾ cups (7 oz/220 g) all purpose (plain) flour
2 eggs
½ cup (2 oz/60 g) freshly grated Parmesan cheese

Cut the hare into pieces and place in a bowl. Add the wine and rosemary and marinate for 24 hours.

Drain the meat, reserving the wine. Place meat in a saucepan with a little salt. Cover and cook over low heat for 10 minutes, then pour off the accumulated liquid. Add the oil, onion, garlic, celery, bay leaves, juniper berries and pepper and cook over moderate heat until onion begins to color, 10 to 15 minutes, stirring constantly.

Pour in the wine and let it evaporate. Add the tomato paste, diluted with a little water, and simmer uncovered for about 1½ hours, adding water as necessary to keep the sauce moist.

Meanwhile, mound the flour on a work surface and make a well in the center. Break the eggs into the well and mix with your hands to form a dough. Knead until smooth and elastic. Roll out the dough thinly and cut into 1-in (2.5-cm)-wide strips.

Discard the bay leaves from the sauce. Bone the meat and chop it coarsely. Return it to the saucepan and reheat, adding more water if required to reach sauce consistency.

Cook the *pappardelle* noodles in boiling salted water until *al dente*. Drain and toss with the sauce. Sprinkle with Parmesan and serve.

SERVES 6

BAKED LASAGNE WITH MEAT BALLS

Marche
LASAGNE ALLA VINCISGRASSI
Baked Lasagne with Meat Balls

In the Marches, the true pasta capital of Italy, only the yolks of eggs are used in making pasta, and a portion of semolina is added to the flour. This makes the dough much harder to knead, but it holds its shape perfectly during cooking and comes out firm and deep yellow in color.

1¾ cups (7 oz/220 g) all purpose (plain) flour
¾ cup (4 oz/125 g) fine semolina
7 egg yolks
7 oz (220 g) sweetbreads
3 oz (90 g) chicken livers
1 bay leaf
3 tablespoons (2 oz/60 g) butter
7 oz (220 g) ground (minced) veal
3 oz (90 g) chopped cooked ham
salt and freshly ground pepper
¼ cup (2 fl oz/60 ml) extra virgin olive oil
½ cup (4 fl oz/125 ml) dry white wine
1 lb (500 g) tomato sauce
7 oz (220 g) *scamorza* or mozzarella, sliced
3 hard-cooked (hard-boiled) eggs, sliced
1 cup (4 oz/120 g) freshly grated Parmesan cheese

BECHAMEL SAUCE

2 tablespoons all purpose (plain) flour
1 tablespoon butter
3 cups (24 fl oz/750 ml) cold milk

Mound 1¾ cups (220 g) flour and the semolina on a board and make a well in the center. Add 6 egg yolks to the well and gradually blend into dry ingredients, then knead to make a smooth, elastic dough.

Roll it out thinly and cut into 4-in (10-cm) squares. Cook a few at a time in plenty of boiling salted water until *al dente*. Lift out with a slotted spoon and place on a clean cloth to drain, without overlapping them.

Drop the sweetbreads into boiling water and blanch for 5 minutes. Peel off membranes and chop the flesh. Sauté the chicken livers and bay leaf in half the butter until livers change color, then chop finely; discard bay leaf. Mix the

chicken livers, veal, sweetbreads and ham with the remaining egg yolk. Add salt and pepper, and mix well.

Form the mixture into walnut-size balls. Roll in flour and brown in the oil and remaining butter in a skillet. Pour in the wine and let it evaporate. Preheat oven to 350°F (180°C). Cover the bottom of a 13 x 9-in (32 x 22-cm) dish (or large round baking dish) with a layer of tomato sauce. Arrange a layer of pasta on top and cover with sliced *scamorza*, a few slices of egg, some of the meatballs, a little tomato sauce, and some Parmesan cheese. Repeat the layers until all the ingredients are used, reserving a few tablespoons Parmesan.

To make the sauce, cook the flour and butter over low heat, stirring until the flour is absorbed. Gradually add the milk, stirring constantly. Boil for one minute, then pour the sauce over the top of the lasagne and sprinkle with the remaining Parmesan.

Bake for 30 minutes. Let rest 5 minutes, then serve.

SERVES 6

Sardegna
GNOCCHI ALLO ZAFFERANO
Gnocchi with Saffron

These small gnocchi are a specialty of the northern Sardinian city of Sassari, where they are called ciciones. *They are made from durum wheat flour (fine semolina), which makes the dough quite difficult to knead, and are served with matured pecorino cheese (in its absence, Parmesan may be used). Saffron is gathered in many parts of Sardinia but is not sold commercially; it is kept for personal use.*

1 lb (500 g) durum wheat (semolina) flour
¼ cup (2 fl oz/60 ml) extra virgin olive oil
½ teaspoon saffron
3 oz (90 g) pork fat, chopped
1 onion, chopped
¼ cup parsley, chopped
7 oz (220 g) ground (minced) pork
7 oz (220 g) ground (minced) lean lamb
1¼ lb (625 g) ripe tomatoes, put through a food mill or
    finely chopped
2 bay leaves
6 fresh sage leaves
salt and freshly ground pepper
¾ cup (3 oz/90 g) grated aged pecorino cheese, optional

Heap the flour on a board and make a well in the center. Add 2 tablespoons oil, the saffron dissolved in a little water, and as much additional water as needed to form a smooth, firm dough. Knead well.

Cut the dough into pieces and with floured hands form into long cylinders about 1 in (2.5 cm) in diameter. Divide into 1¼-in (3-cm) lengths and make a little hollow in the center of each. Arrange the gnocchi on a floured board.

Fry the pork fat, onion and parsley gently in a saucepan with the remaining oil. Add the pork and lamb, and sauté until browned. Stir in the tomatoes, bay leaves, sage and salt and pepper to taste. Cook for about 1 hour or until you have a thick sauce. Cook the gnocchi in plenty of boiling salted water until *al dente*; drain. Arrange on a serving dish. Pour the prepared sauce over, sprinkle with grated cheese if desired and serve.

SERVES 6

CAPPELLETTI IN BROTH

Emilia-Romagna

CAPPELLETTI IN BRODO
Cappelletti in Broth

Filled pasta is a specialty of Emilia-Romagna. Depending on its form, it may be called tortellini, tortelloni, anolini, cappelletti, lasagne *or* cannelloni. Tortellini *and* tortelloni *are square,* anolini *are round with a hole in the center, and* cannelloni *are tubular.*

½ chicken breast (about 4 oz/125 g), chopped
1 tablespoon butter
2 oz (60 g) mortadella
3 oz (90 g) ricotta
1¼ cups (5 oz/155 g) freshly grated Parmesan cheese
3 eggs
pinch of freshly grated nutmeg
salt and freshly ground pepper
1¾ cups (7 oz/220 g) all purpose (plain) flour
6 cups (1½ qt/1.5 l) clear meat broth (stock)

Brown the chicken breast in the butter, seasoning it with salt and pepper; set aside. Chop mortadella finely and combine in a bowl with the chicken, ricotta, 1 cup (4 oz/125 g) Parmesan, 1 egg, nutmeg, salt and pepper and mix well.

Heap the flour in a mound on a board and make a well in the center. Break in the 2 remaining eggs and knead into a soft, smooth dough. Roll out into a thin sheet and cut into 1¼-in (3-cm) circles.

Place a little of the filling in the center of each circle and fold the pasta in half, pressing it around the edges to seal in the filling. Then wind the folded edge around the tip of your index finger and press the two ends together to form a ring.

Bring the broth to boil, drop in *cappelletti* and cook until *al dente*, about 2–3 minutes. Drain and serve, passing the remaining Parmesan cheese separately.

SERVES 6

Piemonte

GNOCCHI DI PATATE
Potato Gnocchi

Potato gnocchi are a Piedmontese specialty, but they are also found in the cuisine of many other northern regions and in Latium. They may be served with meat sauce, pesto, sage leaves fried in butter, tomato sauce or a rich sauce made by melting gorgonzola cheese with a little butter and cream.

RAGÙ

1 carrot
1 celery stalk
1 small onion
10 oz (315 g) fresh or canned tomatoes, peeled and seeded
2 oz (60 g) *pancetta* or rindless bacon
3 oz (90 g) butter
10 oz (315 g) beef tenderloin (fillet), cut into cubes
¼ cup (2 fl oz/60 ml) dry white wine
salt and freshly ground pepper
1 cup (4 oz/125 g) freshly grated Parmesan cheese

GNOCCHI

2 lb (1 kg) baking potatoes
1¾ cups (7 oz/220 g) all purpose (plain) flour
1 egg
salt

PHOTO: FABBRI EDITORI MILANO

POTATO *GNOCCHI*

For the sauce: Cut the vegetables and bacon into small pieces. Melt 1 tablespoon (20g) butter in a saucepan. Add the carrot, celery, onion and meat, browning the meat over medium-high heat. Reduce heat to medium and cook for 10 minutes more. Add wine and tomatoes, season to taste with salt and pepper, and cook over very low heat for 2 hours. Push the sauce through a sieve — do not puree.

For the gnocchi: Boil the potatoes in their skins until tender. Drain and peel them. Put potatoes through a food mill held over a board or other work surface or mash potatoes well. Add the flour, gather the mixture into a mound and make a well in the center. Break the egg into the well, add salt and knead until the mixture forms a smooth, firm dough.

Cut it into pieces and use the palm of your hand to roll each piece into a long sausage shape. Cut these into 2¼-in (3-cm) cylinders, separating them. Roll each of the gnocchi over the concave part of a grater or the prongs of a fork, pressing down lightly with your thumb, and drop them onto a floured board.

Cook the gnocchi a few at a time in boiling salted water, lifting them out with a slotted spoon as soon as they rise to the surface. Spoon the sauce over them, dot with the remaining butter and sprinkle with Parmesan. Serve at once.

SERVES 4–6

TRENETTE WITH PESTO

Liguria

TRENETTE AL PESTO

Trenette with Pesto

Genoese pesto sauce is usually made in a marble mortar by pounding the basil leaves with the rest of the ingredients using a wooden pestle. This prevents the basil from turning black with the heat of the pasta (a reaction usually set off by the steel in a cutting knife). In the absence of a mortar it can be made in a blender.

Trenette are fine ribbon noodles, which can be made at home with 3 cups (13 oz/410 g) flour, two eggs, and sufficient water to make a soft, smooth dough.

Ligurian pasta, unlike that of other regions, contains only a small proportion of egg and is almost white in color.

1 cup fresh basil leaves, tightly packed
2 tablespoons pine nuts
3 garlic cloves, peeled
salt
3 tablespoons grated pecorino cheese
3 tablespoons freshly grated Parmesan cheese
½ cup (4 fl oz/125 ml) extra virgin olive oil
2 medium-size boiling potatoes
1 lb (500 g) green beans, trimmed
13 oz (410 g) noodles

Wash the basil leaves and dry them well.

Combine pine nuts, garlic and basil in a blender. Add a little salt, the cheeses and a small amount of oil, and puree. Pour in remaining oil and blend for a further second or two. Peel the potatoes and cut into julienne strips.

Bring a large saucepan of water to boil, drop in beans and cook for 5 minutes. Add the potatoes, and after 2 minutes add the noodles. When noodles are cooked *al dente*, about 5 minutes, drain mixture and turn out onto a serving plate. Toss with the prepared pesto and serve.

SERVES 4

Friuli-Venezia Giulia

CIALSONS

Pasta with Herbs

Cialsons, little semicircles of filled pasta, are very popular in Friuli. They may be filled in various ways: the most traditional stuffing is based on herbs, but they are also delicious with a filling of spinach, golden raisins (sultanas), cinnamon, a small amount of softened rye bread, and poppyseeds. They are served with a sauce of melted butter and grated aged ricotta, or grated Parmesan cheese.

1¾ cups (7 oz/220 g) all purpose (plain) flour
3 eggs
7 oz (220 g) beet greens or spinach
¼ cup stale rye breadcrumbs, soaked in milk and squeezed dry
pinch of ground cinnamon
pinch of ground cloves
1 tablespoon chopped fresh thyme
1 tablespoon chopped parsley
1 tablespoon juniper berries, ground
salt and freshly ground pepper
3 oz (90 g) butter, melted
¾ cup (3 oz/90 g) freshly grated Parmesan cheese

Heap the flour on a board and make a well in the center. Break 2 eggs into the well and gradually work in flour. Knead until dough is smooth and elastic. Cover while preparing filling.

Boil the beet or spinach leaves in salted water just until wilted. Squeeze dry and chop finely. Mix with remaining egg, the bread, cinnamon, cloves, thyme, parsley and juniper. Season to taste with salt and pepper.

Roll dough out into thin sheets and cut into circles about 2 in (5 cm) in diameter.

Place little mounds of filling onto the pasta circles. Fold them in half to enclose the filling and press the edges together firmly.

Cook the *cialsons* in boiling salted water until *al dente*, about 2-3 minutes, and drizzle with the melted butter. Sprinkle grated Parmesan on top.

SERVES 6

Veneto

RAVIOLI DI BARBABIETOLE

Beet Ravioli

In Italy, beets (beetroot) can be found already cooked in most fruit and vegetable markets. Each evening the vendors bake at home as many beets as they think they will sell the following day. They also cook onions in their skins in the same manner. Baked beets and onions mixed with a dressing of oil and lemon make an excellent salad.

1¾ cups (7 oz/220 g all purpose (plain) flour
salt
3 eggs
1 beet (beetroot), about 10 oz (315 g), baked at 350°F (180°C) until tender
3 oz (90 g) butter
7 oz (220 g) ricotta
freshly ground pepper
½ cup (2 oz/50 g) dry breadcrumbs
3 oz (90 g) freshly grated Parmesan cheese

Sift the flour and a pinch of salt into a mound on a work surface. Make a well in the center and break 2 eggs into it. Work the flour into a soft dough. Form it into a ball, wrap in plastic and let it rest while you prepare the filling.

Peel and slice the beet; puree in a food processor. Melt 3 tablespoons (2 oz/60 g) butter in a saucepan. Add the beet and cook gently for about 10 minutes to gather flavor. Transfer to a bowl and blend in the ricotta, the remaining egg and the breadcrumbs. Adjust the salt and add pepper.

Roll out the dough as thinly as possible with a rolling pin or pasta machine. Cut into circles about 2 in (5 cm) in diameter. Place a little of the beet mixture in the center of each circle. Fold the pasta over the filling and press edges firmly.

Bring a saucepan of water to boil and cook the *ravioli* in it until *al dente*.

Meanwhile, heat the remaining butter in a small saucepan until fairly dark in color. Drain the *ravioli* and place on a serving plate. Pour the melted butter over, sprinkle with cheese and serve.

SERVES 6

Piemonte

AGNOLOTTI ALLA PANNA
Agnolotti with Cream

Stuffed pasta comes in many different forms and under many different names, which all amount to the same thing: agnolotti *in Piedmont,* ravioli *in Tuscany,* tortelli *and* cappelletti *in Emilia-Romagna,* pansoti *in Liguria.*

They can be half-moon shaped, square, hat-shaped or round, and they are filled with a meat mixture or with vegetables, eggs or cheese.

FILLING
10 oz (315 g) young beet greens or spinach leaves
3 oz (90 g) ricotta
3 oz (90 g) leftover roast chicken, finely chopped
3 oz (90 g) cooked ham, finely chopped
¼ cup (1 oz/30 g) freshly grated Parmesan cheese
1 egg
pinch of freshly grated nutmeg
salt and freshly ground pepper

PASTA
2½ cups (10 oz/315 g) all purpose (plain) flour
3 eggs

SAUCE
3 tablespoons (2 oz/60 g) butter
1 cup (8 fl oz/250 ml) cream
¾ cup (3 oz/90 g) freshly grated Parmesan cheese

For the filling: Cook the beet or spinach leaves in boiling salted water just until wilted. Squeeze dry and chop very finely. In a bowl, combine all filling ingredients. Refrigerate.

For the pasta: Combine flour and eggs to form a dough; knead until smooth and elastic. Roll out very thinly. Place small balls of the filling at 2½-in (6-cm) intervals over half the sheet of dough. Fold the dough over to cover filling, pressing with the fingers around each ball. Using a pastry wheel with fluted edge, cut out the *agnolotti* in half-moon or square shapes.

Bring a large pot of water to boil over high heat; drop in the *agnolotti* and cook until *al dente*.

While they are cooking, heat the butter and cream over low heat. Arrange *agnolotti* in a serving dish and pour butter and cream over. Sprinkle with Parmesan and serve.

SERVES 6

PASTA WITH HERBS (top left), *AGNOLOTTI* WITH CREAM (bottom left) AND BEET RAVIOLI (right)

PHOTO: FABBRI EDITORI MILANO

PANSOTI IN WALNUT SAUCE

Liguria

PANSOTI IN SALSA DI NOCI

Pansoti in Walnut Sauce

Pansoti is the Ligurian regional name for ravioli; *and the locally used filling is a very tasty mixture of wild herbs. If these are not available, the* pansoti *may be filled with a mixture of chicory (Belgian endive or green* radicchio), *marjoram and beet greens (or spinach leaves).*

The walnut sauce is usually made in a marble mortar as for pesto, but it can also be done in a blender.

2 cups (8 oz/250 g) all purpose (plain) flour
2 eggs
⅔ cup (3 oz/90 g) dandelion leaves
⅔ cup (3 oz/90 g) borage
⅓ cup (2 oz/60 g) fresh chervil
⅓ cup (2 oz/60 g) fresh marjoram
⅓ cup (2 oz/60 g) fresh chives
2 garlic cloves
3 oz (90 g) ricotta
½ cup coarse stale breadcrumbs, soaked in water and squeezed dry
salt and freshly ground pepper
1 cup (4 oz/125 g) walnuts
¾ cup (3 oz/90 g) freshly grated Parmesan cheese
½ cup (4 fl oz/125 ml) cream
¼ cup (2 fl oz/60 ml) extra virgin olive oil

Heap flour in a mound on a board and make a well in the center. Break 1 egg into well; add sufficient water to make a soft dough. Knead until smooth and elastic. Wrap in plastic and set aside.

Cook herbs in boiling salted water until wilted. Drain and chop with the garlic. Add remaining egg, the ricotta and half the bread. Mix well and season with salt and pepper.

Blanch walnuts in boiling water for 1 minute, then peel off the skins. Place nuts in the blender with remaining bread, 1 tablespoon Parmesan, cream and oil. Blend to a creamy consistency. Transfer sauce to a small saucepan and heat gently.

Roll the pasta dough out with a pasta machine to the second-thinnest setting. Cut into 2½-in (6-cm) squares. Place a small amount of filling in the center of each square and fold the dough back over it to form a triangle, pressing lightly on the edges to seal in filling.

Cook the *pansoti* in plenty of boiling salted water until *al dente*. Serve topped with walnut sauce and remaining Parmesan.

SERVES 6

Abruzzi and Molise

TAGLIERINI ALLA CHITARRA

Pasta alla Chitarra

Pasta alla chitarra is obtained by cutting sheets of pasta dough with a traditional cutter called a "guitar," consisting of two sets of differently spaced wires stretched on a wooden frame, with a tilted board between them to catch the cut pasta.

The same effect can be achieved by preparing a sheet of dough about ¼ in (2 mm) thick and cutting it into strips of that same width so that you have square-shaped rather than cylindrical spaghetti (like long matchsticks). It is also possible to buy pasta alla chitarra *ready made.*

2½ cups (10 oz/315 g) durum wheat (semolina) flour
3 eggs
salt
¼ cup (2 fl oz/60 ml) extra virgin olive oil
1 onion, thinly sliced
7 oz (220 g) *pancetta* or rindless bacon, cut into short julienne strips
2 lb (1 kg) ripe tomatoes, put through a food mill or finely chopped
¼ cup small fresh basil leaves
freshly ground pepper
3 oz (90 g) grated pecorino cheese

Mound the flour on a board and make a well in the center. Break the eggs into the well, add a pinch of salt and work into a dough. Knead for about 10 minutes, letting dough rest for a few minutes halfway through.

Roll out very thinly. If you have a *chitarra*, cut the dough into rectangles the same size as the *chitarra*. Lay each on the wires and pass the rolling pin over it to cut the pasta into strips. In the absence of a "guitar," flour the pastry sheet lightly and allow to dry for a few minutes, then roll up and cut into fine strips using a long, very sharp knife.

Heat the oil in a saucepan over moderate heat, add the onion and *pancetta* and brown for 10 minutes. Add the tomatoes and a little salt and simmer, covered, over very low heat for 1 hour. Just before removing sauce from heat, add the whole basil leaves and a good pinch of pepper.

Cook the pasta in boiling salted water until *al dente*; drain. Serve topped with the sauce and sprinkled with pecorino cheese.

SERVES 6

104

PASTA WITH SARDINES (top) AND *LASAGNE* WITH BREADCRUMBS (bottom)

Sicilia

PASTA CON LE SARDE
Pasta with Sardines

Here is another pasta dish offering a combination of sweet and sour. It is flavored with saffron, which is used in the preparation of many dishes and is a legacy of the Arab invasions.

The sardines found in the Mediterranean are rather small, and do not have much fat.

6 wild fennel fronds, or 2 fennel bulbs
½ cup (2 oz/60 g) raisins
1½ lb (750 g) sardines
1 onion, chopped
½ cup (4 fl oz/125 ml) extra virgin olive oil
¼ teaspoon saffron
½ cup (3 oz/90 g) pine nuts
13 oz (410 g) *bucatini* (thick hollow spaghetti)
salt
¼ cup (1 oz/30 g) breadcrumbs
freshly ground pepper

Chop the fennel; use only the fronds of wild fennel, reserving the stalks, or use the hearts of cultivated fennel bulbs, reserving the outer layers and stalks. Soak the raisins in water to cover for 1 hour; drain. Clean the sardines and open them up; discard the heads and bones.

Sauté the onion in a skillet in ⅔ of the oil until soft. Add the drained raisins, the saffron dissolved in a very small amount of water, the pine nuts and the chopped fennel hearts or fronds. Lay the sardines on top of these ingredients, cover the skillet and cook over low heat for 10 minutes.

Bring a large saucepan of salted water to boil, cover and cook the reserved fennel trimmings in it for 20 minutes. Remove the fennel, add the *bucatini* to the cooking water and cook until *al dente*. Drain and mix them with the remaining oil. Preheat oven to 350°F (180°C). Place a layer of *bucatini* on the bottom of a 9-in (23-cm) dish and cover with half of the sardines. Top with the remaining pasta and then the rest of the sardines. Scatter the breadcrumbs on top, sprinkle with pepper and bake for 20 minutes.

SERVES 6

Friuli-Venezia Giulia

LASAGNE CON UVETTA
Lasagne with Breadcrumbs

The custom of frying breadcrumbs in butter and using them in place of grated cheese as a condiment is found not only in the north (where it probably derives from Austria) but also in the south, for example in Apulia and Sicily.

2½ cups (10 oz/315 g) all purpose (plain) flour
3 eggs
½ cup (2 oz/60 g) fresh breadcrumbs
3 oz (90 g) butter
pinch of ground cinnamon
1½ teaspoons sugar
½ cup (2 oz/60 g) golden raisins (sultanas)

For lasagne noodles, heap the flour on a board and make a well in the center. Break in the eggs and work into a smooth, soft ball. Roll it out thinly and cut into 4-in (10-cm) squares.

Fry the breadcrumbs in half the butter until they begin to color. Stir in the cinnamon and sugar. Soak the raisins in lukewarm water to cover for about 30 minutes. Bring a large pot of salted water to boil, drop in noodles and cook until *al dente*.

Melt the remaining butter in a small skillet. Lift the lasagne out of the water with a slotted spoon and arrange on a serving plate or dish. Scatter the raisins on top. Sprinkle with the melted butter and breadcrumbs and serve.

SERVES 6

PHOTO: GIAN LUIGI SCARFIOTTI

SPAGHETTI WITH EGGS AND BACON

Lazio

SPAGHETTI ALLA CARBONARA
Spaghetti with Eggs and Bacon

In the south of Italy tagliatelle *is replaced by spaghetti, which requires a different sauce.* Tagliatelle *is generally served with butter-based sauces, spaghetti with sauces based on extra virgin olive oil or using some form of bacon or salt pork.*

10 oz (310 g) *pancetta* or rindless bacon, finely diced
1 hot red chili pepper, finely chopped
1¼ lb (600 g) spaghetti
6 tablespoons grated pecorino cheese
6 egg yolks
salt and freshly ground pepper
3 tablespoons freshly grated Parmesan cheese

Combine the *pancetta* and chili pepper in a skillet and cook over low heat until some of the fat has melted. Increase the heat and cook until the *pancetta* browns.

Bring a large pot of salted water to boil and cook the spaghetti in it until *al dente*. Drain, reserving ½ cup water. Transfer to a serving dish.

Mix the pecorino with the reserved spaghetti cooking water. Mix in the egg yolks with a fork, then add a little salt and plenty of pepper. Tip the contents of the skillet over the spaghetti. Add the egg mixture and toss well. Sprinkle with Parmesan and serve.

SERVES 6

DUMPLINGS WITH MEAT SAUCE

Umbria

STROZZAPRETI

Dumplings with Meat Sauce

This is a type of homemade spaghetti containing yeast. In the Campania region the same pasta is known as strangolapreti *(priest strangler); obviously the concept is the same!*

½ oz (20 g) fresh yeast
4 cups (1 lb/500 g) all purpose (plain) flour
salt
¼ cup (2 fl oz/60 ml) extra virgin olive oil
½ onion, chopped
1 celery stalk, chopped
1 carrot, chopped
10 oz (300 g) ground beef (minced steak)
1 bay leaf
3 oz (90 g) fresh mushrooms, sliced
1 lb (500 g) canned peeled tomatoes
pinch of dried thyme
freshly ground pepper

Crumble the yeast into a bowl. Add a couple of table-spoons of flour and sufficient water to form a thick batter. When thoroughly mixed, cover the bowl with a cloth and let stand in a warm place for 1 hour to ferment.

Meanwhile, heat the oil in a saucepan over moderate heat. Add the onion, celery and carrot and sauté until onion is translucent. Add the meat, bay leaf and mushrooms and cook for 10 minutes, stirring occasionally. Add the tomatoes, thyme, salt and pepper and simmer, covered, over low heat for 1 hour.

Shortly before end of cooking time, add the truffle and discard the bay leaf.

While sauce cooks, mound the remaining flour on a board and make a well in the center. Add the yeast and a pinch of salt. Mix in enough water to make a dough; knead and slap it on the board until smooth and elastic. Cut the dough into small pieces and roll them with your hands into long cylinders like fat spaghetti.

Bring a large saucepan of salted water to boil, add the pasta and cook until *al dente*. Drain and serve with the pre-pared sauce.

SERVES 6

Emilia-Romagna

CANNELLONI RIPIENI

Cannelloni

Cannelloni, long cylinders of pasta, may also be filled with spinach and cheese or ham and bechamel. They may be served simply with melted butter and cheese, or with a thin bechamel.

10 oz (315 g) spinach
1¾ cups (7 oz/220 g) all purpose (plain) flour
2 eggs
¼ cup dried mushrooms
½ chicken breast (about 4 oz/125 g)
¼ cup (2 fl oz/60 ml) extra virgin olive oil
1 medium-size onion, chopped
1 medium-size carrot, chopped
1 celery stalk, chopped
1 garlic clove, chopped
¼ cup parsley leaves, chopped
3 oz (90 g) prosciutto, chopped
1 bay leaf
1 whole clove
10 oz (315 g) beef sirloin (fillet steak), chopped
3 oz (90 g) mortadella, chopped
½ cup (4 fl oz/125 ml) dry white wine
1 lb (500 g) plum (egg) tomatoes, put through a food mill or chopped
salt and freshly ground pepper
¾ cup (3 oz/90 g) freshly grated Parmesan cheese

Boil the spinach in a large pot of salted water until wilted. Drain and squeeze dry. Puree in a food processor. Mix spinach with the flour and the eggs and knead into a smooth, soft dough. Wrap in plastic and set aside.

Soak the mushrooms in lukewarm water to cover for 1 hour. Drain and chop. Cut the chicken meat into pieces. Heat oil in a saucepan over moderate heat. Add onion, car-rot, celery, garlic, parsley and prosciutto and sauté for 10 minutes. Add the bay leaf, clove, beef, chicken and mor-tadella. Pour in the wine and let it evaporate. Add the tomatoes and season to taste with salt and pepper.

Cover and cook this sauce over low heat for about 1 hour, or until thickened.

CANNELLONI (top left) AND BREAD *GNOCCHI* (bottom right)

🍴 Roll out the pasta dough very thinly and cut into 4-in (10-cm) squares. Bring a large pot of salted water to boil. Drop in pasta a few squares at a time and cook until *al dente*. Lift each square out with a slotted spoon and place on a cloth to dry.

🍴 Discard the bay leaf from the meat mixture. Place a small amount of mixture in the center of each square of pasta and roll it up to form a cylinder.

🍴 Butter a 9-in (23-cm) baking dish and arrange the *cannelloni* in it. Cover with the remaining meat mixture and sprinkle with Parmesan. Preheat oven to 400°F (200°C). Bake *cannelloni* until heated through, about 20 minutes. Let rest 5 minutes before serving.

SERVES 6

Trentino-Alto Adige

CANEDERLI
Bread Gnocchi

Bread gnocchi are a specialty of the Trentino region. They may be flavored in various ways — with a little chopped liver, with ham, or simply with plenty of parsley. Sometimes they are made with rye rather than white bread. They may be served in a broth or as an accompaniment to meat.

1 stale loaf of firm, coarse-textured bread, 1 lb (500 g)
4 cups (1 qt/1 l) milk
1 shallot, chopped
2 teaspoons chopped fresh chervil
1 tablespoon chopped fresh thyme
pinch of grated nutmeg
salt and freshly ground pepper
4 eggs
8 cups (2 qt/2 l) broth (stock)
3 oz (90 g) butter
½ cup (2 oz/60 g) freshly grated Parmesan cheese

🍴 Cut up the bread and place in a bowl with the milk. Let soak for 30 minutes. Drain and squeeze out all the moisture. Add the shallot, chervil, thyme, nutmeg, salt and pepper. Beat the eggs in a bowl with a little salt. Add to the bread and work the mixture with your hands until all ingredients are well mixed.

🍴 Bring the broth to boil in a wide pan. Form tablespoonfuls of the mixture into balls and drop into the broth. When it returns to boil, reduce heat, cover the pan and simmer for about 10 minutes or until the gnocchi are well puffed up. Remove them one by one with a slotted spoon, arrange on a serving plate and keep warm.

🍴 Meanwhile, heat the butter in a small skillet until it begins to color. Sprinkle grated cheese over the gnocchi; drizzle with butter. Serve at once.

SERVES 6–8

PASTA WITH TURNIP GREENS

Puglia

ORECCHIETTE CON CIME DI RAPA
Pasta with Turnip Greens

Pasta cooked with vegetables is a classic dish of Apulia, a major vegetable-producing region. The vegetables are cultivated beneath the olive trees that cover Apulia's vast rolling plains.

Orecchiette (little "ears" of pasta) are traditionally made by hand. The dough is rolled out into a thin sheet and cut into ¾-in (2-cm) circles, and a little hollow is made in each circle with the finger. They can also now be bought ready made.

½ cup (4 fl oz/100 ml) extra virgin olive oil
1 cup (2 oz/60 g) fresh breadcrumbs
1 lb (500 g) *orecchiette*
1 lb (500 g) turnip greens or spring greens, cleaned
6 cloves garlic, peeled and chopped
1 dried red chili pepper, minced
6 flat anchovy fillets

Heat ¼ cup (2 fl oz/50 ml) olive oil in a skillet over moderate heat. Add the breadcrumbs and stir gently with a wooden spoon until golden brown. Set aside.

Bring a large pot of salted water to boil, drop in the pasta and turnip greens and cook until the pasta is *al dente*.

Meanwhile, in a large, deep skillet sauté the garlic, chili pepper and anchovies in the remaining olive oil until the garlic has colored lightly.

Drain the pasta and turnip greens, add to the skillet and sauté for a couple of minutes. Mix well, sprinkle with the breadcrumbs and serve.

SERVES 6

Emilia-Romagna

ROTOLO DI SPINACI
Spinach Roll

This pasta roll is also popular in other areas of Italy, particularly in Tuscany and the Marches, where the ricotta is especially tasty.

Ricotta is obtained by reboiling the liquid left over from the making of pecorino cheese — hence its name, which means "recooked." It is a very low-fat cheese.

1¾ cups (7 oz/220 g) all purpose (plain) flour
3 eggs
4 lb (2 kg) spinach
1 tablespoon butter
10 oz (315 g) ricotta
1¾ cups (7 oz/220 g) freshly grated Parmesan cheese
¼ cup (2 fl oz/60 ml) extra virgin olive oil
1 small onion, finely chopped
1 carrot, finely chopped
1 celery stalk, finely chopped
2 lb (1 kg) ripe tomatoes, put through a food mill or finely chopped
salt and freshly ground pepper

Heap the flour on a board and make a well in the center. Break 2 eggs into it and work the mixture into a smooth, soft dough. Wrap in plastic and set aside.

Boil the spinach in a large pot of salted water until wilted. Squeeze as dry as possible, then dry it further by sautéing it in the butter in a skillet. Chop spinach finely and mix to a paste with the ricotta, the remaining egg and half the Parmesan cheese.

Heat the oil in a saucepan over moderate heat. Add onion, carrot and celery and sauté until onion is translucent. Add tomatoes and simmer over low heat for about 1 hour, or until thickened to sauce consistency. Add salt and pepper.

Roll the dough out very thinly into a large circle and spread the spinach over it lightly. Roll it up and press the ends together to seal in the spinach. Wrap the roll in cheesecloth and tie at both ends.

Bring a large oval roaster or fish poacher of salted water to boil. Add spinach roll and cook for 20 minutes. Remove from the cloth and slice. Arrange slices on a serving plate sprinkled with the rest of the Parmesan. Pass the tomato sauce separately in a sauceboat.

SERVES 6

Toscana

PANZANELLA
Bread Salad with Tomato

This is another traditional recipe that makes use of leftover bread; it is mixed with tomatoes, onions and olive oil, and sometimes other ingredients such as tuna and olives are added. Tuscan bread is unsalted, which means it stays fresh for a longer period.

8 oz (250 g) week-old firm, coarse-textured bread
3 large ripe tomatoes, peeled and cut into cubes
2 small red onions, minced
4 garlic cloves, chopped
⅓ cup whole fresh basil leaves
3 oz (90 g) canned tuna
2 tablespoons red wine vinegar
salt
⅓ cup (2½ fl oz/90 ml) extra virgin olive oil
freshly ground pepper

Soak the bread in water for a few minutes. Squeeze dry and crumble into a mixing bowl.

Mix the tomatoes, onions, garlic, basil and tuna with the bread.

In a small bowl, mix the vinegar with a pinch of salt until the salt is dissolved. Whisk in the olive oil. Toss with the salad, salt and pepper to taste and serve.

SERVES 6   *Photograph page 4*

Piemonte

FONDUTA CON TARTUFO
Fondue with Truffle

This, together with bagna cauda, *is perhaps the most typical and tasty of Piedmontese dishes. It must be cooked in a double boiler because the cheese and eggs can easily curdle — or, as Italian cooks say,* impazzire, *which means "to go mad." It is most important that* fonduta *be served very hot.*

12 oz (375 g) fontina or Gruyère cheese, thinly sliced
2 cups (16 fl oz/500 ml) cold milk
salt
4 egg yolks
3 tablespoons (2 oz/60 g) butter, softened
1 white truffle (1 oz/30 g)

Place cheese slices in a deep, narrow dish. Cover with milk and let stand for at least 3 hours. Drain, reserving ¼ cup milk. Place cheese in the top of a double boiler with a little salt. Heat over simmering water, stirring constantly with a whisk, until melted and smooth. Heat reserved milk. Mix with egg yolks and butter. Stir rapidly into melted cheese until mixture is smooth and creamy.

Pour into a well-heated serving dish, shave the truffle very thinly over the top and serve at once.

SERVES 6

FONDUE WITH TRUFFLE (left) AND SPINACH ROLL (right)

PHOTO: GIAN LUIGI SCARFIOTTI

Il Centro

Il Centro

There are only five central Italian regions, but these are fittingly acknowledged to constitute the very heart of Italy — and they are all very different. Tuscany is the most famous, an ancient, mellow and harmonious landscape characterized by a graceful way of life. From Tuscany come the best bread and the purest extra virgin olive oil, as well as the classic *chianti* wine. Latium, with Rome as its nerve center, tends towards a more classical but commonsense approach to life and food. "La verde Umbria" is a land of green rolling hills and plains, with produce of great quality, including wonderful olives and black truffles. The Marches is a small, mainly agricultural Adriatic region, whose specialties include fried olives and one of the best Italian white wines, *verdicchio*. And lastly, Emilia-Romagna, distinguished by the rich, buttery, creamy food associated with its fertile farmlands. Several of the best-known Italian gastronomic delights come from Emilia-Romagna — Parmesan, prosciutto and egg pasta like *tortellini*.

Tuscan cuisine has a centuries-old tradition to protect. Gourmets from every age have praised its specialties and appreciated their consistent excellence. In palace and farmhouse, in the hills and on the seashore, it was practically impossible to find a meal that was lacking in grace or was in some way defective. The secret lay in the harmony and restraint, the *divina proportione* that governed the ingredients in the same way as they governed Florentine sculpture and architecture. Tuscany, mistress of culture, could not but be mistress of the kitchen as well. The Tuscans are well aware of this, and any Tuscan will swear that in his house you will dine better than anywhere else in the world: he will be prepared to fight if necessary to establish this "exclusive, universal truth."

SOFT ROLLING HILLS, MEDIEVAL TOWNS, AND GRAY-GREEN OLIVE TREES, TYPIFY THE TUSCAN LANDSCAPE

PREVIOUS PAGES: PERHAPS THE MOST FAMOUS VIEW OF FLORENCE, FROM FORT BELVEDERE
PHOTO: H. SIMEONE HUBER/MARKA

It is true that Tuscan cuisine as a whole is considered excellent. Consequently, it has become a national model for Italians to emulate — just as they refer to the Tuscan language as a model for the Italian language. How can we define Tuscan cooking in a few words? Let us quote Giuseppe Prezzolini, a literary man of the early twentieth century, who wrote that it is "light, lean, tasty and full of character and fragrance, created for people of lively intellect who do not wish to sit around and grow fat; a cuisine that never thought of a risotto, did not create macaroni, and has kept fatty foods at a distance, one that has retained spit and grill." To this perfect description we should add that the purity and natural flavor of the ingredients make it pointless to use tricks and camouflages such as creams, sauces, gravies and excessive seasonings. Tuscan steaks, free range chickens, pigs, white beans, artichokes, peas, game and fish need only one addition to make the most of their natural qualities: extra virgin olive oil, made in the presses of the farms that nestle in the hills around Florence, Siena and Lucca. Without this essential ingredient, the simple Tuscan cooking becomes impossible to imitate, for while there are no secrets to be revealed in the cooking methods, the effect cannot be achieved without the oil's precise nuances.

Many of the dishes also have definite historical reference: they were mentioned in works by Renaissance writers such as Boccaccio, Sacchetti, Redi, Machiavelli or Lorenzo de' Medici, or by famous people who fate decreed should pause in Tuscany for a meal. One such person was the Emperor Charles V, who, when he reached Florence in 1535, "could not but marvel at the splendors of the table" and the excellence of the wine; then there were the guests at Maria de' Medici's wedding, early in the seventeenth century, who were greatly impressed by the magnificence of Florentine banquets.

So what are these fabled gastronomic wonders? They are all dishes of ancient rustic origin; for example, tiny new peas pan-fried in oil with garlic, parsley, prosciutto, pepper and salt; a *fritto misto* of brains, artichokes, zucchini and baby lamb chops; a roast loin of pork; hare in sweet and sour sauce; a Leghorn fish stew; or a simple plate of white beans or bread soup. These are the expressions of a great civilization, which have gradually arrived at their complete and perfect state through the labor and creativity of chefs and housewives who have finely tuned them like precision machines, taking away a pinch of this and adding a touch of that. Although it may not be apparent, Tuscan chefs use the accurate scales of

THE FAMILIAR SIGHT OF A FARMHOUSE IN THE MARCHES PERCHED ON A HILL SURROUNDED BY TREES, GRAPE VINES AND MILES OF NEATLY FURROWED FIELDS

PHOTO JOHN SIMS

PHOTO: HANS WOLF/THE IMAGE BANK

SIENA, THE ANCIENT CAPITAL OF TUSCANY, BOASTS MANY RICH ART TREASURES AND
A MAGNIFICENT CATHEDRAL BUILT BETWEEN THE TWELFTH AND FOURTEENTH CENTURIES

SHOPPING IN THE NARROW STREETS AROUND THE PIAZZA DI SPAGNA IN
ROME IS AN EXCITING EXPERIENCE, ESPECIALLY WHEN YOU DISCOVER
A BOUTIQUE SUCH AS THIS IN THE VIA FRATTINA

PHOTO: RAY JOYCE

the old-fashioned pharmacist, where the last straw could really break the camel's back.

A judicious mixture of the four cardinal virtues — prudence, justice, strength and temperance — was required of the ideal citizen of ancient Rome, whether politician, intellectual, mother or soldier. Not even the cook escaped this rule of life, for he or she needed prudence to use only seasonal produce, justice to respect the natural flavors of foods, strength to stand up to the excesses and affectations of the eating habits of that time, and temperance in regulating quantities and proportions. Today, it could be said that in Rome these noble principles still stand, at least in the kitchen. Many of the ancient recipes have survived intact, save for a few adjustments where ingredients are no longer available, and they have found their way into homes and *trattorie* so that there is a reassuring sense of continuity; nothing that appears on the table in Rome will be improvised or casual. This gastronomic continuity is possible because Romans, both ancient and modern, were and are "market people." The forum, a large market where all the commercial and financial activities of the city took place, was the nerve center of Roman public life. And from this ancient practice of exchange in the marketplace, which of course involved ideas and words as well as goods, comes the typically Roman balanced, commonsense approach to eating.

In Rome's markets there is a hierarchy of displays, which can be traced back to the days when the coats of arms of the city's institutions were

A MAJESTIC TREE-LINED WALK ON THE OUTSKIRTS OF SIENA

flanked by a vine, an olive tree, a fig tree and a few stalks of wheat. Pride of place is given to the fruit and vegetable stands, and so we have the famous vegetable dishes of Rome and Latium: peas with ham, artichokes *alla romana* with garlic and mint, the autumnal broccoli, and *puntarelle,* a particular variety of chicory that is flavored with anchovies and eaten as a salad. There is an old saying that it takes three people to season *puntarelle* — a wise man for the salt, a miser for the vinegar and a genius for the oil. Then there are the reheated spinach, broad beans, and a host of other matchless green vegetable dishes.

Stalls selling fish and meat are few. Fish does not belong in the traditional Roman diet, except on Fridays, when salt cod (otherwise known as the poor man's fish), John Dory, or *palombo* (dogfish) are eaten. Meat is represented by tripe, *guanciale* (pig's cheek), oxtail (*coda alla vaccinara,* oxtail ragout cooked "butcher's style," is famous), and by the very thin slices of veal used for making *saltimbocca* and *piccatine. Abbacchio* (spring lamb), roast kid, and chicken (especially if it is cooked with peppers!) are reserved for Sundays and special occasions.

Eating patterns in this region still follow the weekly and seasonal agricultural calendar. The menu is organized around the consecration of feast days, with a meat dish once a week, tripe on Sundays, *gnocchi* on Thursdays, pancakes on St. Joseph's day, lamb at Easter, homemade *fettuccine* on Sundays, pasta and broccoli in autumn,

baked artichokes in spring, and for the feast of St. John, snails stewed with tomatoes, garlic, anchovies, mint and pecorino cheese. Spaghetti was admitted to the Roman table around 1800, and *alla carbonara* has become one of the most famous ways of serving it. Rice is used sparingly, notably for *supplì* (rice croquettes) and in stuffed tomatoes.

Because it is situated in the heart of the peninsula, with no outlet to the sea, Umbria has always been subject to some degree of influence from its neighbors. Economically and politically it was formerly dependent on the Papal States, and anyone traveling from Rome to the Adriatic coast had to pass through it. Reflected in its cooking is the contradiction between its original poor, peasant lifestyle and the more open, pleasure-oriented one that was imported. The former tradition goes back to the Franciscan and Benedictine orders, which first appeared in these parts; the second, modeled on life at the Roman court, was popular among country squires and the lords of the local castles who wanted to feel that they were the equals of the Papal aristocracy. These two very different styles resulted in two very different approaches to food: one simple and austere, using very few ingredients, and the other richer and more sophisticated. Today, Umbrian cuisine reflects this dual tradition, alternating between the rustic and the refined, with centuries-old peasant recipes on the one hand and sophisticated dishes from the provincial courts on the other.

There are some first courses that belong to a very ancient tradition and come under the heading of "poor" cuisine: thick soup made from spelt (an ancient cereal grain), onion soup, *tegamaccio* (a soup made with fish from Lake Trasimeno) and *ciriole ternane,* thick spaghetti with a cooked oil and garlic dressing. Conversely, some of the thrush dishes of more aristocratic origin include the salmis of wood pigeon, pheasant with olives and lamb on the spit.

There is, however, a common thread between these two culinary "schools," and that is olive oil, without question the most widely used of Umbria's agricultural products. The oil here is much stronger in taste than the Tuscan variety, giving all the varied dishes a common taste, a unifying basic element, which the palate cannot fail to detect.

The overall picture is of a nucleus of starchy foods and vegetables, with meats as a secondary addition. The purity of the ingredients is so fundamental that Umbrian cuisine is widely reputed for its health-giving properties.

Pork processing is considered to be a typically Umbrian activity. People involved in the butchering and preparation of sausages are known in Rome and Tuscany as *norcini* (literally, inhabitants of Norcia), and the Umbrians have been famous for their expertise in this field since medieval times.

So far the gastronomic picture does not contain any particular marvels other than the simplicity

THE GRAPE HARVEST IN THE TUSCAN PROVINCE OF CHIANTI. THESE WILL BE USED TO MAKE THE FAMOUS CHIANTI WINE ENJOYED ALL OVER THE WORLD

and rectitude of some of its dishes. But apart from the oil, there is one exclusive, rare and precious ingredient in Umbrian cuisine, and that is the black truffle. Found near Norcia, it has darkish flesh and a flavor that transforms a plate of *taglierini alla francescana,* a quick *frittata,* or a slice of toasted black bread into a dish worthy of a king. In the old days the truffle was thought to have magical powers, and certainly the addition of a few wafer-thin slices is all that is needed to turn ordinary dishes into memorable meals.

The full-flavored cuisine of the Marches is based essentially on the quality of the raw ingredients: meat, dairy foods, pork products, vegetables and fish of all kinds. It is a quality protected with care and dedication by the local gastronomes, who are determined to guard the rich culinary tradition of their region. In this sense it may be considered a conservative cuisine, for its recipes have remained strictly the same for centuries, some of them dating back to Roman times. It is thanks to the women that this heritage has been treasured and preserved, the traditional secrets of the kitchen being passed on from mother to daughter. It is said that when a girl from the Marches was betrothed, her future mother-in-law

would put her to the test in the kitchen: if she could "draw out the dough with elbow grease," in other words roll it out more and more thinly until her arms ached, she could be considered the ideal wife for the son of the house.

Given such a background, what could possibly be the number-one specialty of the region, if not *tagliatelle*? Actually, it is known here as *vincisgrassi*. It is in fact *lasagne*, but was renamed in the Napoleonic era by a prince called Windisch-Graetz, who pronounced the dish sublime and officially adopted it as part of the refined cuisine of his court. What he tasted is a kind of pasta pie with a sauce of chicken livers, chicken meat, lamb brains, mushrooms, truffles, Parmesan cheese, cream and prosciutto, covered with bechamel and baked in the oven. Another exclusive dish of which the *Marchigiani* are justly proud is the famous *porchetta al forno,* a young pig boned and roasted whole, well flavored with herbs and spices. It has now been adopted in other regions. The Marches also boast a first in fish cookery with *brodetto,* born of the inventiveness of local fishermen in two of the coastal towns, Porto Recanati and Ancona, who vie with each other to produce the best version. Those from Recanati

THE SPECTACULAR PIAZZA SAN PIETRO AS SEEN FROM THE ROOF OF SAINT PETER'S BASILICA. THE VIA DELLA CONCILIAZIONE LEADING INTO THE PIAZZA WAS COMPLETED IN 1937 AND IS A FITTING APPROACH TO BERNINI'S MASTERPIECE

begin by coating the fish in flour and seasoning it with saffron. The Anconans use neither of these, but add a little vinegar. Both variations use anything from twelve to twenty types of fish, and begin with a lightly fried mixture of oil, onion, garlic and parsley.

This is only the beginning of a very long list of dishes: pasta with sauces and pasta in soups, main dishes of meat and fish according to choice. But they all have in common a kind of mania that is exclusive to the *Marchigiani* — a fixation for stuffing. Everything is diligently stuffed, from chickens to pecorino *ravioli*, from cauliflower to olives. Yes, such is their skill in this perennial art that they even stuff olives — following an age-old recipe, of course, which no one is prepared to challenge. "The olives should be filled with very finely ground veal, pork, chicken breast, pure pork mortadella, prosciutto sautéed in butter and oil, with Marsala, truffles and nutmeg, grated Parmesan, all blended together with beaten eggs and meat sauce; dredge them lightly in flour, dip them in beaten egg, coat them in breadcrumbs and fry them in plenty of boiling oil." The ingredients are always the same, but the proportions are left to the individual cook, like an alchemist with a magic formula.

Pasta sfoglia — pasta dough, made with flour and fresh eggs and hand rolled — is the sovereign specialty of the cuisine of Emilia and Romagna. It is the product of a highly sophisticated craft that has been practiced for centuries. It involves the ritual motions of an art as surely as goldsmithing or cabinetmaking, but what the apprentices learn from the master cook is how to knead dough, roll it out and cut it into a thousand different shapes.

Lasagne, tagliatelle, taglierini, quadrucci, ravioli, cappelletti, tortellini — all these are famous names and they account in great measure for the world renown of Emilian cuisine. Consider the *tortellino*: it is a small square of dough filled with a mixture of pork loin, beef sirloin, turkey or chicken breast, mortadella, prosciutto, egg, grated Parmesan, nutmeg and beef marrow. The varying proportions of these ingredients constitute the difference between the Emilian school of cooking and those of Bologna, Modena, Parma, Reggio and Romagna, all linked by the universal cornerstone of stuffed pasta, but traditionally divided on the question of the correct filling. It is said that the *tortellino* derived its characteristic shape from the navel of the beautiful daughter of an Emilian country innkeeper; the Cardinal of Bologna's cook, traveling to Rome with his master, is supposed to have fallen in love with her and been inspired by his love to invent *tortellini*. There are similar stories about the origins of other Emilian dishes, ranging from *pasticcio di lasagne* to meat sauce and from veal scallops to *fritto misto*, and they are all tales of love and homage to female beauty. True or false, they all have an obvious meaning: in this area, historically among the most prosperous in Italy, one of the things that helps to inspirit the cooking is the people's vitality and zest for living. They sit down to the table with enthusiasm and feeling, with an instinctive love of gastronomy that makes every meal a banquet.

It is also said that in Emilia-Romagna people eat a lot. It would be more correct to say they eat well — in other words, they know how to eat and how to choose the best of what the soil so generously offers. And this is confirmed by the numerous specialties of the cuisine. For instance, how many possible "interpretations" are there of a piece of pork? The answer is many, and all of the highest order. As one sixteenth-century author enthusiastically wrote, pork products "are eaten raw, they are eaten cooked, and they sharpen the appetite at any hour of the day": mortadella from Bologna, Parma ham, salamis, sausages, the pigs' trotters of Modena. In short, there is a whole world of tastes here that have understandably moved beyond regional and national borders.

And so has another specialty of this region — *parmigiano reggiano,* perhaps the most famous cheese in the world, known for at least a thousand years for its exquisite taste. It is an ideal food in any diet and for everybody, be they one month or one hundred years old.

There is another "slice" of this regional cuisine that is less well known — that of the Romagna coast — where we find fish (gratinéed, served with sauce or cooked with herbs), game (roasted or casseroled), traditional farmhouse first courses like *passatelli, malfatti* and ricotta-filled *cappelletti,* and *piada,* a crisp round *focaccia* that is eaten hot and filled with the famous pork products of the region.

NOXIAAEGYPTIORVMDVMSER
INNOCENSPREMIEGOLVMBA
QVAEPACISOLEAMGESTA
ETVIRTVVMLILIISRET
OBELISCVMPROTROPHEO
ROMAETRIVM

BERNINI'S FOUNTAIN OF THE FOUR RIVERS ADORNS
THE PIAZZA NAVONA, ONE OF ROME'S MOST BEAUTIFUL SQUARES

I Secondi

CHEESE PANCAKE

Friuli-Venezia Giulia

FRICÒ

Cheese Pancake

A fricò is a very tasty cheese pancake. The mountain cheese of this area is low-fat and rather dry; either fontina or Swiss Gruyère may be used in its place.

1¼ lb (625 g) fontina or Gruyère cheese
3 tablespoons (2 oz/60 g) butter
1 medium onion, finely chopped
2 eggs, well beaten
salt and freshly ground pepper

Remove the rind from the cheese and slice it thinly. Melt the butter in a 10-in (25-cm) cast iron skillet over low heat. Add the onion and cook until very tender and translucent. Add the cheese and beaten eggs.

Continue cooking over low heat until the cheese forms a crust on the bottom, about 20 minutes. With the aid of a lid, turn the pancake and cook the other side. Drain on paper towels for 1 minute. Transfer to a platter and serve.

SERVES 6

Friuli-Venezia Giulia

FRITTATA ALLA VERDURA

Vegetable Frittata

Vegetable frittatas are very popular all year round. Here, as almost everywhere else in Italy, the vegetables used vary according to the season. In summer there are zucchini, peas or beans; in winter the popular radicchio, fennel *or* celery.

3 oz (90 g) sliced *pancetta* or rindless bacon
1¼ lb (625 g) *radicchio*, fennel, zucchini (courgettes)
  or spinach
2 tablespoons extra virgin olive oil
salt and freshly ground pepper
6 eggs, beaten

Lay the *pancetta* slices in a cast iron skillet and cook over low heat until crisp. Remove from the pan and crumble. Cut the vegetable in pieces and place in the skillet. Cook over medium heat in the oil until it begins to wilt. Season with salt and pepper and mix with the eggs and bacon in a bowl.

Pour egg mixture into the hot bacon fat and cook on one side, then tip the frittata onto a flat lid and slide it back into the pan to cook the other side. Remove from heat while the center is still soft. Transfer frittata to a serving plate and serve immediately.

SERVES 6

Umbria

FRITTATA AI TARTUFI NERI

Black Truffle Frittata

Black truffles are a specialty of Norcia, a small town in Umbria. They are used in stuffings or as a topping for pasta, served sliced over eggs cooked in butter, and added to pâtés — especially pâtés based on prosciutto.

Though they are harvested more or less at the same time of year, they have a less intense flavor than the white truffles of Alba.

6 eggs
salt and freshly ground pepper
2 large baking potatoes, boiled, peeled and sliced
1 medium-size black truffle, diced
1 slice (3 oz/90 g) cooked prosciutto, diced
2 tablespoons extra virgin olive oil
additional black truffle, thinly sliced (optional)

Beat the eggs with a little salt and pepper in a bowl. Stir in potatoes, truffle and prosciutto.

Heat the oil in a nonstick skillet and pour in the egg mixture. When one side of the frittata has cooked, turn it with the aid of a flat lid, and finish cooking the second side. Transfer to a serving plate. If desired, scatter some more sliced truffle on top of the frittata before serving.

SERVES 6

Sicilia

FRITTATA DI CAVOLFIORE

Cauliflower Frittata

Many kinds of cauliflower are grown in Sicily. In addition to the white variety, there are violet types and very tender and tasty green ones.

2 lb (1 kg) cauliflower
¼ cup (2 fl oz/60 ml) extra virgin olive oil
salt and freshly ground pepper
6 anchovy fillets in oil, chopped
6 eggs
2 tablespoons drained capers

Bring a large saucepan of salted water to boil. Remove the tough stalks of the cauliflower. Separate the florets and cook for 10 minutes in the boiling water. Drain and cool. Heat the oil in a skillet or non-stick pan. Add cauliflower, salt, pepper and anchovies and sauté over medium-high heat for a few minutes.

Beat the eggs in a small bowl; add the capers and salt and pepper. Pour this mixture over the cauliflower. Cook until the frittata is golden on the bottom. Invert onto a lid, then slide it back off the lid into the pan and cook the other side. Transfer the frittata to a serving plate and serve immediately.

SERVES 6

VEGETABLE FRITTATA (top left), BLACK TRUFFLE FRITTATA (top right)
AND CAULIFLOWER FRITTATA (bottom)

Basilicata

SPIEDINI DI PROVOLA
Cheese on Skewers

Basilicata is a very mountainous and rather infertile region. The most common cheese found in this area is provola, *a buffalo cheese that is often smoked over burning straw so that it will keep longer.*

7 oz (220 g) *pancetta* or rindless bacon, in a single piece
7 oz (220 g) smoked *provola* cheese
1 medium eggplant (aubergine)
7 oz (220 g) spicy Italian sausage
¼ cup bay leaves
¼ cup (2 fl oz/60 ml) extra virgin olive oil
salt and freshly ground pepper

Cut the bacon, cheese and eggplant into cubes; slice the sausage into rounds.

Thread pieces of eggplant, bacon, cheese and sausage alternately on 6 skewers, adding a bay leaf after each piece. Place kebabs over very hot coals. Mix the oil with salt and pepper. Grill for 20 minutes, turning frequently and basting with the seasoned oil almost constantly. Serve hot.

SERVES 6

CHEESE ON SKEWERS GARNISHED
WITH PARSLEY AND BASIL

Calabria

PIZZA DI SALSICCIA
Italian Sausage Pizza

Like most of the sausages of southern Italy, those of Calabria are spicy hot. This pizza, which is very rich and filling, is planned as a main course rather than a first course.

2 oz (60 g) dried *porcini* mushrooms or champignons
½ oz (15 g) fresh yeast or 1 envelope dry yeast
4 cups (1 lb/500 g) all purpose (plain) flour
1 lb (500 g) spicy Italian pork sausage, sliced
salt and freshly ground pepper
½ cup (4 fl oz/125 ml) extra virgin olive oil
1 tablespoon chopped parsley

ITALIAN SAUSAGE PIZZA

Soak the dried mushrooms in lukewarm water until softened. Dissolve yeast in ½ cup (4 fl oz/125 ml) lukewarm water. Heap the flour in a mound on a board and make a well in the center. Add yeast mixture and sufficient water to form a dough. Knead until smooth and elastic and shape into a ball. Cover dough with a towel and let rise until doubled in volume.

Knead the dough once more, briefly. Roll it out on a floured baking sheet into a circle ⅜ in (1 cm) thick.

Drain and finely chop the mushrooms. Cover dough with the mushrooms and sliced sausage. Drizzle with oil and bake in a preheated 475°F (250°C) oven for about 20 minutes or until crust is golden brown. Sprinkle with parsley and serve immediately.

SERVES 6

Liguria

TORTA PASQUALINA
Savory Easter Pie

This typical Ligurian dish is mainly served around Easter time, because that is when artichokes are the most tender and tasty. The artichokes grown in this region are very small.

1 lb (500 g) tender beet or spinach leaves
3 baby globe artichokes
½ cup (4 fl oz/125 ml) extra virgin olive oil
7 eggs
¾ cup (3 oz/90 g) freshly grated Parmesan cheese
7 oz (220 g) ricotta
2 tablespoons chopped fresh marjoram
2 tablespoons chopped fresh borage
salt and freshly ground pepper
2½ cups (10 oz/315 g) all purpose (plain) flour
1 egg yolk
extra virgin olive oil

Cook the beet leaves and the artichokes separately in boiling water just until tender. Coarsely chop the beet leaves; slice the artichokes. Sauté them briefly in a skillet with half the oil. Mix in 1 egg, the Parmesan, ricotta, marjoram, borage, and salt and pepper.

Heap the flour on a board and make a well in the center. Add remaining oil and sufficient water to make a smooth, soft dough. Divide the dough into 18 pieces and roll each out into a very thin round, large enough to cover the bottom of a 9-in (23-cm) pie dish.

Stack 9 of these sheets in the pie dish, brushing each with extra oil. Top with the vegetable and ricotta mixture, and make 6 hollows in it. Break an egg into each of the hollows and cover with the rest of the pastry sheets, brushing each with oil as before.

Brush the top of the pie with 1 egg yolk beaten with 1 tablespoon water. Bake in a preheated 350°F (180°C) oven until golden brown, about 1 hour. Serve hot or cold.

SERVES 6

Campania

PARMIGIANA DI MELANZANE
Baked Eggplant with Mozzarella

This is perhaps one of the most famous dishes of southern Italy — typical of the Campania region, but also popular in Sicily. It is a pan-Mediterranean dish; similar versions are to be found in Yugoslavia, Greece and Turkey.

2 lb (1 kg) eggplants (aubergines)
salt
oil for frying
4 garlic cloves, peeled and crushed
¼ cup (2 fl oz/60 ml) extra virgin olive oil
2 lb (1 kg) ripe tomatoes, peeled and chopped
freshly ground pepper
10 oz (315 g) mozzarella, sliced
¼ cup chopped fresh basil leaves

Wash the eggplants, cut off their tops and slice them crosswise. Sprinkle with salt and arrange the slices on a plate. Top with a weight and prop the plate at an angle so that most of the eggplant juices will drain out. Let drain for about 2 hours.

Dry the eggplant and fry in ½ in (1 cm) of smoking-hot oil until golden. Drain eggplant on paper towels.

Meanwhile, heat the garlic in the olive oil, add the peeled tomatoes and some salt and pepper, and cook this sauce for about 30 minutes to reduce it.

Spread a couple of tablespoons of the tomato sauce in a baking dish. Add a layer of the eggplant slices and a few slices of mozzarella. Scatter some basil on top. Continue layering ingredients until all are used, finishing with a sprinkle of basil leaves. Bake in a preheated 400°F (200°C) oven for 20 minutes. Serve hot.

SERVES 6

SAVORY EASTER PIE

PHOTO: FABBRI EDITORI MILANO

BAKED EGGPLANT WITH MOZZARELLA

131

STUFFED CABBAGE LEAVES

Lombardia

INVOLTINI DI VERZA RIPIENI
Stuffed Cabbage Leaves

In winter, when cabbage leaves are tender, they are filled with a variety of the tastiest ingredients — sausages, meats of all kinds, prosciutto, mortadella — or simply with boiled rice flavored with herbs, Parmesan cheese and eggs to make a lighter vegetarian dish.

12 cabbage leaves
5 oz (155 g) ground (minced) pork
5 oz (155 g) ground (minced) beef
2 fresh pork sausages, peeled and mashed
½ cup (1 oz/30 g) fresh breadcrumbs, soaked in milk and
   squeezed dry
1 egg, beaten
¾ cup (3 oz/90 g) freshly grated Parmesan cheese
1 sprig fresh thyme, chopped
2 tablespoons butter
salt and freshly ground pepper
¼ cup (2 fl oz/60 ml) light (single) cream or half and half
   (half milk and half cream)

Blanch the cabbage leaves for 1 minute in boiling salted water. Drain, lay them flat on a cloth and press lightly on the stalks to flatten. Remove the hard, thick central stalk to make rolling easier.

Mix the pork, beef, sausage, breadcrumbs, egg, Parmesan and thyme. Spread this mixture on the cabbage leaves, roll them up and secure with a toothpick.

Melt the butter in a skillet and arrange the rolls in it. Cook over moderate heat for 20 minutes, turning them once very carefully and moistening them occasionally with a little water. Season with salt and pepper.

Pour the cream into the pan and boil until slightly thickened. Serve immediately.

SERVES 6

Marche

BRODETTO DI SOGLIOLE
Adriatic Sole Soup

Brodetto is the name given to fish soup in the Marches and on the Adriatic coast. This brodetto marchigiano is a soup made only from sole, the most plentiful type of fish in those sandy depths. The fish used for this dish are generally not too large.

1 lb (500 g) fish bones and trimmings
1 carrot, coarsely chopped
1 celery stalk, coarsely chopped
½ cup parsley
4 cups (1 qt/1 l) water
salt and freshly ground pepper
¼ cup (2 fl oz/60 ml) extra virgin olive oil
2 garlic cloves, chopped
3 anchovy fillets, chopped
½ cup (4 fl oz/125 ml) dry white wine
4 ripe tomatoes, peeled and coarsely chopped
¼ teaspoon saffron, dissolved in a small amount of water
2 lb (1 kg) sole fillets
6 slices firm, coarse-textured bread

Combine fish scraps, carrot, celery, half the parsley, water, salt and pepper in a large saucepan and bring to simmer. Cook for 30 minutes over low heat.

Chop the remaining parsley. Heat oil in a saucepan. Add the chopped parsley, garlic and anchovy fillets and cook gently. Add the wine and cook until it evaporates. Add the tomatoes, the strained fish stock and the saffron and cook for about 10 minutes or until slightly thickened. Add the fillets of sole and cook for 3 to 5 more minutes.

Toast the bread in the oven until golden. Place one slice in the bottom of each soup bowl, pour the soup over and serve.

SERVES 6

ADRIATIC SOLE SOUP

SOUSED SARDINES (left) AND SARDINES STUFFED WITH RAISINS AND PINE NUTS (right)

Veneto

SARDE IN SAOR
Soused Sardines

The Venetian saor *is essentially the same as the* carpione *of Neapolitan cooking: in this case, however, golden raisins and pine nuts are added. The fish is marinated in boiled vinegar for a day before it is eaten.*

2 lb (1 kg) fresh sardines
1 cup (4 oz/125 g) all purpose (plain) flour
oil for deep frying
salt
¼ cup (2 fl oz/60 ml) extra virgin olive oil
2 onions, sliced
1 cup (8 fl oz/250 ml) red wine vinegar
pinch of ground cinnamon
freshly ground pepper
2 tablespoons pine nuts
2 tablespoons golden raisins (sultanas), soaked in
   lukewarm water

❧ Clean the sardines and remove the heads. Open the fish flat, wash and dry them and dredge in flour.
❧ Deep fry the fish in very hot oil until crisp. Drain on paper towels. Season with salt. Heat the olive oil in a non-aluminum saucepan and fry the onions until translucent. Add the vinegar and season with cinnamon and pepper. Boil for 2 minutes, then remove from heat.
❧ Arrange the sardines in layers in a bowl, scattering pine nuts and the drained raisins between layers. Slowly add the onion mixture. Marinate for at least 24 hours, then drain and serve garnished with parsley, if desired.

SERVES 6

Sicilia

SARDE A BECCAFICO
Sardines Stuffed with Raisins and Pine Nuts

In Sicilian cooking, raisins are often combined with fish as well as with meat. Sicily is known for the variety of grapes it produces, including the Pantelleria muscat which is world famous for its sweetness.

2 lb (1 kg) fresh sardines
½ cup (3 oz/90 g) raisins
½ cup (3 oz/90 g) pine nuts
3 tablespoons fine dry breadcrumbs
2 garlic cloves, chopped
freshly ground pepper
2 tablespoons extra virgin olive oil
1 cup (4 oz/125 g) all purpose (plain) flour
oil for frying

❧ Clean and bone the sardines, remove the heads and tails, and wash and dry the fish.
❧ Soak the raisins in a cup of lukewarm water until soft. Drain and pat dry. Mix raisins with the pine nuts, breadcrumbs, garlic, pepper and olive oil. Stuff the sardines with this mixture, then reclose them and coat thoroughly with flour.
❧ Pour oil into skillet to the depth of 1 in (2.5 cm). Heat oil, then add the sardines and fry for 5 minutes or until nicely browned on both sides. Drain fish on paper towels and sprinkle with salt. Arrange on a dish and serve.

SERVES 6

Liguria

SPIGOLA AL SALE
Sea Bass Baked in Salt

This method of cooking produces a particularly tasty fish that retains all its natural flavor. The fish used must be fairly large; salmon makes a good alternative to sea bass.

The salt forms a hard crust around the fish that is easily broken away at the end of cooking.

1 sea bass, salmon or grouper 4 lb (2 kg), cleaned
3 fresh rosemary sprigs
salt and freshly ground pepper
8 lb (4 kg) coarse sea salt
1 cup (4 oz/125 g) all purpose (plain) flour
¼ cup (2 fl oz/60 ml) extra virgin olive oil
2 tablespoons butter
juice of 1 lemon
1 tablespoon chopped parsley

Into the cavity of the fish put a sprig of rosemary and a sprinkle of salt and pepper. Cover the bottom of an oval casserole with sea salt and lay the fish on this, placing a sprig of rosemary underneath it and another on top. Cover the fish completely with the rest of the sea salt.

Mix the flour to a thin paste with a little water. Brush the surface of the salt with the paste. Bake fish in a preheated 400°F (200°C) oven until the salt begins to brown, about 30 minutes.

Bring casserole to the table and break the salt block. Remove the fish and transfer to a serving dish. Heat the oil and butter; before they begin to sizzle, stir in salt, pepper, lemon juice and parsley. Pour into a sauceboat and serve with the fish.

SERVES 6

Sicilia

TEGLIA DI PESCE SPADA
Marinated Swordfish

Swordfish is one of the most common Sicilian fish. It is mainly caught in the channel that divides Sicily from Africa, and is sold fresh in the markets in autumn and winter. The fish is often grilled and served with oil, lemon juice and capers, which grow wild on the island and are preserved in salt.

6 swordfish steaks (tuna fish or snapper cutlets), about 7 oz (220 g) each
salt and freshly ground pepper
1 cup (8 fl oz/250 ml) dry white wine
1 fresh rosemary sprig
4 garlic cloves, finely chopped
¼ cup (2 fl oz/60 ml) extra virgin olive oil
2 tablespoons fine dry breadcrumbs
3 tablespoons drained capers, chopped
juice of 1 lemon

Place the swordfish steaks in a bowl and season with salt and pepper. Pour in the wine. Finely chop the rosemary leaves and add to fish with the garlic. Coat steaks well and marinate for at least 1 hour.

Drain fish, reserving marinade. Brush a skillet with a little of the oil and heat it. Sprinkle fish with breadcrumbs and capers, add to skillet and cook on both sides until nearly cooked through, basting from time to time with marinade.

Whisk the rest of the oil with the lemon juice in a small bowl. Pour over the fish and cook for a few more minutes. Serve hot.

SERVES 6

OCTOPUS *SANTA LUCIA*

Campania

POLPO ALLA LUCIANA
Octopus Santa Lucia

Octopus are found in large numbers hidden in the grottoes of Campania. They are considered a delicacy, and there are many ways of preparing them.

1 octopus, about 2 lb (1 kg)
¼ cup (2 fl oz/60 ml) extra virgin olive oil
salt and freshly ground pepper
3 garlic cloves, chopped
¼ cup parsley, chopped
a small piece of chili pepper
juice of 1 lemon
1 tablespoon chopped parsley

Clean the octopus, removing the sac, eyes and mouth. Pound it with a meat mallet for about 10 minutes to soften the fibers.

Preheat oven to 225°F (105°C). Place the octopus in a ceramic casserole just large enough to hold it. Pour the oil over it and sprinkle with salt, pepper, garlic, parsley and chili pepper. Cover the casserole with a sheet of waxed paper and tie a piece of string tightly around the outside. Cover the casserole and bake until the octopus is tender, about 2 hours.

Remove the lid and waxed paper and place the casserole on a napkin-covered serving plate. Sprinkle with the lemon juice and scatter the extra parsley over the top. Serve hot.

SERVES 6

Campania

POLPETIELLI AFFOGATI
Stewed Baby Octopus

Polpetielli are tiny octopus weighing no more than 10 oz (315 g) each. This recipe is also sometimes used for baby squid or cuttlefish (ink removed); it may be served hot, lukewarm or cold. Whatever the seafood, it must be cooked for a long period over a very gentle flame. It is best to use a terracotta pan or casserole, which will diffuse the heat.

2 lb (1 kg) baby octopus
salt
1 whole red chili pepper
1 tablespoon chopped parsley
1 small tomato, peeled and cut into strips
⅓ cup (3 fl oz/100 ml) extra virgin olive oil
1 lemon, cut into wedges

Remove the eyes, mouths and ink sacs from the octopus and wash them several times; do not dry. Beat them lightly with a mallet to tenderize. Place in a terracotta casserole and season with salt. Add the whole chili pepper, parsley, tomato and oil.

Cover tightly and cook over very gentle heat for 2 hours or until octopus is very tender. Remove from heat and let rest briefly.

Discard the chili pepper. Serve the octopus in the casserole, passing the lemon wedges separately.

SERVES 6   *Photograph page 155*

Sardegna

ARAGOSTE AL FINOCCHIO
Lobster with Fennel

The jagged coast of Sardinia, with its tall cliffs and blue-green sea, is a favorite refuge of lobsters. They are caught in abundance by local fishermen and cooked with fennel, which grows plentifully in the wild.

salt
juice of 1 lemon
1 tablespoon fennel seeds
½ cup (4 fl oz/125 ml) extra virgin olive oil
freshly ground pepper
1 large bunch of wild fennel
6 small lobsters whole

Dissolve salt to taste in the lemon juice. Mix in the fennel seeds, oil and pepper.

Make a bed of fennel on a preheated grill and lay the lobsters on top. Grill for 15 minutes, turning from time to time and brushing often with the marinade.

Arrange lobsters on a platter and serve, serving the rest of the marinade separately.

SERVES 6

LOBSTER WITH FENNEL

Campania

FRITTO MISTO DI PESCE
Mixed Fried Seafood

This dish is usually made of tiny baby squid, cuttlefish rings and tails of scampi, or langoustines. It is served crisp and piping hot, garnished with lemon wedges and little sprigs of parsley.

10 oz (315 g) baby squid
10 oz (315 g) cuttlefish (or substitute medium to large squid)
10 oz (315 g) *scampi* tails or large shrimp (prawns), shelled
1 cup (4 oz/125 g) all purpose (plain) flour
oil for deep frying
6 lemon wedges
salt

Clean the squid and cuttlefish, removing the eyes, beaks and transparent quills. Leave the baby squid whole. Cut the bodies of the cuttlefish into rings and separate the tentacles.

Wash all the seafood and dry it well. Dredge each piece in flour. Heat a good quantity of oil in a large cast iron skillet and fry the seafood a few pieces at a time. Drain on paper towels, sprinkle with salt and serve at once, accompanied with slices of lemon.

SERVES 6

Toscana

SEPPIE IN ZIMINO
Squid in Zimino

This is a famous Tuscan dish that is also found in other regions such as Liguria. It is excellent served as an accompaniment to polenta.

"In zimino" means that the squid is cooked with vegetables — usually spinach or beet greens.

1 tablespoon extra virgin olive oil
½ onion, chopped
1 garlic clove, minced
1 dried red chili pepper, minced
¼ cup chopped parsley
½ celery stalk, chopped
1 lb (500 g) squid, cleaned and cut into rings, including the tentacles
1 teaspoon all purpose (plain) flour
½ cup (1½ oz/45 g) dried mushrooms, soaked for 30 minutes, drained and chopped
2 tomatoes, chopped
1 lb (500 g) fresh spinach, chopped
1 cup (8 fl oz/250 ml) dry white wine
salt and freshly ground pepper

TROUT WITH CREAM SAUCE

⚏ Heat the olive oil in a saucepan over medium heat. Add the onion, garlic, chili pepper, parsley and celery and sauté until the onion is lightly colored.

⚏ Add the squid and cook for 10 minutes over medium heat. Sprinkle in the flour, and stir to blend. Add the mushrooms, tomatoes, spinach and wine. Season with salt and pepper. Cover and simmer ½ hour.

⚏ Uncover and simmer until liquid is thickened to sauce consistency. Transfer to a platter and serve hot.

SERVES 6

SQUID IN ZIMINO

Trentino-Alto Adige

TROTELLE ALLA PANNA
Trout with Cream Sauce

Trout are to be found in abundance in the rivers of the very mountainous Trentino area on the Austrian border. They are bought alive, cleaned at the last moment and cooked in a vegetable stock.

1 large carrot, cut into several pieces
1 celery stalk, cut into several pieces
several parsley sprigs, 2 thyme sprigs and 1 bay leaf tied
   into a bunch
a small piece of onion
3 tablespoons (2 oz/60 g) butter
1 cup (8 fl oz/250 ml) sour cream
salt
6 trout, about 8 oz (250 g) each, cleaned
2 tablespoons chopped parsley

⚏ In a saucepan, bring 4 in (10 cm) of salted water to boil with the carrot, celery, herbs and onion. Cover and simmer for 30 minutes.

⚏ Meanwhile, melt butter in a skillet, add the sour cream and a little salt and bring slowly to boil, stirring constantly. Simmer until reduced to a thin sauce consistency. Set aside and keep warm.

⚏ Place the trout in the vegetable stock and poach gently just until flesh is opaque and easily flakes when tested with a fork, about 10 minutes. Lift out and drain briefly. Arrange trout on a serving plate, pour the sauce over them, sprinkle with parsley and serve.

SERVES 6

Veneto

ANGUILLA ALL'UVETTA
Eel with Golden Raisins

Eels are bred in the delta of the River Po and form an important part of many dishes in the cooking of the Venetian region, particularly around the area of Chioggia, a charming little port that resembles a miniature Venice. Eels are often served with polenta.

¼ cup (2 fl oz/60 ml) extra virgin olive oil
7 oz (220 g) fresh *porcini* mushrooms or champignons, sliced
salt and freshly ground pepper
juice of ½ lemon
2 tablespoons golden raisins (sultanas)
2 lb (1 kg) eels, skinned
1 tablespoon butter
1 onion, sliced
1 carrot, sliced
2 garlic cloves, minced
1 tablespoon all purpose (plain) flour
1 cup (8 fl oz/250 ml) red wine
1 tablespoon brandy
1 whole clove
several parsley sprigs, 1 rosemary sprig and 2 bay leaves
    tied into a bunch
¾ cup (6 fl oz/200 ml) water

Heat 2 tablespoons oil in a skillet over moderate heat. Add mushrooms and sauté for 5 minutes. Add salt and pepper and squeeze lemon juice over the mushrooms. Cover raisins with lukewarm water and let soak until needed. Cut the eel into chunks; wash and dry them.

Heat remaining oil with the butter in a skillet. Add the onion and carrot and sauté over moderate heat until onion is translucent. Add the pieces of eel and brown over high heat for 10 minutes. Remove the eel. Add the garlic to the skillet and stir just until fragrant. Stir in the flour, then add the wine, brandy, clove, herbs and water. Cover and cook over low heat for 1 hour.

Strain the sauce through a sieve and transfer sauce to a saucepan. Add the mushrooms, the drained raisins and the eel, and simmer for a few minutes to blend flavors. Serve at once.

SERVES 6

EEL WITH GOLDEN RAISINS SERVED WITH POLENTA

TUNA STEAKS WITH CAPERS

COSTOLETTE DI TONNO AI CAPPERI

Tuna Steaks with Capers

Sicilian fishing expeditions are known as bloody "massacres." Numerous boats surround the schools of fish, enclosing them in a vast net. Then the tuna are killed with harpoons and hauled aboard the boats.

6 tuna steaks, about 7 oz (220 g) each
salt and freshly ground pepper
1 cup (8 fl oz/250 ml) dry white wine
1 fresh rosemary sprig, finely chopped
6 garlic cloves, finely chopped
¼ cup (2 fl oz/60 ml) extra virgin olive oil
2 tablespoons dry fine breadcrumbs
juice of 1 lemon
1 tablespoon drained capers, chopped

☙ Place the tuna steaks in a nonaluminum bowl. Salt and pepper them. Add the wine, rosemary and garlic, and turn steaks to coat evenly. Let marinate at least 1 hour. Drain tuna and pat dry; reserve marinade.

☙ Coat a grill or corrugated cast iron pan with some of the oil and heat it. Grill the tuna on both sides, basting frequently with the reserved marinade. Sprinkle the cooked tuna with breadcrumbs.

☙ In a small bowl, whisk the remaining oil with the lemon juice, capers, and salt and pepper. Transfer the tuna to a serving plate. Drizzle sauce over it and serve.

SERVES 6

141

CRAB WITH LEMON GARNISHED WITH MAYONNAISE, CAPERS AND FISH ROE

Veneto

GRANSEOLA AL LIMONE
Crab with Lemon

Granseole are large, very tender spider crabs found only in Venice, where they are considered a delicacy. They are served simply with lemon so as not to overwhelm their flavor.

6 spider crabs or small green crayfish (lobsters)
18 lettuce leaves
½ cup (4 fl oz/125 ml) extra virgin olive oil
juice of 1 lemon
2 tablespoons chopped parsley
salt and freshly ground pepper

Bring a saucepan of salted water to boil and drop in the crabs (still alive, if possible). Cook for 10 minutes or until pink in color, then let cool in the water. Make a circular cut beneath the upper shells of the main body and take out the flesh (or halve lobsters lengthwise). Remove the entrails and stomach, reserving the coral if there is any. Clean out the inside of each shell and wash well.

Place 3 lettuce leaves on each plate. Top with the crab shells. Mix the crabmeat with the oil, lemon, parsley and a little salt and pepper. Return the flesh to the shells, scatter the coral (if any) over it and serve.

SERVES 6

Lombardia

OSSI BUCHI IN GREMOLATA
Stewed Veal Shanks with Lemon

Gremolata is a mixture of parsley, anchovies and lemon rind traditionally sprinkled over these ossi buchi, or veal shanks. The dish is generally served over saffron rice, which produces a perfect marriage of flavors. It is a good idea to ask the butcher to cut the meat from the central part of the shank, where the bone is smaller.

The bone marrow is lifted out with a toothpick so that its taste can be savored.

6 pieces veal shank (*ossi buchi*) cut about 1 in (2.5 cm) thick
1 cup (4 oz/125 g) all purpose (plain) flour
2 tablespoons butter
½ cup (4 fl oz/125 ml) dry white wine
salt and freshly ground pepper
1 anchovy fillet, chopped
juice of 1 lemon
grated rind of ½ lemon
2 tablespoons chopped parsley

Dredge the veal shanks in flour, shaking off excess. Melt the butter in a wide skillet, arrange the veal shanks in it side by side, and brown them on one side over medium heat. Turn carefully and brown the other side.

Pour in the wine and allow to evaporate completely. Add salt and pepper, cover and simmer the meat for about 1½ hours, adding water a little at a time to keep some liquid in the bottom of the pan. Add the anchovy and the lemon juice and rind. Sprinkle with parsley and serve.

SERVES 6

STEWED VEAL SHANKS WITH LEMON

Val d'Aosta

COSTOLETTE ALLA VALDOSTANA
Veal Chops Valdostana

Fontina, typical of this region, is a very tasty mountain cheese made from cow's milk. It is used in the preparation of numerous dishes, the most famous being a fondue served with the white truffles of Alba sliced on top.

6 veal chops or cutlets with bone
6 thin slices fontina or Gruyère cheese
2 eggs
salt and freshly ground pepper
¾ cup (3 oz/90 g) fine dry breadcrumbs
3 oz (90 g) butter

Cut the chops in half almost to the bone, creating a pocket for stuffing. Insert 1 slice of cheese in each chop and close the meat over it, pressing firmly, to seal edges.
Beat egg with salt and pepper. Dip each chop in egg to coat both sides, then coat with breadcrumbs. Season with salt and pepper. Heat the butter in a pan and brown the chops over a medium heat for about 5 minutes on each side. Drain the chops on paper towels and serve.

SERVES 6

LITTLE VEAL ROLLS WITH MARJORAM ACCOMPANIED BY BROCCOLI AND TOMATO (right) AND VEAL CHOPS VALDOSTANA SERVED WITH SAUTÉED CHAMPIGNONS AND CUCUMBER SLICES (left)

Liguria

INVOLTINI ALLA MAGGIORANA
Little Veal Rolls with Marjoram

Marjoram is characteristic of the Liguria region, where it grows wild in the fields and is used in many fillings for meat, pasta and vegetables.

1⅔ lb (800 g) small, thin slices of veal (escalopes)
½ cup (1 oz/30 g) firm, coarse-textured breadcrumbs, soaked in milk and squeezed dry
3 tablespoons chopped fresh marjoram
1 egg
3 oz (90 g) prosciutto, chopped
salt and freshly ground pepper
1 tablespoon butter
½ cup (4 fl oz/125 ml) dry white wine

Pound the veal slices with a mallet until thin and flat. Combine the bread, marjoram, egg, prosciutto, salt and pepper.
Place a small amount of this filling on each veal slice and roll it up to seal in the filling. Fasten with a toothpick. Melt the butter in a skillet and brown the veal rolls over high heat for about 10 minutes. Pour in the wine and stir to scrape up browned bits. Cook over very low heat until juices are thickened to sauce consistency, about 20 minutes.
Arrange the rolls on a serving dish, pour the sauce over and serve.

SERVES 6

continue cooking over low heat for 30 minutes, adding water a little at a time to keep some liquid in the bottom of the pan.

☙ Arrange the chops on a serving dish. Scrape up the browned pan juices, adding a little more water if necessary. Pour over the chops. Serve accompanied with boiled baby carrots sautéed in butter and parsley.

SERVES 6

VEAL CHOPS WITH SAGE (top) AND MILANESE VEAL CHOPS (bottom)

Lombardia

NODINI ALLA SALVIA
Veal Chops with Sage

These chops are cut from the saddle, where there are no protruding ribs. The meat from this part of the animal is fatter than that used for veal scallops, and so is more suitable for cooking over a long period of time. When cooked it takes on a dark golden color. It is important to cook these chops in an aluminum skillet so that a brown coating forms on the bottom; this is to be blended with added water from time to time.

2 tablespoons butter
½ cup (1 oz/30 g) fresh sage
6 veal chops, about 1 in (2.5 cm) thick
2 tablespoons all purpose (plain) flour
¼ cup (2 fl oz/60 ml) Marsala
salt and freshly ground pepper

☙ In a wide heavy aluminum skillet, heat the butter with the sage, then add the chops and brown on both sides over high heat. Sprinkle chops with flour. Pour in the Marsala and let it evaporate. Add salt and pepper, cover pan and

Lombardia

COSTOLETTE ALLA MILANESE
Milanese Veal Chops

Outside Italy, these are known as "Viennese chops" (Wiener schnitzel). It is difficult to know who gave the recipe to whom; Lombardy was in fact under Austrian domination for a long period.

1 egg
salt and freshly ground pepper
6 veal chops (cutlets) with bone, cut from the rib side of the loin
¾ cup (3 oz/90 g) fine dry breadcrumbs
3 oz (90 g) butter
1 lemon, cut into wedges

☙ Beat the egg on a plate with salt and pepper. Flatten the chops and dip each one in the egg. Coat with breadcrumbs, pressing them well to make them adhere.

☙ Heat the butter in a skillet over low heat and cook the chops for 5–7 minutes on each side until light golden. Arrange on a serving plate, garnish with lemon slices or wedges and serve.

SERVES 6

Toscana

LINGUA AL DRAGONCELLO
Tongue in Tarragon Sauce

In most parts of Italy, boiled meat is served with a green sauce based on chopped parsley. In Tuscany, particularly in the area around Siena, the parsley is replaced by tarragon, which is the characteristic herb of the area.

1 veal tongue, about 1⅔ lb (800 g)
2 tablespoons fresh breadcrumbs, soaked in red wine vinegar and squeezed dry
½ cup (4 oz/125 g) chopped fresh tarragon
1 tablespoon chopped drained capers
1 hard-cooked (hard-boiled) egg, chopped
3 anchovy fillets in oil, chopped
½ cup (4 fl oz/125 ml) extra virgin olive oil
salt and freshly ground pepper

☙ Bring a large saucepan of salted water to boil. Add the tongue and simmer for 30 minutes. Peel off the skin, return the tongue to the saucepan and simmer for a further 1½ hours.

☙ Mix the breadcrumbs, tarragon, capers, egg, anchovies, oil, salt and pepper and blend well. Slice the tongue and arrange on a serving plate. Cover with the sauce and serve.

SERVES 6   *Photograph page 149*

VEAL WITH MARSALA SERVED WITH WHITE RICE (left) AND VEAL SCALLOPS WITH PROSCIUTTO AND SAGE SERVED WITH CAULIFLOWER (right)

Lombardia

PICCATA AL MARSALA
Veal with Marsala

This piccata *is usually served on top of a Milanese risotto, (see* risotto alla zafferano, *page 84), making an elegant one-dish meal. This is one of the rare cases of rice being served with meat; it is normally not done.*

Another meat dish traditionally served with risotto is ossi buchi in gremolata *(see page 142).*

1½ lb (750 g) veal rump roast, cut into 3-in (8-cm) round
   scallops (escalopes)
1 cup (4 oz/125 g) all purpose (plain) flour
3 tablespoons (2 oz/60 g) butter
salt and freshly ground pepper
½ cup (4 fl oz/125 ml) Marsala
1 tablespoon chopped parsley

Pound the meat until very thin. Dredge it in flour on both sides, shaking off excess. Melt the butter in a large skillet over high heat. Add the meat and brown on both sides. Season with salt and pepper. Pour in Marsala a little at a time.

Cover the skillet and cook over low heat 25 minutes, adding water as needed to keep meat from drying out. Add parsley and cook 5 minutes longer. Serve immediately.

SERVES 6

Lazio

SALTIMBOCCA ALLA ROMANA
Veal Scallops with Prosciutto and Sage

There are two versions of this dish found in Latium: the veal may be rolled up around the ham, or the ham and sage may be placed on top of each piece of veal and secured with a toothpick before the scallops are cooked in butter and white wine.

6 slices prosciutto, halved
12 fresh sage leaves
12 veal scallops (escalopes) about 1½ lb (750 g)
1 tablespoon butter
½ cup (4 fl oz/125 ml) dry white wine
salt and freshly ground pepper

Place ½ slice of prosciutto and a sage leaf on each veal slice. Roll up each piece and secure with a toothpick.

Melt the butter in a heavy skillet and brown the veal rolls well. Add the white wine and cook until reduced to several tablespoons, scraping browned bits from the bottom of the pan. Cover and cook over low heat for 20 minutes, adding water a tablespoon or so at a time to keep meat from drying out. Serve rolls hot.

SERVES 6

STUFFED COLD VEAL

Liguria

CIMA ALLA GENOVESE
Stuffed Cold Veal

This dish is usually accompanied with cooked vegetables dressed with light Ligurian olive oil, which has a special, delicate aroma. The broth (stock) in which the veal was cooked is used to make a light soup with the addition of 7 oz (220 g) of homemade soup pasta (taglierini).

1 piece of veal breast, about 1¼ lb (625 g)
3 oz (90 g) sweetbreads
3 oz (90 g) ground (minced) pork tenderloin (fillet)
3 oz (90 g) pork fat
¼ cup parsley leaves, chopped
1 bay leaf
3 oz (90 g) cooked peas
1 tablespoon shelled pistachio nuts
2 tablespoons freshly grated Parmesan cheese
1 tablespoon chopped fresh marjoram
1 dinner roll or 1 cup (2 oz/60 g) firm, coarse-textured
    breadcrumbs, soaked in milk and squeezed dry
salt and freshly ground pepper
1 egg
1 tablespoon dry Marsala
2 hard-cooked (hard-boiled) eggs shelled
1 small onion, peeled and halved
1 carrot, coarsely chopped
1 celery stalk, coarsely chopped

⁂ Ask the butcher to cut a pocket in the veal so that it is open at one end and closed at the other.
⁂ Soak the sweetbreads in cold water to cover for at least 1 hour, changing water several times. Transfer sweetbreads to a saucepan and cover with cold water. Bring slowly to boil and simmer, uncovered, 3 to 5 minutes. Drain. Remove the membrane. Coarsely chop sweetbreads. In a bowl, mix them with the pork, pork fat, parsley, bay leaf, peas, pistachios, Parmesan, marjoram, bread, salt and pepper. Stir in the raw egg and the Marsala.

⁂ Place a few spoonfuls of the stuffing mixture in the pocket of the meat, pushing it well down to the bottom. Put in one of the cooked eggs and some more stuffing, then the second egg and the remaining stuffing.
⁂ Sew up the opening in the meat, using a large needle and heavy thread. Then tie the meat with string in loops along its length, like a salami. Fill a large saucepan with enough water to cover the meat. Add onion, carrot and celery and bring to boil. Add the meat and simmer gently for 2 hours, partially covered.
⁂ Drain the meat. Cover with a plate and top with a weight. Refrigerate for 3 hours before slicing and serving.

SERVES 6

Piemonte

FRITTO MISTO ALLA PIEMONTESE
Piedmontese Sweet and Savory Fritters

The "mixed fry" of Piedmontese cooking is justly famous because it is made up of a variety of ingredients, including amaretti and sweet semolina cakes. The Piedmontese fritto misto *is cooked in clarified butter.*

2 cups (16 fl oz/500 ml) milk
2 tablespoons sugar
½ cup (3 oz/90 g) fine semolina
1 egg yolk
½ calf's brain
7 oz (220 g) sweetbreads
6 thin slices veal, about 2½ in (6 cm) in diameter
6 slices calf's liver, about 2½ in (6 cm) in diameter
6 amaretti biscuits
1 cup (4 oz/125 g) all purpose (plain) flour
2 eggs, well beaten
2 cups (8 oz/250 g) fine dry breadcrumbs
1 lb (500 g) butter, clarified
salt

PIEDMONTESE SWEET AND SAVORY FRITTERS

Piemonte

STRACOTTO AL BAROLO
Beef Braised in Barolo Wine

Barolo is a fine, long-lived wine from Piedmont. For this dish it is best to use a wine that is at least five years old; this gives a thicker and tastier sauce.

2 lb (1 kg) braising beef
2 carrots, cut into several pieces each
1 medium onion, coarsely chopped
2 celery stalks, cut into several pieces
½ cup parsley
2 bay leaves
1 tablespoon juniper berries
1 teaspoon peppercorns
½ cup diced lard
½ bottle (1½ cups/12 fl oz/375 ml) aged Barolo (red) wine
1 tablespoon butter
1 tablespoon extra virgin olive oil
salt

Bring the milk to boil in a saucepan with the sugar. Add the semolina all at once and cook for 20 minutes, stirring constantly. Remove from heat and mix in 1 egg yolk. Spread mixture about ⅜ in (1 cm) thick on a wet board. When it has cooled, cut into circles about 2 in (5 cm) in diameter.

Boil the brain and sweetbreads in water to cover for 10 minutes. Remove membranes. Place on a plate and top with a weight; cool completely. Cut into slices ⅜ in (1 cm) thick. Dredge the semolina cakes, meats and amaretti first in the flour, then in the beaten eggs and finally in the bread-crumbs.

Heat the butter in a 10-in (25-cm) cast iron skillet and fry the fritters a few at a time. Drain on paper towels, transfer to a serving dish and serve piping hot.

SERVES 6

Combine the meat, all the vegetables, the herbs and the wine in a bowl. Cover and marinate in the refrigerator for at least 24 hours.

Remove the meat and dry well; reserve marinade. Make little cuts on the surface of the meat and fill them with lard. Brown the meat thoroughly in hot butter and oil in a flameproof casserole. Preheat oven to 350°F (180°C). Lift out the marinade vegetables with a slotted spoon and add to the meat. Add 1 cup of the wine and salt to taste. Cover and braise in the oven for about 3 hours, adding more wine as needed to keep meat from drying out.

Remove meat when done and place on a platter. Put the vegetables and wine through a food mill or grind to a textured puree in food processor. Reheat this and pour over the meat. Serve at once.

SERVES 6

BEEF BRAISED IN BAROLO WINE

HOT PEPPER STEAKS

Lazio

BISTECCHE ALL' ARRABBIATA
Hot Pepper Steaks

These large pieces of meat, beaten very thin with a meat mallet, are called "frenzied steaks" because they are liberally sprinkled with chili peppers.

It is important to use a very heavy cast iron skillet for this dish — otherwise the steaks will be just like meat cooked on a grill.

6 beef sirloin steaks, about 5 oz (155 g) each
2 tablespoons extra virgin olive oil
2 red chili peppers, minced
3 garlic cloves, minced
salt and freshly ground pepper

Pound the steaks with a meat mallet until they are about ¼ in (0.5 cm) thick. Heat the oil over high heat in a large cast iron skillet. Add the red peppers and garlic.
Place the steaks on top and cook for about 1 minute on each side. Add salt and pepper at the end of cooking. Serve accompanied with sautéed vegetables. Garnish with lemon slices and rosemary if desired.

SERVES 6

Lazio

CODA ALLA VACCINARA
Oxtail Ragout

This simple but very tasty dish has a long cooking time so that all the fat in the oxtail can melt out gradually. The oxtail stock, strained and clarified, makes excellent aspic.

4 lb (2 kg) oxtail pieces
2 carrots
1 celery stalk, cut into several pieces
2 medium onions
¼ cup parsley
2 bay leaves
2 oz (60 g) fatty prosciutto
2 tablespoons extra virgin olive oil
salt and freshly ground pepper
¾ cup (6 fl oz/200 ml) dry white wine
1 lb (500 g) peeled tomatoes
1 fresh thyme sprig
2 whole cloves
pinch of lemon peel

Combine oxtail, 1 carrot, celery, 1 onion and parsley in a large saucepan. Add enough salted water so that the pieces of meat float.

OXTAIL RAGOUT (top) AND TONGUE IN TARRAGON SAUCE GARNISHED WITH PARSLEY (recipe page 144)

❧ Bring to boil; simmer over low heat for 4 hours, skimming frequently. When the meat is tender, drain; strain and reserve the stock.

❧ Finely chop the remaining carrot and onion, the bay leaf and the prosciutto. Heat the oil in a saucepan. Add chopped ingredients and oxtail and sauté over moderate heat until browned. Add salt and pepper and stir well. Add the wine, tomatoes, thyme, cloves and lemon peel and simmer for 30 minutes, adding reserved stock as required. Transfer to a serving dish and serve hot.

SERVES 6

FEGATO DI VITELLO ALLA VENEZIANA

Calf's Liver Venetian Style

It is essential for the success of this famous dish that the liver be tender and that it be cooked very briefly over very high heat, so that it does not become hard and dry. It is best to cook the onions separately and add them at the last moment.

1⅔ lb (800 g) calf's liver
13 oz (410 g) onions, thinly sliced

3 tablespoons (2 oz/60 g) butter
½ cup (4 fl oz/125 ml) dry white wine
salt and freshly ground pepper

Slice the liver very thinly, and cut into medium pieces. Fry the onions in half the butter in a skillet until golden. Add the wine and salt and pepper, cover and braise the onions until tender over low heat. Remove onions and keep warm.

Melt the rest of the butter in the skillet, add the liver and sauté over high heat just until cooked through. Add salt to taste, then mix in the onions. Serve immediately, garnished with chopped parsley if desired.

SERVES 6

CALF'S LIVER VENETIAN STYLE

150

STEAKS WITH TOMATO, GARLIC AND OREGANO SAUCE

Campania

BRACIOLE ALLA PIZZAIOLA

Steaks with Tomato, Garlic and Oregano Sauce

This sauce is called pizzaiola *because the beef is cooked like a pizza with oil, garlic, oregano and tomatoes.*
    Braciole are very thin, wide slices of beef without bone.

¼ cup (2 fl oz/60 ml) extra virgin olive oil
1 garlic clove, peeled

6 thin slices of beef, 5 oz (155 g) each
1 lb (500 g) tomatoes, peeled and coarsely chopped
salt and freshly ground pepper
1 tablespoon chopped fresh oregano (or 2 teaspoons dried oregano)

Heat the oil with the garlic in a cast iron skillet over high heat. Add the meat and brown on both sides. Add the tomatoes, season with salt and pepper and bring to boil.
Turn down the heat. Sprinkle the oregano over the meat and tomatoes, partially cover the pan and cook for 20 minutes more to reduce the sauce before serving.

SERVES 6

STEWED TRIPE (left) AND FRIED KEBABS (right)

Abruzzi and Molise

TRIPPA IN UMIDO
Stewed Tripe

Tripe is made up of many parts: the first stomach or paunch, the second stomach, considered the best eating, which looks like honeycomb; the spongy, wrinkled third stomach; and the "reed" or fourth stomach. It must be boiled for a long time to soften before it can be used. In Abruzzi, sheep tripe is highly favored.

2 lb (1 kg) tripe
¼ cup (2 fl oz/60 ml) extra virgin olive oil
1 carrot, finely chopped
1 onion, finely chopped
1 garlic clove, finely chopped
1 celery stalk, chopped
3 plum (egg) tomatoes, peeled
1 teaspoon fennel seeds
6 tablespoons freshly grated pecorino cheese
1 tablespoon chopped parsley
salt and freshly ground pepper

Cook the tripe in plenty of boiling water until tender. Drain and cut into strips or small pieces.

Heat the oil in a large saucepan over medium heat. Add the carrot, onion, garlic and celery and sauté until tender. Stir in the tomatoes, tripe and fennel seeds and cook, covered, over low heat for 30 minutes. Adjust the seasoning and sprinkle with the grated cheese and parsley. Mix well, turn out onto a platter and serve.

SERVES 6

Emilia-Romagna

STECCHI FRITTI
Fried Kebabs

Fried meat on skewers is found in the cooking of other Italian regions as well as in Emilia. It is enjoyed in Liguria and in the south, where the meats are replaced by mozzarella or provola cheese, small onions and pieces of bell pepper (capsicum).

8 oz (250 g) chicken livers
8 oz (250 g) lean veal, cut into cubes
8 oz (250 g) sweetbreads
5 tablespoons (3 oz/90 g) butter
8 oz (250 g) sweet Italian sausage
¼ cup fresh sage leaves
¼ cup bay leaves
½ cup (2 oz/60 g) freshly grated Parmesan cheese
1 cup (2 oz/60 g) fresh breadcrumbs (crusts trimmed),
   soaked in milk and squeezed dry
2 eggs
grated rind of ½ lemon
salt and freshly ground pepper
grated nutmeg
2 cups (8 oz/250 g) fine dry breadcrumbs
oil for deep frying

Cut chicken livers into pieces the size of the veal cubes. Blanch the sweetbreads for 5 minutes in boiling water. Drain and remove membrane. Cut into cubes.

Melt 2 tablespoons butter in a skillet, add veal and sweetbreads and sauté until lightly browned. Add 2 tablespoons water, cover and cook over low heat for 20 minutes. Melt 2 tablespoons butter and sauté the chicken livers over high heat until browned. Sauté sausage pieces in the remaining 1 tablespoon butter until browned.

Thread pieces of veal, sweetbreads, chicken livers, sausage, sage and bay leaves alternately on skewers. Mix Parmesan with the moistened breadcrumbs. Beat the eggs with the lemon rind, salt, pepper and nutmeg and add to the bread mixture.

Dip each brochette into the egg mixture then roll in fine breadcrumbs to coat. Heat oil to 350°F (180°C), just before the smoking point; deep fry the kebabs until golden brown on all sides. Drain on paper towels and serve at once, garnished with parsley.

SERVES 6

FILLET STEAK WITH MARROW GARNISHED WITH PARSLEY

Lombardia

CASSOELA
Milanese Stewed Pork

This is traditionally prepared when a pig is killed. The cabbage serves to absorb the fat that melts into the stew as it cooks. Cassoela is almost always served with polenta.

10 oz (315 g) pork rind
1 tablespoon extra virgin olive oil
1 tablespoon butter
2 large onions, sliced
10 oz (315 g) Italian pork sausage
2 lb (1 kg) pork spareribs, chopped
½ cup (4 fl oz/125 ml) dry white wine
2 celery stalks, sliced
2 carrots, sliced
2 lb (1 kg) white cabbage, finely shredded
6 cups (1½ qt/1.5 l) meat broth (stock)
salt and freshly ground pepper

Boil the pork rind in salted water to cover for 1 hour. Drain and cut into strips.

Heat the oil and butter in a skillet, add onions and fry gently until translucent. Add the pork rind, sausage and spareribs and sauté for a few minutes. Add the wine and let it evaporate.

Remove the pork rind, sausage and ribs and set aside. Add the celery, carrots and cabbage to the onion in the pan. Pour a cup of stock over them and simmer for 1 hour.

Place the meats on top of the vegetables. Add salt, pepper and the remaining broth and cook for another 30 minutes or until tender. Serve hot with polenta.

SERVES 6

Piemonte

FILETTO AL MIDOLLO
Fillet Steak with Marrow

Piedmontese meat is famous for its exceptional quality. The Piedmont region is full of pastureland and the animals roam free to enjoy the abundance of food.

6 slices beef marrow, about ⅜ in (1 cm) thick
6 beef fillet steaks, about 5 oz (155 g) each
salt and freshly ground pepper
2 tablespoons butter, room temperature
2 tablespoons chopped fresh parsley
½ cup (4 fl oz/125 ml) brandy

Bring a small saucepan of water just to simmer. Drop in the marrow slices and simmer for 2 minutes, then drain and keep warm.

Tie around the circumference of the steaks with string so they will keep their shape during cooking. Season with salt and pepper. Cook on a very hot grill or in a corrugated cast iron pan without added fat for about 2 minutes on each side. Transfer to a serving dish and keep warm.

Cream the butter with the parsley. Spread this mixture on the steaks and place a slice of marrow on each. Warm the brandy in a small saucepan, ignite and pour over the steaks. Serve at once.

SERVES 6

MILANESE STEWED PORK SERVED WITH POLENTA

SPIT-ROASTED BOAR

Calabria

CINGHIALE ALLO SPIEDO
Spit-roasted Boar

Until a few years ago, boar were protected in Italy because they were becoming rare. Now they are multiplying rapidly, and often pose a threat to crops — particularly vines and young woodland shoots — and so it is permissible to hunt them in season.

1 fresh rosemary sprig
1 bay leaf, finely chopped
2 garlic cloves, finely chopped
1 tablespoon fennel seeds
salt and freshly ground pepper
1 leg of milk-fed boar or pork, about 4 lb (2 kg)
¼ cup (2 fl oz/60 ml) extra virgin olive oil

☙ Prepare a large charcoal fire and let coals burn to gray-ash stage.
☙ Chop the rosemary leaves finely and mix with the bay leaf, garlic, fennel seeds and plenty of salt and pepper.
☙ Clean the boar and singe off hairs. Make incisions all over the leg and insert the prepared seasoning mixture. Skewer the meat on the spit, rub its entire surface with the oil, salt it all over and set it close to the coals.
☙ Cook on the rotating spit for about 1½ hours, until well browned, basting from time to time with the oil. Remove from the spit and cut into serving pieces.

SERVES 6

Emilia-Romagna

COTECHINO CON LENTICCHIE
Pork Sausage with Lentils

A cotechino is a large pork sausage made by stuffing a pork casing with a mixture of ground meat and fat. Before it is cooked it must be pricked all over with a fork; it is then wrapped in a fine cloth and tied securely.

Sometimes a zampone is served in place of the cotechino. This consists of the same mixture stuffed into a pig's trotter, which has been boned and hollowed out.

3 cups (18 oz/560 g) lentils
3 oz (90 g) *pancetta* or rindless bacon, finely chopped
3 bay leaves
1 *cotechino* Italian pork sausage, about 2 lb (1 kg)
salt and freshly ground pepper
1 cup (8 fl oz/250 ml) water

☙ Soak the lentils in cold water to cover for 12 hours. Discard any that float to the surface, and drain the rest.
☙ Cook the bacon in a large saucepan over medium-high heat until crisp. Add the lentils and bay leaves, season with salt and pepper and pour in 1 cup water. Cover and cook until all is absorbed, about 30 minutes. Discard the bay leaves. Wrap the sausage in a fine cloth and simmer gently in water to cover for 1½ hours. Drain, remove the cloth, slice and place on a platter. Arrange the warmed lentils around sausage and serve.

SERVES 6

Toscana

FEGATELLI DI MAIALE AL FINOCCHIO
Pork Liver with Fennel

This is a specialty of Chianti and the area around Siena, where fennel grows wild in every field and where pigs are allowed to roam free to feed on acorns from the oaks that abound there.

1 piece of caul fat
1⅔ lb (800 g) pork liver
6 garlic cloves
salt and freshly ground pepper
3 tablespoons fennel seeds
6 thick slices firm, coarse-textured bread
24 bay leaves
¼ cup (2 fl oz/60 ml) extra virgin olive oil

☙ Soak the caul fat for about 1 hour in a bowl of luke-warm water to soften it. Drain well and pat dry with a kitchen towel. Lay the caul on a table or board. Divide it and the liver into 12 pieces.
☙ Mash the garlic with a little salt, plenty of pepper and fennel seeds; coat the liver with this mixture. As each piece is coated, wrap it in a piece of the caul fat. Cut the bread as neatly as possible into 18 equal pieces.
☙ Thread the ingredients onto 6 metal skewers, beginning with a piece of bread, then a bay leaf, a piece of liver, another bay leaf, bread, bay leaf, liver, bay leaf, and finally another piece of bread.
☙ Preheat oven to 350°F (180°C). Line the skewers up on a shallow baking dish with each end of the skewers resting on the sides of the dish so that the meat does not touch the bottom. Brush with a little olive oil, paying special attention to the bread. Bake until liver is cooked through, about 40 minutes, turning often and basting frequently with the remaining oil. Transfer the skewers to a platter and serve.

SERVES 6

PORK LIVER WITH FENNEL (top), PORK SAUSAGE WITH LENTILS (bottom right)
AND STEWED BABY OCTOPUS (bottom left, recipe page 136)

Puglia

INVOLTINI DI MAIALE
Cheese-stuffed Pork Rolls

Provola *is typically a southern cheese. It has a slightly oval shape and a knob on top where it has been tied in its little bag and hung for the whey to drain.* Provola *is often smoked.*

1¼ lb (625 g) pork tenderloin (fillet), thinly sliced
3 oz (90 g) *provola* cheese, sliced
3 oz (90 g) anchovies in oil, coarsely chopped
2 tablespoons extra virgin olive oil
salt and freshly ground pepper

Flatten the meat well with a mallet. Place a small piece of cheese and a scrap of anchovy fillet in the center of each slice. Roll up and secure with a toothpick.

Heat the oil in a saucepan over high heat. Add the pork rolls and brown on all sides. Add a very little salt and some pepper, pour in a small amount of water, turn down the heat and cook slowly until all liquid is absorbed and a brown film has formed on the bottom of the saucepan. At this point remove the rolls, arrange them on a serving dish and keep warm.

Pour a little more water into the saucepan and bring to boil, scraping up browned bits. Simmer for a moment, then pour this sauce over the meat rolls. Serve garnished with parsley if desired.

SERVES 6

Basilicata

MAIALE ALL' ALLORO
Pork with Bay Leaves

In Basilicata, where the soil is rather unproductive, the farmers breed pigs, lambs, poultry and rabbits. Small villages cling to the mountaintops, rugged cliffs line the coast and the sea is deep and stunningly beautiful. Its most famous tourist city is Maratea.

2 tablespoons extra virgin olive oil
1 loin of pork, about 2 lb (1 kg)
1 tablespoon juniper berries, finely chopped
2 whole cloves
about 10 bay leaves
2 medium onions, chopped
salt and freshly ground pepper
1 cup (8 fl oz//250 ml) dry white wine

Heat the oil in a saucepan just large enough to hold the meat. Add pork and brown over moderate heat for about 10 minutes. Add juniper berries, cloves, bay leaves, onions, salt and pepper.
Lower the heat and cook the meat until very tender, about 1½ hours, adding ½ cup wine a little at a time.
Slice the meat and arrange on a serving dish. Pour the remaining wine into the pan and bring to boil, scraping up browned bits. Put this sauce through a sieve and pour it over the meat. Serve immediately.

SERVES 6

Toscana

ARISTA DI MAIALE AL ROSMARINO
Pork with Rosemary

Chine of pork is the loin section with the bones. It is advisable to have the butcher prepare it so that the meat is cut almost completely away from the bone.

1 fresh rosemary sprig
6 garlic cloves, crushed
salt and freshly ground pepper
1 chine of pork, about 2½ lb (1.25 kg)
2 tablespoons extra virgin olive oil
1 tablespoon butter
½ cup (4 fl oz/125 ml) dry white wine

Finely chop the rosemary leaves. Mix rosemary and garlic with salt and plenty of pepper. Rub the meat well with this mixture and tie it securely to the bone. Place the meat in a Dutch oven or aluminum saucepan with the oil and butter. Bake in a preheated 400°F (200°C) oven for 1½ hours, turning frequently.
Untie the meat and remove the bone. Arrange meat in slices on a serving dish. Pour wine into the pan and bring to boil, scraping up browned bits and season to taste. Serve this sauce with the meat.

SERVES 6

PORK WITH ROSEMARY

LAMB AND CARDOONS

LAMB PATTIES WITH MINT

Abruzzi and Molise

AGNELLO AI CARDI
Lamb and Cardoons

Lamb is more or less the only meat eaten in Abruzzi, which is a very mountainous and rather poor region. It is generally cooked over charcoal or roasted in the oven, but often vegetables like fennel, artichokes or cardoons are cooked with it.

½ cup (4 fl oz/125 ml) extra virgin olive oil
3 lb (1.5 kg) boneless lamb, cut into serving pieces
salt and freshly ground pepper
2 lb (1 kg) cardoons (or celery)
¼ cup (1 oz/30 g) all purpose (plain) flour
3 anchovy fillets, mashed
1 onion, chopped
½ cup (4 fl oz/125 ml) dry white wine

Heat half the oil in a large, deep skillet over low heat. Add the lamb and season with salt and pepper. Cover with a tight-fitting lid and cook for 1 hour.

Meanwhile, clean the cardoons, discarding stringy parts. Cut cardoons into small pieces and cook for 5 minutes in a saucepan of boiling water with the flour sprinkled over the surface. Drain and rinse cardoons, then sauté for 10 minutes in the remaining oil with the anchovies and onion.

Add cardoons to the lamb. Stir in wine and cook for a few more minutes. Adjust salt and pepper and serve.

SERVES 6

Sardegna

POLPETTE D'AGNELLO ALLA MENTA
Lamb Patties with Mint

Wild herbs, with their strong flavor, are almost the only seasoning used in Sardinia. Meat, fish and soups are given a boost with mint, wild fennel, rosemary and bay leaves, which grow freely on the mountain slopes and along the coast.

1⅔ lb (815 g) ground (minced) lamb
½ cup (1 oz/30 g) firm, coarse-textured breadcrumbs, crusts trimmed, soaked in milk and squeezed dry
1 egg, beaten
½ onion, minced
2 garlic cloves, crushed
3 tablespoons chopped fresh mint
salt and freshly ground pepper
3 tablespoons extra virgin olive oil

Place the lamb in a bowl and mix it with the bread, egg, onion, garlic and mint. Add salt and pepper to taste and mix well. Using your hands, form the mixture into 6 balls, flattening them slightly between the palms.

Heat the oil in a skillet and sauté the patties over fairly high heat until browned on both sides. Season with salt and pepper and serve. Garnish with extra mint if desired.

SERVES 6

Basilicata

AGNELLO AL FORNO
Oven-roasted Lamb

In this region meat is cooked simply in olive oil and lard; but it is flavored with numerous herbs, including the oregano that grows wild here.

3 lb (1.5 kg) lamb, with bone
2 tablespoons extra virgin olive oil
3 tablespoons (2 oz/60 g) lard
1 tablespoon chopped fresh oregano
1⅔ lb (815 g) baking potatoes, peeled and cut into small uniform pieces
10 oz (310 g) tomatoes, peeled and chopped
10 oz (310 g) pearl (baby) onions, peeled
½ cup (2 oz/60 g) grated pecorino cheese
salt and freshly ground pepper

Cut the lamb into small pieces. Heat the oil and lard in a deep skillet. Add all remaining ingredients and stir well. Bake in a preheated 350°F (180°C) oven for 1 hour, stirring often. Serve hot.

SERVES 6

OVEN-ROASTED LAMB SERVED WITH BROCCOLI

Sardegna

AGNELLO AL FINOCCHIO
Lamb and Fennel

The Sardinians have special expertise in the breeding of sheep. Their lambs are particularly tender because they are slaughtered when very young, weighing no more than 20 lb (10 kg). Lamb is almost the only meat eaten on the island of Sardinia.

1 shoulder of lamb, about 3 lb (1.5 kg)
¼ cup (2 fl oz/60 ml) extra virgin olive oil
1 onion, chopped
salt and freshly ground pepper
1 lb (500 g) canned peeled tomatoes
1 lb (500 g) small wild fennel stalks, or 2 fennel bulbs with leaves

Wash and dry the lamb and cut it into pieces.

Heat the oil in a large skillet, add the onion and lamb and sauté over moderate heat until the lamb is browned. Add salt, pepper and tomatoes, cover and cook over low heat for 10 minutes.

Trim the fennel and cut into small pieces. Add to the lamb and cook uncovered until the meat is very tender, for about 1½ hours, adding a little water if necessary. Adjust the seasoning. Arrange the lamb in a dish and serve.

SERVES 6

Lazio

COSTOLETTE D'AGNELLO A SCOTTADITO
Grilled Lamb Chops

The Romans love these lamb chops, which are quite small and cut ⅜ in (1 cm) thick. They are cooked either on a grill or in a very hot cast iron skillet that has been lightly sprinkled with table salt.

1⅔ lb (815 g) lamb chops (cutlets) with bone
juice of 1 lemon
¼ cup (2 fl oz/60 ml) extra virgin olive oil
salt and freshly ground pepper

Place the chops on a plate and squeeze half the lemon juice over them. Add the oil, salt and pepper. Let the chops marinate for about 1 hour, turning from time to time.

Pat the meat dry and cook for just a few minutes on each side on a very hot grill or in a cast iron skillet that has been lightly sprinkled with salt. Arrange the chops on a serving plate, season with salt and pepper and squeeze the rest of the lemon juice over them. Serve at once.

SERVES 6

LAMB AND FENNEL (left) AND GRILLED LAMB CHOPS SERVED WITH SLICED CUCUMBER, LEMON AND FENNEL (right)

STUFFED TURKEY ROLL GARNISHED WITH FRESH BASIL

Emilia-Romagna

ROLLÈ DI TACCHINO ALLA BOLOGNESE

Stuffed Turkey Roll

Stuffed meats are a common feature of the cooking of Emilia-Romagna. Sometimes a single large slice of turkey or veal is stuffed, sometimes small individual rolls called involtini *are served, and sometimes an entire* cotechino *(a large sausage made by filling a pork casing with ground pork and spices) is rolled into a slice of meat. In each case the filling is flavored with plenty of* parmigiano reggiano, *the Parmesan cheese from the district of Reggio-Emilia.*

2 eggs
½ cup (2 oz/60 g) freshly grated Parmesan cheese
salt and freshly ground pepper
3 tablespoons extra virgin olive oil
10 oz (315 g) spinach, chopped
pinch of freshly grated nutmeg
1 slice turkey, about ⅜ in (1 cm) thick and about 1¼ lb (600 g)

1 tablespoon chopped fresh rosemary
3 oz (90 g) thinly sliced *pancetta* or rindless bacon
1 tablespoon butter
1 cup (8 fl oz/250 ml) dry white wine

❧ Beat the eggs in a bowl with the Parmesan cheese; season with salt and pepper. Pour into a cast iron skillet which has been heated with a tablespoon of olive oil. Cook the omelet on both sides.

❧ Heat another tablespoon of oil in a large saucepan, add spinach and cook over low heat until wilted. Sprinkle with the nutmeg and add salt to taste. Arrange the omelet, spinach, rosemary and *pancetta* on top of the turkey. Roll up the meat and tie it securely, enclosing the filling completely.

❧ Heat the butter and the remaining oil in a large ovenproof skillet and brown the turkey roll on all sides over high heat. Pour in half the wine and let it evaporate. Transfer the turkey to a preheated 350°F (180°C) oven for 1 hour.

❧ Lift out the meat and keep warm. Pour the rest of the wine into the pan and bring to boil, scraping up browned bits. Slice the meat and pour the pan juices over the slices before serving.

SERVES 6

Trentino-Alto Adige

ANITRA ALLE PRUGNE
Duck with Prunes

The cooking of the Trentino region shows considerable Austrian influence, and often meat — especially duck and game such as roebuck, deer and hare — is cooked with prunes, cranberries or red currants, or accompanied by stewed chestnuts.

7 oz (220 g) dried prunes
1 duck, about 3 lb (1.5 kg)
salt and freshly ground pepper
1 lemon, sliced
½ cup (4 fl oz/125 ml) dry white wine
stewed chestnuts as an accompaniment

Soak the prunes in lukewarm water to cover. When they are nicely swollen, drain and pit them.

Preheat oven to 350°F (180°C). Wash the duck and discard the heart and liver; pat dry. Rub inside and out with salt and pepper. Stuff the duck with the prunes and lemon slices. Sew up the cavity and place in a buttered flameproof baking dish.

Roast for 2 hours or until joints rotate easily, basting the duck frequently with the fat that melts in the baking dish. Lift out the duck, cut it into serving pieces and arrange on a platter. Remove prunes from cavity and keep warm; discard lemon.

Discard the fat from the baking dish and pour in the wine, scraping up browned bits and stirring over moderate heat until slightly thickened. Pour sauce over the duck, arrange the prunes and chestnuts around it and serve.

SERVES 6

Emilia-Romagna

CAPPONE BOLLITO IN SALSA VERDE

Boiled Capon with Green Sauce

Boiled capon is a northern Italian dish that is traditionally eaten at Christmas. It may be accompanied by green sauce or mostarda di Cremona, or simply served with extra virgin olive oil mixed with a little lemon juice, salt and pepper.

1 capon (or 1 large chicken), about 5 lb (2.5 kg), cleaned
1 carrot, cut into several pieces
1 celery stalk, cut into several pieces
1 small onion, stuck with 1 clove
several parsley sprigs tied into a small bunch, plus ½ cup (2 oz/60 g) loose parsley
1 tablespoon fresh breadcrumbs, soaked in red wine vinegar and squeezed dry
1 garlic clove, minced
2 anchovy fillets, mashed
½ cup (4 fl oz/125 ml) extra virgin olive oil
1 tablespoon drained capers
1 hard-cooked (hard-boiled) egg, chopped
salt and freshly ground pepper

Place the capon in a saucepan with cold salted water to cover; bring to boil. Add the carrot, celery, onion and bunch of parsley and poach over low heat for 2 hours.

Meanwhile, mince the rest of the parsley. Mix with breadcrumbs, garlic and anchovies. Add the oil, capers and egg; season with salt and pepper.

Lift the capon out of the cooking stock and arrange on a platter. Pour the sauce into a sauceboat and serve separately.

SERVES 6

Puglia

POLLO ARROSTO
Roast Chicken

Chickens in Italy are usually lean and rather small. Country housewives often raise them for family consumption, and sometimes they sell them. Chickens bred in this way, known as farmyard or free-range chickens, are the tastiest.

1 chicken, about 3 lb (1.5 kg)
1 lemon
salt and freshly ground pepper
1 fresh rosemary sprig
2 tablespoons extra virgin olive oil
½ cup (4 fl oz/125 ml) dry white wine

162

Clean the chicken; wash and dry it well. Wash the lemon but do not peel it: place it inside the chicken. Salt and pepper the inside of the chicken and sew up the cavity with thread.

Chop the rosemary leaves, add a little salt and rub the chicken all over with this mixture. Place the oil in a shallow ovenproof skillet, add the chicken and brown on all sides over moderate heat. Transfer it to a preheated 350°F (180°C) oven and roast for 1½ hours.

Take out the stitching and discard the lemon. Place the chicken onto a serving dish and keep warm. Pour the wine into the skillet and boil for a few minutes, scraping up browned bits. Pour this sauce into a gravy boat and serve separately.

SERVES 4

Toscana

Fritto Misto alla Fiorentina
Florentine Meat and Vegetable Fritters

The Florentine "mixed fry" consists of chicken, rabbit and vegetables such as artichokes, zucchini and zucchini flowers. Unlike the Piedmontese version, this one is cooked in extra virgin olive oil, which makes it crisper.

½ chicken
½ rabbit
2 small zucchini (courgettes)
2 globe artichokes, leaf tips trimmed
juice of 1 lemon
6 zucchini (courgette) flowers, optional
2 eggs
1 cup (4oz/125g) all purpose (plain) flour
extra virgin olive oil for frying
salt and freshly ground pepper

Cut the chicken and rabbit into smallish pieces, the zucchini into short strips and the artichokes into small wedges. Remove chokes from artichokes. Place the artichokes in a bowl of water with lemon juice added to prevent them from turning brown.

Open the zucchini flowers and remove the pistils. Beat the eggs well in a shallow bowl with salt and pepper. Dry all the vegetables well. Dredge all the items to be fried in flour, then coat with egg.

Fry a few pieces at a time until crisp and golden; do not let pieces stick to bottom of pan. Drain on paper towels and serve piping hot.

SERVES 6

FLORENTINE MEAT AND VEGETABLE FRITTERS

STEWED QUAIL

Marche

QUAGLIE IN UMIDO
Stewed Quail

The Marches is a rather hilly region that, like all of central Italy, has a wealth of game. Quail are hunted in winter and spring, and the wild ones are much tastier than those bred domestically.

They may be served on a bed of polenta or risotto, making a rich one course meal.

7 oz (200 g) *pancetta* or rindless bacon, finely chopped
12 quail, cleaned and trussed
½ cup (4 fl oz/125 ml) dry white wine
4 ripe tomatoes, peeled and chopped
salt and freshly ground pepper
4 lb (2 kg) fava beans or broad beans, shelled

Brown half the *pancetta* in a large saucepan. Add the quail; pour the wine over them and allow it to evaporate. Add the tomatoes, season with salt and pepper, and cook over low heat for 20 minutes.

While the birds are cooking, fry the remaining *pancetta* in another saucepan. Add the shelled beans and a little salt, cover and cook over low heat for a few minutes until beans are almost tender. Tip this mixture over the quail and continue cooking for 5 minutes to blend flavors. Transfer to a serving dish and serve.

SERVES 6

Puglia

CONIGLIO ALLA BARESE
Bari-style Rabbit

Raisins and pine nuts feature in many traditional meat and pasta dishes of southern Italy. The pine nuts are found in the ripe cones that fall from umbrella pines. They are protected by a husk that must be broken with care so that the nuts may be extracted whole.

½ cup (3 oz/90 g) golden raisins (sultanas)
1 rabbit, about 4 lb (2 kg)
¼ cup (2 fl oz/60 ml) extra virgin olive oil
2 tablespoons sugar
1 tablespoon all purpose (plain) flour
½ cup (4 fl oz/125 ml) white wine vinegar
salt and freshly ground pepper

1 tablespoon chopped fresh thyme
2 bay leaves
1 fresh rosemary sprig
1 cup (8 fl oz/250 ml) meat broth (stock)
½ cup (3 oz/90 g) pine nuts

Soak the raisins in lukewarm water to cover until needed. Cut the rabbit into pieces; wash and dry well. Heat the oil in a large skillet, add the rabbit pieces and brown over moderate heat.

Pour off excess fat from the pan. Sprinkle in the sugar, flour, vinegar, salt and pepper and simmer until the liquid is completely absorbed. Add the thyme, bay leaves and rosemary.

Pour in the broth and add the drained raisins. Cover and simmer for 40 minutes. Discard the rosemary, scatter the pine nuts over and serve.

SERVES 6

Marche

CONIGLIO ALL' ANCONETANA
Stuffed Rabbit

Stuffed rabbit is a specialty of Ancona. Sometimes the filling is enriched with chopped black olives and a couple of chopped anchovy fillets.

1 rabbit, about 2½ lb (1.25 kg)
3 garlic cloves
3 oz (90 g) prosciutto
3 oz (90 g) firm, coarse-textured bread
½ cup (4 fl oz/125 ml) milk
salt and freshly ground pepper
pinch of ground nutmeg
½ cup chopped fennel tops
¼ cup (2 fl oz/60 ml) extra virgin olive oil
grated rind of 1 lemon

Wash the rabbit thoroughly under running water. Reserve the heart and liver. Finely chop together the rabbit heart and liver, 1 garlic clove and half the prosciutto. Crumble the bread into a small bowl. Add the milk, a pinch each of salt and pepper and the nutmeg and let soak.

Add 2 peeled garlic cloves to a small amount of lightly salted water in a large saucepan. Add the fennel, cover and steam for 15 minutes. Discard the garlic cloves. Drain the fennel and squeeze dry, reserving the cooking liquid; chop finely with the remaining prosciutto.

Place the fennel and prosciutto in a saucepan with half the oil and the lemon rind and cook over low heat for 10 minutes to blend the flavors.

Squeeze the bread dry. Remove fennel mixture from the heat and add the bread and the rabbit heart and liver. Stir until smooth.

Preheat oven to 350°F (180°C). Fill the cavity of the rabbit with the prepared stuffing and sew up the opening. Place in an oiled baking dish and season with salt and pepper. Bake 1½ hours, basting every now and again with the fennel cooking liquid.

When the rabbit is almost cooked, turn up the heat to 425°F (220°C) to brown it for 5 minutes. The rabbit is cooked if the juices run clear when pierced with a skewer. Cut the rabbit into serving pieces and arrange them on a platter to serve.

SERVES 6

STUFFED RABBIT (top) AND BARI-STYLE RABBIT SERVED WITH SPAGHETTI

Piemonte

LEPRE IN SALMÌ
Salmis of Hare

A hare may be eaten after it has been hung to age for three days. The fur must be left on during this time, but the entrails are removed as soon as the hare is killed.

An excellent pâté can be made by putting any leftover meat through a sieve and mixing it with butter and herbs.

1 hare
2 cups (16 fl oz/500 ml) dry red wine
½ cup (4 fl oz/125 ml) vinegar
1 carrot, coarsely chopped
1 celery stalk, coarsely chopped
1 small onion, coarsely chopped
¼ cup parsley
1 fresh rosemary sprig
2 bay leaves
¼ cup fresh sage
1 teaspoon whole black peppercorns
salt
2 tablespoons all purpose (plain) flour
2 tablespoons extra virgin olive oil

Skin the hare and discard the head and feet. Cut hare into serving pieces and place in a large bowl with all remaining ingredients except flour and oil. Let marinate in a cool place for at least 24 hours, turning several times.

Drain meat, reserving marinade. Dry the pieces of meat and sauté them in the oil in a large saucepan. Sprinkle with flour and salt. Add the marinade, including vegetables, and simmer, covered, over low heat for 2 hours.

Drain the meat and arrange the pieces on a serving platter. Sieve the cooking juices with the vegetables and boil briefly to reduce if necessary. Pour over the hare and serve.

SERVES 6

Trentino-Alto Adige

CAPRIOLO AL RIBES
Roebuck with Red Currant Sauce

Game served with a sweet fruit sauce is a specialty of this region, where the Austrian influence is so strong that many of the inhabitants use German as their everyday language and the names of all the towns are written in both German and Italian.

4 lb (2 kg) roebuck or venison leg
1 bottle (24 fl oz/750 ml) dry red wine
1 onion, sliced
1 carrot, sliced
1 celery stalk, sliced
1 tablespoon juniper berries
2 whole cloves
1 fresh rosemary sprig
2 bay leaves
7 oz (220 g) pork fat, chopped
1 tablespoon all purpose (plain) flour
salt and freshly ground pepper
1 can (1 lb/500 g) red currant jam
2 tablespoons *grappa* or brandy

Bone the meat and cut into large cubes. Place in a bowl with the wine, vegetables and flavorings and marinate for at least 24 hours.

Drain and dry the meat, reserving marinade. Lard the meat with half the chopped pork fat, inserting the fat with a larding needle or pressing a piece of fat into a slit cut in each meat cube. Melt the remaining pork fat in a large nonaluminum saucepan, add the meat and brown lightly on all sides. Strain in the wine from the marinade and cook, uncovered, over low heat for 1½ hours.

Stir in the flour and taste for salt and pepper. Continue cooking until sauce is reduced to desired consistency. Combine red currant jam and *grappa* in another non-aluminum saucepan and bring just to boil. Pour into a sauceboat and serve with the meat.

SERVES 6

OPPOSITE PAGE: ROEBUCK WITH RED CURRANT SAUCE
BELOW: SALMIS OF HARE

PHOTO: FABBRI EDITORI MILANO

PHEASANT WITH OLIVES

Veneto

PICCIONI RIPIENI
Stuffed Pigeons

Pigeons are often served on their own as a main dish, with a risotto flavored with either fresh mushrooms or peas. In this case the bread is eliminated.

3 pigeons (Cornish hens or squab)
3 oz (90 g) cooked ham, thinly sliced, chopped
½ cup breadcrumbs, without crusts, soaked in milk and
   squeezed dry
1 egg
1 tablespoon chopped onion
2 oz (60 g) pork fat, chopped
6 fresh sage leaves, chopped
1 tablespoon juniper berries, crushed
salt and freshly ground pepper
3 fresh rosemary sprigs
2 tablespoons extra virgin olive oil
1 tablespoon butter
1 cup (8 fl oz/250 ml) dry white wine
6 slices firm, coarse-textured bread

Clean the pigeons and take out the livers. Mix the ham, bread, egg, onion, pork fat, sage, juniper berries, salt and pepper. Stuff the pigeons with this mixture, adding a whole sprig of rosemary to each.

Grease a shallow pan with the oil and butter and brown the pigeons over moderate heat. Pour in a little wine, lower the heat and cook, covered, for 1 hour, adding the remaining wine a little at a time.

Meanwhile, toast the slices of bread until golden. Arrange on a serving dish. Cut the pigeons in half and place a half on each slice of bread. Pour the cooking juices over and serve.

SERVES 6   *Photograph page 4*

Umbria

FAGIANO ALLE OLIVE
Pheasant with Olives

Pheasant is cooked during the hunting season, which runs from September to March. The flesh of the newly killed pheasant is rather leathery, so it must be hung to age for five or six days before it is cleaned. Before cooking, the entrails and all the feathers must be removed.

2 oz (60 g) sliced *pancetta* or rindless bacon
1 pheasant, dressed
1 cup (4 oz/125 g) pitted black olives
1 tablespoon fennel seeds
1 tablespoon butter
2 tablespoons extra virgin olive oil
salt and freshly ground pepper
1 tablespoon juniper berries, crushed
½ cup (4 fl oz/125 ml) dry white wine
¼ cup (2 fl oz/60 ml) meat or chicken broth (stock)

Wrap the bacon slices around the breast of the pheasant and tie it securely. Stuff the bird with the olives and fennel seeds, and sew up the cavity.

Heat the butter and oil in an ovenproof skillet over moderate heat and brown the pheasant slowly for 20 minutes. Season with salt, pepper and juniper berries. Add the wine and let it evaporate. Add the broth and roast in a 375°F (190°C) oven for 1 hour, basting frequently with the pan juices.

Cut the bird into serving pieces and arrange the olive stuffing around it. Place pan over moderate heat and use a little water to help scrape up browned bits from the bottom. Pour this sauce through a sieve over the bird and serve.

SERVES 6

Umbria

COLOMBACCI IN SALMI
Salmis of Wood Pigeon

Like their neighbors the Tuscans, the Umbrians are great hunters, and they are very fond of wild pigeons, which have tastier flesh than domestic birds. This method of marinating makes them quite delicious.

3 wood pigeons (Cornish hens or squab)
1½ cups (12 fl oz/375 ml) dry red wine
1 carrot, sliced
1 celery stalk, sliced
½ onion, sliced
extra virgin olive oil
salt and freshly ground pepper
3 oz (90 g) prosciutto, chopped
1 shallot, chopped
2 bay leaves
a few juniper berries
three tablespoons extra virgin olive oil
½ cup (4 fl oz/125 ml) broth (stock)
¼ cup (2 fl oz/60 ml) Marsala

Clean the birds and reserve the livers. Place the birds in a bowl and add the wine, carrot, celery and onion. Turn to coat birds well and let marinate for 24 hours. Drain and dry them, reserving the vegetables. Brush with olive oil, add salt and pepper and roast on a spit for about 40 minutes or place in a baking dish and cook in a hot oven (400°F/200°C), basting occasionally, for 1 hour or until juices run clear when birds are pierced with a skewer.

Combine the prosciutto, shallot, bay leaves, juniper berries and reserved livers in a saucepan with 3 tablespoons oil and sauté over high heat for several minutes. Pour in the broth, the reserved vegetables and Marsala and reduce the heat. Add salt and pepper, cover and simmer for 30 minutes.

Cut the pigeons in half and transfer to a shallow pan. Force the cooking juices and vegetables through a sieve, add to the pigeons and simmer for a further 10 minutes before serving.

SERVES 6

Il Sud

Il Sud

S outhern Italy is very different in character from both the northern and the central regions. It is truly a Mediterranean land dominated by the presence of the sea, and specializing in hearty, spicy food — pasta, tomatoes, eggplants, fish, lamb and pork.

Campania is famous for Naples and its pizza, Pompeii, Capri and the romance and gaiety of its people. Abruzzi, the Molise, and Calabria are proud mountain areas where life is simple and frugal. Basilicata, another mountainous region, is different — there the hunter tradition mixes with an Eastern influence to produce very interesting dishes of mutton and pork. In Apulia, by way of contrast, vegetables and pasta reign supreme.

"The difference between the king and me is that the king eats as much spaghetti as he likes, while I eat as much as I've got." This old Neapolitan saying illustrates the unique character of Campanian cuisine: popular traditions and aristocratic traditions, having overcome ancient differences, find that they have a common bond in the higher ideal of pasta (leaving aside the size of the portions, of course). All Neapolitans are united in the name of macaroni and spaghetti, and the phenomenon appears to be quite contagious. This simple and natural food has conquered the rest of the country and become the dominant feature of Italy's gastronomic culture. Without spaghetti and tomato sauce, or macaroni and meat sauce (two of the specialties of this region), something very important is lacking and there is likely to be a feeling of unease and unhappiness. This is not simply an old wives' tale or representation of a stereotype: it is part of a real need for an identity. Consequently, any betrayal of, or offense against,

THE AMALFI COASTLINE IS AMONG THE MOST BEAUTIFUL IN EUROPE. SUSPENDED HIGH ABOVE THE SEA IS RAVELLO (left) AND ON THE WATER'S EDGE IS POSITANO (previous pages), SHROUDED IN EVENING MIST

173

spaghetti on the part of the cook is naturally not to be tolerated. A plate of inferior spaghetti — overcooked, with an unsatisfactory sauce — causes frustration and disappointment, and, like a character in a romantic serial, an Italian who suffers such an offense never forgets it.

So in order to avoid such psychological complications, Italians reserve for spaghetti and macaroni the kind of special treatment they have had for centuries in the kitchens of Naples and Campania: they are always prepared with the same care and dedication as they would receive on grand occasions. Obligatory partners for pasta are those special Italian tomato-based sauces, robust of flavor yet at the same time refined, which have conquered the world. A variation of the tomato-and-dough combination, which again originated in Naples but now belongs to an international cuisine, is the pizza. The pizzas you find in Campania are always delicious, and always different from the thousands of imitations scattered around the planet.

The imagination and creativity of Neapolitan cooks is expressed not only in these traditional epicurean delights, but in at least eighty other typical regional dishes, which include first courses, main courses, vegetables and cheeses (we have only to think of mozzarella and all its possible uses).

In this vast panorama we give special mention to *fritto alla napoletana* or *fritto di casa,* the glory of the Neapolitan housewife, which brings together at least twenty varieties of fish, vegetables and organ meats in a joyful and unforgettable blend of tastes and flavors; and *sfogliatelle,* sweet pastries with ricotta, sugar, eggs and candied fruit, which in ancient days were always made at home until they became public domain in the eighteenth century.

The regions of the Abruzzi and the Molise consist of 60 percent mountains, 30 percent hills, and the remaining 10 percent a short strip of lowland along the coast. This means that the *Abruzzesi* and *Molisani*, from time immemorial, have lived difficult, solitary lives, the only prospects of employment being sheep rearing, farming or fishing — or emigration for anyone seeking further opportunities.

But here more than anywhere the old saying, "They have made a virtue out of necessity" holds good — and in matters culinary above all. Indeed, limited economic resources have ensured that the cooks of Abruzzi, forced to use a given number of foods and ingredients according to the meager local production, have concentrated all their skills and care on perfecting a few superb gastronomic specialties, which reach truly great heights. What is more, many of the best chefs in Italy come from families of cooks in this region, who have passed on from father to son the secrets of this ancient and refined cuisine. One of these, unfortunately anonymous, was responsible for the invention of *maccheroni alla chitarra* somewhere around 1700: a very fine sheet of pasta is laid over a square or

MANY OF THE FARMING METHODS USED IN CALABRIA ARE THE SAME AS THOSE USED CENTURIES AGO

PHOTO: PAOLO CURTO/THE IMAGE BANK

COLORFUL FISHING BOATS ON A TINY BEACH ALONG THE AMALFI COAST LEAVE LITTLE
ROOM FOR PEOPLE TO STRETCH OUT ON THE PEBBLY BEACH AND ENJOY THE SUN

THE CALABRIANS ARE A MOUNTAIN PEOPLE WITH A STRONG
CULINARY TRADITION THAT RECALLS THE LIVES OF THE SHEPHERDS OF OLD

PHOTO: SANTI VISALLI/THE IMAGE BANK

A TOBACCO FARM IN CAMPANIA

PHOTO: MARIO FINOTTI/ACTION PRESS

rectangular wooden frame fitted with wires (the "guitar") and then pressed down with a rolling pin, which cuts it into the four-cornered *fettuccine* characteristic of this region. We are told that the modern *chitarra* has ancient forebears, first the *retroncelo* and later the *caratturo* (both now found only in antique collections), which made four-cornered pasta strips rather wider than our *maccheroni alla chitarra* today.

Another element typical of this cuisine is the red chili pepper, regarded as a "poor" condiment in comparison with imported spices; it is used in nearly every dish from soups to roasts and vegetables. And along the coast there is the renowned *brodetto di pesce*, considered to be the father of all the other fish soups of the Adriatic coast.

This is a land of shepherds and their flocks, so it has a tradition of lamb cooked in many different ways — roasted, braised, even made into meat sauce; of cheeses — *scamorza* and *caciocavallo*, which find poor imitations all over the country; of full-flavored mountain ham; of liver sausage and mortadellas, and all the other "derivations" of pork. The general rule in this cuisine is moderation and simplicity; the ancient custom of wasting nothing, never throwing anything away, seems still to be followed. There is one first course, for instance, made up of leftovers from the pantry at the end of winter — a few chickpeas, a few lentils, a bit of bacon, one or two

175

vegetables and some pasta, all cooked for hours with the bone from the prosciutto (by this time quite bare). But in the midst of this traditional frugality there is one momentous exception: the *panarda,* a dinner on a grand scale with at least 30 courses. Any guest who accepts an invitation to the *panarda* must try everything, or risk seriously offending the hostess.

A string of mountains between the Tyrrhenian and Ionian Seas, with only 9 percent of its area low-lying, where "the rivers are torrents, the mountain slopes subject to landslides, the forests destroyed": this is how Calabria was described at the beginning of the century by travelers who had penetrated as far as the southernmost point of the Italian peninsula. They were struck not only by the violence of nature here, but by the theme of escape which seemed to dominate the character of the people. The events of the past centuries have left an indelible mark: long ago when trade was flourishing in the Greek colonies of Croton and Sybaris the Calabrians began leaving the mountains to move down to the sea. Subsequently, they returned to the mountains to escape the Saracen pirates, and later went down once more to the sea and beyond, in search of better living conditions.

In the midst of this constant movement, a closed and isolated patriarchal society continued to operate, so that inevitably each new generation lived exactly the same way as the one before it. At the present time this picturesque region, fragrant with bergamot (of which the entire national production comes from this area), cedar (90 percent of national production) and olive trees, has the unhappy distinction of having the lowest per capita income in the country, despite its intense economic growth in recent years.

It is interesting to note that the only secure possession the people of Calabria could take with them and rely on in a foreign country was the dietary tradition of their ancestors. As soon as finances permitted, they recreated the lost atmosphere of their homeland around substantial quantities of *ragù* and *stracotto* (beef larded with *pancetta* and cooked in wine with carrots, leeks, dried mushrooms, onions, tomatoes, nutmeg and cloves). Thus Calabrian cuisine is a function of a collective memory, in which the dishes are evidence of time recaptured. How far back, for example, can we trace the taste of their cabbage soup (lamb or beef broth with cabbage and pecorino)? Or *pancotto* (broth, stale bread, garlic, bay leaves, celery and parsley)? Or mushroom soup, or *lagane* (handmade *fettuccine* cooked in milk and sprinkled with pecorino)? Each dish speaks of seasons, harvests and simple living on the edge of survival, where natural fruits of the earth and sea (snails, fish, game, figs, olives and almonds) were considered signs of the benevolence of the gods. Similarly, kid meat and cheeses recall the lives of the shepherds of old, while the many varieties of homemade pasta call to mind images of the fam-

THE TINY WHITEWASHED HOUSES IN MONTE SANT' ÀNGELO, APULIA, CONTRAST WITH THE MORE COLORFUL BUILDINGS OF THE SEASIDE VILLAGES

ily gathered around the table as the women of the household worked the dough. The eggplant too — the most-used vegetable in this region — belongs to the same culinary world, whether it is cooked in vinegar and sugar, sautéed with garlic, stuffed, or baked with cheese.

The region of Basilicata has two official names. One, Lucania, is derived from the earliest inhabitants of the area in pre-Roman times, the Lucanians. The other is more recent, dating back to the time of the Greek-Byzantine domination of the area; *basileus* is the Greek word for king, and the name Basilicata meant a province of the empire. Thus the original pastoral-warrior civilization was replaced by the sophisticated and decadent Eastern tradition — with noteworthy results, at least in the kitchen.

On the one hand we have some ancient recipes, typical of a primitive society of hunters, which have remained unchanged — such as hare marinated in wine and flavored with garlic and bay leaves, and partridge cooked with olives. On the other hand, there are flavors and taste combinations from the Near East that have come into general use in dishes like *tagliolini* with milk and saffron, or almond milk flavored with cinnamon. Another feature of Lucanian cuisine is that it has remained a private affair within the family — or at the very most, a village affair. This is because of the physical structure of the region, which is all hills and mountains with isolated villages clinging to their tips. In the past, communication was not always possible and, in general, the people could not leave the village even if they wished.

Hence the traditions of the local cuisine have remained in the custody of household kitchens.

Two of the most popular dishes are boned lamb with celery, onions and rosemary, and *gnumariddi*, lamb offal and sweetbreads cooked with garlic, onions and cheese. As in Abruzzi and inland Apulia, mutton is the principal meat. Then there is pork, which is also made into sausages and hams of some repute; and for special occasions, such as weddings, christenings and religious ceremonies, chicken stuffed with eggs, pecorino and chicken livers. The remainder of the diet consists of vegetables, mostly baked in the oven and eaten in vast quantities as a substitute for meat, which is too costly for family budgets in this ungenerous land: eggplants with olives, anchovies and capers; potatoes baked with onions and pecorino; mixed dishes of vegetables including peppers, zucchini, broccoli and tomatoes. Or else pasta: hard wheat *fusilli* with ricotta, and *strascinati* — traditional pasta served with a sauce of chickpeas, green peas or lentils.

Apulian cuisine is something of an anomaly in relation to the other regional cuisines. The pasta-meat-vegetable relationship here is in fact reversed: vegetables, produced in vast quantities throughout the region, come first, and the other foods follow. Peppers, eggplants, broccoli, spinach, artichokes, broad beans, tomatoes, peas and other produce unquestionably have the leading role in the Apulian diet, with the other foods making up the entourage. The tutelary deity linking the many-faceted vegetable world with the lesser world of the other foods is olive oil, more acidic and therefore stronger-flavored than the Tuscan oil. So what does one eat with the vege-

tables? Pasta first of all, in particular *orecchiette*, the typical pasta of this region. The women make these "little ears" of wheat-and-water dough following a ritual that goes back many hundreds of years. Vegetables are also used in soups, notably the *maritata*, for which chicory, fennel, celery and escarole are boiled, layered alternately with pecorino and pepper and covered with broth; in *calzoni* and *panzerotti*, pastry rolls with various fillings that are baked in the oven or fried; and in the impressive pies made with kid meat, chicken, beef, potatoes, onions, zucchini, tomatoes and cheese, which may be served as either first or second courses.

This cuisine has the same basic structure as that of Naples, with a baroque overlay: the dishes are complex, and preparation is lengthy and often done in several stages. The Apulians even go so far as to stuff figs, and fillings feature in all their traditional cakes and pastries for religious and agricultural festivals, such as Christmas and Easter. The plentiful fish, mollusks and crustaceans of this region are known for their quality; the waters here are largely pollution-free and teeming with life. Italy's major oyster beds are located here, the oysters being brought into the harbor from the larger bay every season. Even fish do not escape the piepan, where they are alternated with layers of vegetables and Middle Eastern-derived flavorings. Cheeses — mozzarella, *scamorza*, *caciocavallo* and pecorino — are produced in large quantities inland, as is mutton, which is cooked with garlic and herbs in the same manner as the ancient Italian cooks.

THE EVENING ATMOSPHERE OF THE *PIAZZA* IS UNIQUE. PIAZZA UMBERTO 1, ON THE ISLAND OF CAPRI, IS ONE OF THE MORE CHIC, FREQUENTED BY TOURISTS FROM ALL OVER THE WORLD.

Le Verdure

ACETO DI VINO
OLIO DI SEMI
OLIO DI OLIVA
OLIO DI SANSA
E DI OLIVA

PHOTO: GIAN LUIGI SCARFIOTTI

IN THE FAMOUS MARKET AT CAMPO DEI FIORI, THE COOKS OF ROME DECIDE ON THE MENU FOR THE DAY, WATCHED OVER BY THE STATUE OF GIORDANO BRUNO

Le Verdure

A CORNER SHOP IN FLORENCE OFFERS
AN INVITING DISPLAY TO TEMPT THE PASSING SHOPPER

A small vegetable garden protected by a wall or hedge, where edible herbs can be grown for household consumption: this has a remote origin, going back to the time when our nomadic food-gathering ancestors turned to farming and ceased to be migratory. But the model is the Garden of Eden. On the fifth day of Creation, the Lord said, "Behold, I have given you every herb bearing seed, which is on the face of all the earth, and every tree, in which is the fruit of a tree yielding seed: to you it shall be for meat."

When was the vegetable garden first heard of in Italy? It is impossible to say exactly, but certainly the ancient Latin authors were already writing about it with some technical expertise. As far back as that time the beneficial (or harmful) effects of certain vegetables on the human body were known. And so doctors and farmers had a complementary involvement in the *hortus*, one being concerned with health, the other with nourishment, and both beginning with the same raw materials.

The vegetable garden in Roman dwellings was within the house; limited in size, it produced vegetables, fruit and herbs. From the fall of the Roman Empire up to the early Middle Ages there was a distinct drop in the quality of vegetables grown, and many varieties survived only in the

PHOTO: RAY JOYCE

PREVIOUS PAGES: ITALIAN CUISINE IS BASED ON THE AVAILABILITY
OF FRESH LOCAL PRODUCE LIKE *ZUCCHINI* FLOWERS, *RADICCHIO* AND
PORCINI MUSHROOMS   PHOTO: RAY JOYCE

PHOTO: JOHN SIMS

COLORFUL CABBAGES SET AGAINST THE BACKGROUND OF A CANAL IN MANTOVA

"DO NOT TOUCH THE MERCHANDISE" — A DISPLAY OF SPICES IN RAVENNA

PHOTO: WEINBERG-CLARK/THE IMAGE BANK

kitchen gardens of monasteries and castles. During the Renaissance, it became the custom to establish permanent vegetable gardens at the gates of the cities. But large fields of vegetable crops such as we are accustomed to seeing today are relatively recent, dating from the end of the eighteenth and the beginning of the nineteenth centuries; only then did agriculture begin to be seen in terms of mass production. Today, Italy produces 200 million tons of vegetables a year, spread over about 50 different varieties. Most of this enormous quantity of fresh vegetables finds its way to our tables via mass distribution networks, but a considerable portion still comes from small family-run market gardens. Thus, as we approach the year 2000, the earthly paradise is still part of our lives.

While we are on the subject of vegetable growing, we must mention the Old World and the New — in other words, the world before and after the discovery of America. Up to the beginning of the sixteenth century, produce from the kitchen garden remained more or less the same as it had been in the beginning, except for contributions from the East brought in during Roman times and in the Middle Ages.

From a list given in *Tacuinum Sanitatis*, a late-fifteenth-century work, it appears that many of the vegetables in use at that time were the same as those we use today: lettuce, with which the ancients suggested diners should *claudere coenas* (finish dinner) because it would do them good; cabbage; spinach, which it was recommended should be cooked without water so as not to lose the nutrients; celery; leeks; turnips, to be pickled; fennel; onions; asparagus; pumpkin; garlic; basil; parsley; chickpeas; eggplants (aubergines); and salads, the favorite food of young girls. With the discovery of new lands, the vegetable garden was enriched with potatoes, tomatoes, peppers (capsicums) and beans, as well as numerous varieties of fruits and cereals. The penetration of these new items was not easy, meeting resistance from age-old eating habits and from conservatives who accused the new vegetables of causing horrible diseases such as leprosy and consumption. It took a war and subsequent famine around 1700 to persuade people to assuage their hunger with potatoes. After that came tomatoes, grown from seeds imported by Christopher Columbus and destined to become the most popular vegetable in Italy, the most suitable accompaniment for pasta, meat and other vegetables in the form of sauce.

Let us look at a few suggestions for preparing vegetables. Firstly they must be shiny, bright in color and firm to the touch: this is why housewives touch before they buy, amid protests from the shopkeeper! They may be boiled, stewed or marinated. The proper way to boil them is to use only a small amount of salted water — except for potatoes, which require a cold-water start — and to cook them uncovered so they do not lose their bright color. Artichokes, cardoons and salsify are boiled in water and lemon juice with a tablespoon of flour added, to prevent them from darkening. Remember not to cook vegetables for too long; they must always retain a certain firmness. Steaming is also an excellent way to keep in the flavor.

Stewed vegetables, on the other hand, involve the use of oil or butter without the addition of water, because the vegetables exude their own juices during cooking. For stewing it is preferable to use a terracotta pan with a lid. In this way the vegetables cook slowly and evenly and do not stick to the pan.

To marinate asparagus, artichoke hearts and so on, mix three parts salted water to one part olive oil, and add a bouquet garni*, some black peppercorns and coriander seeds. Bring this marinade to simmer and cook it for 20 minutes. Remove it from the heat, immerse the vegetables in it and leave them to marinate for 48 hours.

A bouquet garni is generally called mazzetto di odori *(small bunch of herbs), but it may also be known as* dote *(dowry) — it was something on which the bridegroom's family could rely in moments of crisis. In cooking, the "dowry" is composed of those elements which give flavor and fragrance to any food — a few pieces of celery, onion, carrot, parsley, basil and bay leaf tied together. Other herbs and seasonings may be added to this traditional mixture according to individual taste, as in making up a bouquet of flowers.*

BELL PEPPERS IN THE MAREMMA DISTRICT OF TUSCANY

PHOTO: GERT VON BASSEWITZ/SUSAN GRIGGS AGENCY

Abruzzi and Molise

CARDI FRITTI AL POMODORO
Fried Cardoons with Tomato Sauce

The cardoon is a thistlelike vegetable that grows easily even in the cold climate of the Abruzzi mountains. It is very popular in almost all the regions of Italy.

¼ cup (2 fl oz/60 ml) extra virgin olive oil
3 garlic cloves, chopped
1 lb (500 g) ripe tomatoes
salt and freshly ground pepper
3 lb (1.5 kg) cardoons, Swiss chard stalks or celery
juice of 1 lemon
1 cup (4 oz/125 g) all purpose (plain) flour
1 egg, beaten with a pinch of salt
oil for deep frying
2 tablespoons chopped parsley

Heat the oil in a skillet over medium heat. Add the garlic and sauté until fragrant. Add the tomatoes, season with salt and pepper and cook over low heat for about 30 minutes or until sauce is quite dense.

Clean the cardoons, removing the leaves and peeling the outer strings. Cut into small pieces, and as each is prepared drop it into a bowl of water acidulated with the lemon juice.

Bring plenty of salted water to boil in a large saucepan. Drop in the cardoons and cook until tender but firm. Drain, rinse under cold running water and dry.

Heat oil to 350°F (180°C), or just before smoking point. Dredge the cardoons in flour and dip in the egg. Deep fry until crisp and golden on all sides. Drain the cardoons on paper towels, transfer to a serving plate and keep hot. Stir the parsley into the hot tomato sauce, pour it into a sauceboat and serve separately.

SERVES 6

RADICCHIO WITH BACON

Veneto

RADICCHIO ALLA PANCETTA
Radicchio with Bacon

The radicchio *from Castelfranco Veneto is round like a ball, with slightly wrinkled leaves that are variegated white and dark red. It is not as tender as the variety grown in Treviso, but it is easier to find and less expensive.*

2 tablespoons extra virgin olive oil
3 oz (90 g) smoked *pancetta* or rindless bacon, cut into strips
1 onion, sliced
2 lb (1 kg) Castelfranco *radicchio* or Belgian endive
salt and freshly ground pepper

❧ Heat the oil in a skillet over low heat. Add the *pancetta* and onion and sauté for 15 minutes, stirring frequently.
❧ Trim the *radicchio* and discard the root. Cut into lengthwise wedges. Add to the skillet and season with salt and pepper. Cook over low heat, turning carefully, for 5 minutes. Transfer to a serving dish and serve.

SERVES 6

Veneto

RADICCHIO DI TREVISO ALLA GRIGLIA
Grilled Radicchio Lettuce

The radicchio of Treviso is a specialty of this region. It is kept for a few days covered in sand so that the stalks whiten. This particular type of radicchio *has long, smooth leaves which are red at the tips. It is either grilled or sautéed in butter or used as a stuffing for entrées, meat or fish.*

2 lb (1 kg) *radicchio di Treviso* or Belgian endive
3 tablespoons extra virgin olive oil
salt and freshly ground pepper

❧ Trim the *radicchio* and discard the root. Cut into quarters lengthwise.
❧ Coat a flattop grill with the oil and heat until very hot. Grill the *radicchio* for a few minutes on each side. Remove from heat and let it rest, covered, for a minute. Transfer to a serving plate, season with salt and pepper, and serve.

SERVES 6

GRILLED RADICCHIO LETTUCE

PHOTO: FABBRI EDITORI MILANO

Sicilia

FAGIOLINI ALLA PEPERONATA

Green Beans with Tomato and Bell Pepper Sauce

In Sicily, the tomato reigns everywhere. It is added to meat, fish, pasta and other vegetables. The tomatoes of this region are particularly flavorful and have a very thin skin, because they are left to ripen on the plant in the hot Sicilian sun and are picked only when ready to eat.

2 ripe tomatoes
2 yellow bell peppers (green capsicums)
3 tablespoons extra virgin olive oil
1 onion, sliced
2 garlic cloves, chopped
1¼ lb (625 g) green beans
salt and freshly ground pepper
2 tablespoons chopped fresh oregano

❧ Drop the tomatoes into a saucepan of boiling water for a few seconds, then peel and chop them. Halve and seed the peppers, then cut into strips.

❧ Heat the oil in a skillet, add the onion and garlic and sauté until the onion is golden. Add the peppers and cook gently for 5 minutes. Add the tomatoes and cook over medium-low heat for 30 minutes.

❧ Meanwhile, trim the beans and cook for 2 minutes in a large pot of boiling salted water. Drain and add to the other vegetables. Season with salt and pepper and finish cooking for a few more minutes. Transfer to a serving plate, sprinkle with the oregano and serve.

SERVES 6

Campania

PEPERONATA

Pepper and Tomato Stew

Peperonata is an excellent accompaniment to meat or fish, and it can also be used as a sauce for spaghetti, rigatoni or penne. Sometimes it is enriched with capers and anchovy fillets.

3 ripe tomatoes
6 red and yellow bell peppers (capsicums)
¼ cup (2 fl oz/60 ml) extra virgin olive oil
1 onion, sliced
2 garlic cloves, chopped
salt
1 tablespoon chopped fresh oregano
a few fresh basil leaves

❧ Plunge the tomatoes and peppers into boiling water for a few seconds; drain and peel. Chop the tomatoes; seed and slice the peppers.

❧ Heat the oil in a skillet over medium heat. Add the garlic and onion and sauté until translucent. Add the pepper slices and salt to taste, and cook for a few minutes. Add the tomatoes and oregano. Cover, reduce heat and cook slowly for 30 minutes, stirring from time to time. Add the basil and cook for a few minutes more to blend flavors. Transfer to a bowl and serve.

SERVES 6

GREEN BEANS WITH TOMATO AND BELL PEPPER SAUCE (left) AND PEPPER AND TOMATO STEW

BROCCOLI RABE COOKED IN OIL

Abruzzi and Molise

BROCCOLETTI ALL'OLIO
Broccoli Rabe Cooked in Oil

Broccoli rabe (broccoli di rapa) is a typical autumn and winter vegetable. It even stands up well to the cold climate of the mountains in Abruzzi. The greens are often served sautéed with raisins and pine nuts.

3 lb (1.5 kg) broccoli rabe (rape) or turnip tops
¼ cup (2 fl oz/60 ml) extra virgin olive oil
2 garlic cloves, chopped
3 tablespoons coarse breadcrumbs
juice of 1 lemon
salt and freshly ground pepper

❧ Trim the greens and separate the tough stalks from the tips. Bring a saucepan of salted water to boil and add the stalks. When they are almost tender, add the tips and cook another minute or two. Drain.

❧ Heat the oil in a skillet over medium heat. Add the garlic and breadcrumbs and fry gently until fragrant. Add the greens, lemon juice and salt and pepper and cook, covered, for 5 minutes. Transfer to a bowl and serve.

SERVES 6

Liguria

POMODORI ALLA MAGGIORANA
Tomatoes with Marjoram

Marjoram, which is also known in this region as "lost herb," is the basis of most stuffings in Ligurian cooking, along with borage. The herb grows very easily, and it can be dried for winter.

6 ripe tomatoes
3 tablespoons fresh marjoram leaves, chopped
3 tablespoons fine dry breadcrumbs
1 garlic clove, chopped
salt and freshly ground pepper
¼ cup (2 fl oz/60 ml) extra virgin olive oil

❧ Cut the tomatoes in half. Squeeze them gently to eliminate seeds. Sprinkle salt over the cut sides and invert them to drain. Mix the marjoram, breadcrumbs and garlic. Season with salt and pepper. Turn tomatoes cut sides up and sprinkle with the marjoram mixture. Drizzle with 3 tablespoons oil.

❧ Preheat oven to 350°F (180°C). Use the remaining oil to grease a baking dish. Arrange the tomato halves in it and bake for 30 minutes. Serve hot.

SERVES 6

TOMATOES WITH MARJORAM (top) AND CARROTS WITH MARSALA

Sicilia

CAROTE AL MARSALA
Carrots with Marsala

Marsala is a typical Sicilian dessert wine, very fragrant and quite sweet. It is used all over Italy, even in the cooking of many meat dishes. There is also a dry version which is normally served as an aperitif.

2 tablespoons extra virgin olive oil
1½ lb (750 g) carrots, peeled and sliced
salt and freshly ground pepper
1 teaspoon sugar
¼ cup (2 fl oz/60 ml) dry Marsala

Heat the oil in a large saucepan. Add the carrots and sauté over high heat for a few minutes. Season with salt and pepper, add a few tablespoons of water and continue cooking over low heat until almost tender.

Just before removing them from the stove, raise the heat and sprinkle the sugar over the carrots, stirring so that they become lightly caramelized. Sprinkle with Marsala and let it evaporate. Transfer carrots to a serving plate if desired and serve at once.

SERVES 6

CHESTNUTS AND BRUSSELS SPROUTS IN BUTTER

Trentino-Alto Adige

CASTAGNE E CAVOLINI AL BURRO

Chestnuts and Brussels Sprouts in Butter

Chestnuts are now relatively rare in Europe as a result of a disease that struck years ago, killing the trees. They are sold in the streets, cooked in their skins on a brazier set up on a special cart.

1¼ lb (615 g) chestnuts
2 tablespoons butter
1 celery stalk, cut into strips
10 oz (315 g) Brussels sprouts, quartered
½ cup (4 fl oz/125 ml) dry white wine
salt

⚟ Preheat oven to 350°F (180°C). Place the chestnuts on a baking sheet and bake for 10 minutes. Remove the shells and the inner skins. Place the chestnuts in a skillet with the butter, celery and sprouts and sauté over low heat for 5 minutes. Add the wine and salt and bring to boil. Cover and cook until sprouts are tender and all liquid is absorbed, about 10 minutes. Serve hot.

SERVES 6

Sicilia

CAVOLFIORE ALL' ACCIUGA

Cauliflower with Anchovy Sauce

The cauliflowers grown in Sicily are mainly of the green variety, which are sweeter than white ones.

1 cauliflower, about 3 lb (1.5 kg)
½ cup (4 fl oz/125 ml) extra virgin olive oil
3 garlic cloves, chopped
3 tablespoons dry breadcrumbs
6 anchovy fillets in oil, mashed
salt and freshly ground pepper

⚟ Trim the cauliflower, removing tough stems. Cook it in boiling salted water until crisp-tender — the water must barely touch the tips so that they do not break; drain. Transfer to a serving dish and keep warm.
⚟ Heat the oil in a skillet over medium-high heat. Add the garlic, breadcrumbs and anchovies and cook for 2 minutes, stirring constantly. Pour sauce over the cauliflower and serve.

SERVES 6

Liguria

MELANZANE AL FUNGHETTO

Sautéed Eggplant

The term al funghetto *means the vegetables are cooked very briefly, like mushrooms, and are flavored with garlic and parsley. The eggplants must be firm and not too large; choose oval rather than round ones because they have fewer seeds.*

If eggplants are not to be fried they should not be salted and left to drain, because they lose too much moisture and with it some flavor.

1½ lb (750 g) eggplants (aubergines)
2 garlic cloves, chopped
¼ cup (2 fl oz/60 ml) extra virgin olive oil
salt
2 tablespoons chopped parsley

⚟ Cut the tops off the eggplants and cut them first into thick slices, then into cubes.
⚟ Fry the garlic gently in the oil in a large skillet. Add the eggplant and cook over moderate heat just until tender. Season with salt, sprinkle parsley over and serve.

SERVES 6

Val d'Aosta

CIPOLLINE ALLA FONTINA

Onions in Cheese Sauce

Cipolline are round, flat and rather small onions, similar to pickling onions. They have a golden brown outer skin, which is removed. They are very sweet and have long a shelf life, and so are popular in winter. If they are unavailable, pearl (baby) onions may be used instead.

2 lb (1 kg) small onions with skin on
½ tablespoon butter
1 tablespoon all purpose (plain) flour
2 cups (16 fl oz/500 ml) milk
a pinch of powdered clove
salt and freshly ground pepper
3 oz (90 g) fontina or Gruyère cheese, thinly sliced
2 tablespoons chopped parsley

⚟ Bring a large saucepan of salted water to boil. Drop in the onions and boil gently for 20 minutes. Drain and peel them; keep warm.
⚟ Melt the butter in a wide skillet. Add the flour and mix well. Gradually pour in the milk, stirring constantly. Bring to boil and season with clove, salt and pepper. Add the cheese and allow it to melt, then stir in the parsley. Pour over onions and serve.

SERVES 6

CAULIFLOWER WITH ANCHOVY SAUCE (top), SAUTÉED EGGPLANT (center)
AND ONIONS IN CHEESE SAUCE (bottom)

Sicilia

CIPOLLINE ALL' UVETTA

Onions with Tomatoes and Raisins

Many of the traditional dishes of Sicily combine raisins with savory foods. In comparison to the cuisines of other regions, Sicilian cooking has always been elaborate, with a rich variety of flavors.

2 lb (1 kg) pearl (baby) onions
4 ripe plum (egg) tomatoes
salt and freshly ground pepper
1 whole clove
¼ cup (1 oz/30 g) raisins
1 tablespoon butter
1 tablespoon extra virgin olive oil
3 tablespoons sugar
¼ cup (2 fl oz/60 ml) red wine vinegar

Blanch onions in boiling water to cover for 10 minutes. Drain and peel. Blanch tomatoes in boiling water for a few seconds. Peel and puree. Combine pureed tomatoes with salt, pepper and clove and simmer for 30 minutes to thicken.

Soak raisins in water to cover for 30 minutes. Drain. Place the onions in a nonaluminum saucepan with butter and oil and sauté for 5 minutes over medium-high heat. Add reduced tomatoes and simmer for 30 minutes over very low heat.

Dissolve sugar in the vinegar and boil for several minutes. Add to onion mixture with raisins. Simmer until sauce is reduced to desired consistency and serve.

SERVES 6

Emilia-Romagna

CIPOLLE RIPIENE AL PROSCIUTTO

Onions with Ham Stuffing

In Emilia, where many excellent pork products are made, in addition to the famous Parmigiano-Reggiano *cheese, vegetables are often served with a stuffing or flavoring of some kind of sausage, salami or prosciutto. Parma ham is famous throughout the world for its sweet, delicate flavor.*

6 large white onions, peeled
3 oz (90 g) cooked prosciutto, finely chopped
6 tablespoons freshly grated Parmesan cheese
1 egg, beaten
2 tablespoons coarse breadcrumbs (crusts trimmed),
 - soaked in milk and squeezed dry
salt and freshly ground pepper
1 tablespoon butter
¼ cup (2 fl oz/60 ml) meat broth (stock)

Cook the onions in boiling salted water for 15 minutes. Rinse them under cold running water; drain and dry. Cut a slice from the top of each and scoop out the centers with a spoon so that you have 6 little "bowls." Place them upside down while preparing the filling.

Finely chop half the scooped-out onion. Add the cooked prosciutto, cheese, egg and bread; season with salt and pepper. Mix well and fill the onion shells with the stuffing.

Preheat oven to 350°F (180°C). Grease a baking dish with some of the butter and arrange the onions in it. Dot with the remaining butter and moisten onions with the broth. Bake for 40 minutes, basting the onions from time to time with the pan juices. Serve hot.

SERVES 6

ONIONS WITH TOMATOES AND RAISINS (left) AND ONIONS WITH HAM STUFFING (right)

BEET GREENS WITH ANCHOVIES

Marche

BIETOLINE ALL' ACCIUGATA

Beet Greens with Anchovies

Young beet greens can be used for this dish in spring; substitute turnip greens during autumn and winter.

(1 kg) young beet greens or turnip greens
6 anchovy fillets in oil, mashed
6 garlic cloves, chopped

3 tablespoons extra virgin olive oil
salt and freshly ground pepper

Wash the beet greens several times; drain. Place in a saucepan with a very small amount of salted water and cook over high heat for 2 minutes. Drain and squeeze dry.
Mix the anchovy fillets and garlic. Heat the oil in a skillet over medium heat. Add the garlic mixture and fry until fragrant. Add the beet greens and season with salt and pepper. Cook, covered, over low heat for 5 minutes. Serve at once.

SERVES 6

PEAS WITH HAM (left) AND BEAN SALAD WITH TUNA (right)

Joscana

PISELLI AL PROSCIUTTO
Peas with Prosciutto

In late spring, peas are a real specialty in Tuscany. They are very sweet, and are picked while small so they are especially tender.

3 tablespoons extra virgin olive oil
1 small onion, very thinly sliced
3 oz (90 g) *prosciutto*, cut into narrow strips
4 cups (1 lb/500 g) peas
salt and freshly ground pepper
½ cup (4 fl oz/125 ml) boiling water
2 tablespoons chopped parsley

Heat the oil in a skillet over medium heat. Add the onion and prosciutto and sauté until onion is translucent. Add the peas, salt, pepper and boiling water and cook uncovered until peas are tender.

Transfer to a heated bowl and scatter the parsley on top before serving.

SERVES 6

Joscana

INSALATA DI FAGIOLI AL TONNO
Bean Salad with Tuna

The beans used for this dish are the small, white oval-shaped ones called cannellini. *They are very similar to Great Northern beans, with a rather thin skin. If they are dried they need to be soaked overnight before cooking so they will not wrinkle, and cooked over low heat barely covered with water — which they will have absorbed by the end of the cooking time.*

1 lb (500 g) dried *cannellini* beans
½ cup fresh sage leaves
½ cup (4 fl oz/125 ml) extra virgin olive oil
7 oz (220 g) canned tuna in oil
juice of 1 lemon
freshly ground pepper
½ onion, thinly sliced
salt

Soak the beans in water to cover overnight. Drain, cover with fresh cold water and bring to simmer with the sage and a tablespoon of oil. Simmer until tender, about 1½ hours. Drain off any water that remains and discard the sage. Let the beans cool.

Lightly break up the tuna with a fork. Toss with the lemon juice and plenty of pepper. Place the beans in a salad bowl and pour the remaining oil over them. Add onion and toss. Season with salt and pepper. Scatter the tuna on top and serve.

SERVES 6–8

Trentino-Alto Adige

MELE AL BURRO
Apples Cooked with Butter and Wine

Grown in the valleys and at the foot of the high mountains, apples are the major specialty of the Trentino region. Together with turnips, chestnuts and cabbages, they are a great resource for winter. They are served as both vegetable and fruit, often in pureed form.

1 tablespoon butter
6 large Golden Delicious apples, peeled, cored and sliced
pinch of cinnamon
½ cup (4 fl oz/125 ml) dry white wine
juice of ½ lemon
pinch of salt

Melt the butter in a skillet, add the apples and cook over medium heat for a few minutes, sprinkling with the cinnamon. Add the wine, lemon juice and salt and cook over low heat until the apples are tender but not mushy and the liquid has evaporated. Serve hot.

SERVES 6–8

Friuli-Venezia Giulia

CAVOLO ROSSO ALL' ACETO
Red Cabbage with Vinegar

The cooking of Friuli-Venezia Giulia shows the influence of Austria, and here cabbage is cooked in the Austrian manner — first in vinegar, then sweetened with red currant jelly. It is very good with roast turkey or goose.

1 red cabbage, about 2 lb (1 kg)
1 tablespoon butter
salt and freshly ground pepper
½ cup (4 fl oz/125 ml) red wine vinegar
½ cup (4 oz/125 g) red currant jelly

Discard the outer leaves of the cabbage and shred the rest finely. Melt the butter in a large nonaluminum sauce-

APPLES COOKED IN BUTTER AND WINE (top), RED CABBAGE WITH VINEGAR (center) AND CABBAGE STEWED IN WINE (bottom)

pan, add the cabbage and mix well. Add salt and pepper to taste, and pour in the vinegar.

Cover the saucepan and cook the cabbage over low heat for 1 hour, stirring occasionally.

Add the red currant jelly and let it melt. Continue cooking uncovered until all the liquid is absorbed. Serve hot.

SERVES 6

Lombardia

VERZA IN UMIDO
Cabbage Stewed in Wine

The cabbages grown in Lombardy are the round ones with dark, slightly wrinkled leaves. They become tastier and more tender after the first frost. Other types of cabbage can also be used for this recipe, whether they be red, white or green.

1 cabbage, about 2 lb (1 kg)
3 oz (90 g) *pancetta* or rindless bacon
1 tablespoon butter
1 cup (8 fl oz/250 ml) dry white wine
salt and freshly ground pepper
½ cup (4 fl oz/125 ml) white wine vinegar

Discard the tough stalks and damaged outer leaves of the cabbage. Shred cabbage finely; wash and drain it.

In a large nonaluminum saucepan, sauté the *pancetta* in the butter until golden. Add the cabbage and wine; season with salt and pepper. Cover and cook over low heat for 30 minutes or until liquid is absorbed. Stir in the vinegar and cook for another 20 minutes. Serve hot.

SERVES 6

LEEKS IN RED WINE SAUCE (top) AND BEET STALKS WITH BECHAMEL SAUCE (bottom)

Piemonte

PORRI AL VINO ROSSO
Leeks in Red Wine Sauce

Leeks are mainly a winter vegetable. They are always full of soil, so it is a good idea to make cuts in the green part to make washing them easier. They are also excellent boiled and served with bechamel sauce and grated Parmesan cheese.

2 lb (1 kg) leeks
1 tablespoon butter
½ cup (4 fl oz/125 ml) red wine
1 beef bouillon (stock) cube

❧ Remove the root and a little of the green part of the leeks. Quarter the green section lengthwise, cutting until you reach the white part. Wash well and shake off water.
❧ Melt butter in a large skillet. Add the leeks, cover and sauté for a few minutes over low heat. Pour in the wine, add the lightly crumbled bouillon cube and cover the pan once more. Reduce the heat and braise leeks for 10 minutes. Lift them out of the pan with a slotted spoon, arrange on a serving plate and keep hot.
❧ Boil the sauce over moderate heat until reduced to about ¼ cup (2 fl oz/60 ml). Pour it over the leeks and serve. Sprinkle with chopped parsley if desired.

SERVES 4–6

Lombardia

COSTE ALLA BESCIAMELLA
Beet Stalks with Bechamel Sauce

Bechamel is a white sauce widely used in the north of Italy over vegetables such as fennel, asparagus tips, celery and cardoons, and also on fish fillets and in pasta dishes. It can be flavored with dried porcini *mushrooms (or champignons), tomato paste or parsley.*

3 lb (1.5 kg) beet greens or Swiss chard (silverbeet)
2 tablespoons butter
freshly ground pepper
2 tablespoons all purpose (plain) flour
2 cups (16 fl oz/500 ml) milk, heated to boiling
grated nutmeg
¾ cup (3 oz/90 g) freshly grated Parmesan cheese
1 hard-cooked (hard-boiled) egg
salt

❧ Remove the green leaves from the vegetables and reserve for another use. Cut the white stalks into small pieces and blanch in a saucepan of boiling salted water for 2 minutes. Drain.
❧ Melt 1 tablespoon butter in a skillet. Add a sprinkling of pepper. Stir in beet stalks and sauté until just tender, about 5 minutes. Transfer to a baking dish.
❧ For bechamel sauce, melt the remaining butter in a

GREENS WITH AMARETTI

saucepan over low heat. Stir in the flour and cook for 1 minute. Add the boiling milk and mix well. Stir in the nutmeg, cheese, and salt and pepper to taste.

Preheat oven to 400°F (200°C). Pour the sauce over the beet stalks and bake for 15 minutes. Sieve the hard-cooked egg over the top and bake for 5 minutes longer. Serve hot.

SERVES 6

Piemonte

ERBETTE AGLI AMARETTI

Greens with Amaretti

Erbette *(literally "young grasses" but also a translation of "herbs") is a typical spring vegetable of the Piedmont. It resembles Swiss chard (or silverbeet) but has a slender green stalk. Beet* greens or spinach can easily be substituted. In other parts of Italy these greens are called *bietoline.*

1 tablespoon dried *porcini* mushrooms or champignons
2 lb (1 kg) greens
2 tablespoons butter
salt and freshly ground pepper
3 oz (90 g) amaretti biscuits

Soak the mushrooms in lukewarm water until soft, then drain and chop them. Cook the greens in a large saucepan of boiling salted water for 1 minute. Drain and squeeze out all moisture.

Place greens in a pan with the butter. Add the mushrooms, season with salt and pepper and cook gently for 10 minutes to blend flavors. Transfer to a serving dish, crumble the amaretti over the top and serve.

SERVES 6

BEANS AND TOMATO

Toscana

FAGIOLI ALL'UCCELLETTO

Beans and Tomato

Fagioli all'uccelletto is one of the most famous of Tuscan winter dishes. It is usually served with mildly spiced sausages, which are sautéed in a cast iron skillet for a few minutes with a tablespoon of olive oil.

1 lb (500 g) *cannellini* beans
6 tablespoons extra virgin olive oil
3 garlic cloves, crushed
¾ cup fresh sage
4 ripe tomatoes, peeled and chopped
salt and freshly ground pepper

Cook the beans as in the recipe for bean salad with tuna on page 194.

Heat the oil in a skillet over medium heat. Add the garlic and sage and sauté until fragrant. Add the tomatoes and simmer gently for 20 minutes. Add the beans, cover and cook over very low heat for 30 minutes. Season with salt and pepper. The finished dish should have the consistency of a soup.

SERVES 6

Liguria

TEGLIA DI PATATE E FUNGHI

Baked Potatoes and Mushrooms

Potatoes done this way are very simple to prepare and may also be served as a first course. When porcini *mushrooms are in season they are used fresh instead of dried, sautéed briefly in a little olive oil. Alternatively, the mushrooms may be replaced by fried slices of fresh artichoke.*

1 cup (3 oz/90 g) dried *porcini* mushrooms or champignons
5 tablespoons extra virgin olive oil
2 lb (1 kg) baking potatoes, peeled and thinly sliced
2 onions, sliced
salt and freshly ground pepper
1 cup (4 oz/125 g) freshly grated Parmesan cheese
2 cups (16 fl oz/500 ml) milk

Soak the mushrooms in lukewarm water to cover for 1 hour. Drain and sauté in 1 tablespoon oil over low heat for 5 minutes. Heat 2 tablespoons oil in a saucepan over low heat. Add onions, cover and cook until tender. Season with salt and pepper.

Preheat oven to 350°F (180°C). Layer the potatoes, onions and mushrooms alternately in a large oiled baking dish; sprinkle each layer with Parmesan, salt and pepper. Pour the milk over the potatoes and bake for 1 hour, or until all the liquid is absorbed and a light golden crust has formed on top. Let rest for 5 minutes before serving.

SERVES 6

Piemonte

SEDANO AL MIDOLLO

Celery with Marrow Sauce

Beef marrow is found in the bones of the animal's hooves. It is used in the preparation of many dishes, sometimes raw and sometimes previously boiled. Whether raw or cooked, it is easily extracted from the bones with slight pressure of the fingers.

1 carrot, sliced
½ onion, sliced
3 bunches celery
1 cup (8 fl oz/250 ml) broth (stock)
salt and freshly ground pepper
1 bay leaf
½ cup (4 fl oz/125 ml) Marsala
2 marrow bones, about 2 in (5 cm) long
1 teaspoon fresh lemon juice

Combine the carrot and onion in a large saucepan. Cut the celery into 2½-in (6-cm) lengths. Place on top of the carrot mixture and pour in broth. Season with salt, pepper and bay leaf. Cover and cook over low heat for 30 minutes. Add the Marsala and lower the heat as far as possible so that the contents of the saucepan are just kept hot.

Meanwhile, cover the bones with water in another saucepan. Bring to boil and cook over low heat for 15 minutes. Push the marrow out of the bones and chop it. Add to celery mixture with lemon juice and salt and pepper to taste. Simmer for another few minutes before serving.

SERVES 6

Lazio

FAVE AL GUANCIALE

Broad Beans and Bacon

Broad beans are good only when they are very fresh and the pods are not too thick. They generally are ready for picking in May and June, and do not last long.

Guanciale is bacon made from pig's cheek, but it may be replaced by pancetta *or ordinary bacon.*

3 oz (90 g) *guanciale, pancetta* or pork fat, chopped
1 small onion, sliced
6 lb (3 kg) broad beans, shelled
3 ripe tomatoes, peeled and chopped
salt and freshly ground pepper

Fry the meat slowly in a saucepan with the onion until onion is translucent. Add the beans and cook for a few minutes over low heat. Add the tomatoes, season to taste with salt and pepper, and continue cooking until all the liquid is absorbed. Transfer to a bowl and serve.

SERVES 6

BROAD BEANS AND BACON (top), CELERY WITH MARROW SAUCE (bottom left) AND BAKED POTATOES AND MUSHROOMS (bottom right)

Lazio

CARCIOFI ALLA GIUDEA
Deep-fried Artichokes

This Roman specialty is a major attraction of the Piperno, a restaurant in the city's traditional Jewish quarter. The secret of the dish is that the oil must be hot but not too hot, to allow time for the inside of the artichokes to cook without burning the outside.

6 medium-large globe artichokes
juice of 1 lemon
salt and freshly ground pepper
oil for deep frying

Clean the artichokes, removing the tough outer leaves and trimming the stalks. As each one is prepared, immerse it in a bowl of cold water mixed with the lemon juice to prevent darkening. Drain the artichokes and dry them well. Rap them on a work surface so that the leaves open slightly; pull the leaves back. Season the inside of the artichokes with salt and pepper.

Heat the oil in a deep skillet to 300°F (150°C). Plunge the artichokes upside down into the oil and fry for about 10 minutes or until crisp and golden, turning them often and pressing them against the bottom of the pan to open the leaves. Drain artichokes on paper towels and serve.

SERVES 6

Toscana

INSALATA VERDE
Green Salad

In Italy, green salads are always dressed with oil, vinegar and salt. Sometimes pepper is also added. The Tuscan green salad consists solely of lettuce, or else of lettuce leaves and Castelfranco radicchio, slightly bitter rucola or arugula, and leaves of parsley, salad burnet or other herbs as desired.

3 oz (90 g) head lettuce
3 oz (90 g) lamb's lettuce or other leaf lettuce
3 oz (90 g) *radicchio*
¼ cup parsley leaves
¼ cup mint leaves
¼ cup arugula (rocket cress) leaves or dandelion greens, optional
salt
1 tablespoon red wine vinegar
¼ cup (2 fl oz/60 ml) extra virgin olive oil

Trim the salad greens and the herbs and wash them well. Dry them with care and place in a salad bowl.
Dissolve salt in the vinegar and sprinkle over the salad. Pour the oil over and mix well. Serve at once.

SERVES 6

DEEP-FRIED ARTICHOKES

GREEN SALAD

LENTIL SALAD

Basilicata

INSALATA DI LENTICCHIE
Lentil Salad

In this region, as in Calabria, it is easier to find dried legumes (pulses) than fresh vegetables. The only vegetables that grow in summer are tomatoes, bell peppers (capsicums) and eggplants (aubergines), and these are often mixed with dried beans, chickpeas or lentils in soups or salads.

1 lb (500 g) lentils
1 onion, halved
2 bay leaves
3 tomatoes, cut into wedges
1 tablespoon chopped parsley
salt and freshly ground pepper
2 tablespoons red wine vinegar
¼ cup (2 fl oz/60 ml) extra virgin olive oil

Soak the lentils in cold water to cover for about 12 hours. Discard any that float to the surface. Drain the rest, and place them in a saucepan. Cover with water and cook over low heat until tender, adding the onion and bay leaves.

Discard the onion and bay leaves, drain the lentils and transfer to a salad bowl. Let cool.

Sprinkle the tomatoes with salt and arrange around the lentils. Scatter the parsley over them. Dissolve salt in the vinegar, add the oil and pepper and continue to stir this dressing as you pour it over the lentils and tomatoes.

SERVES 6

Puglia

FUNGHI ALLA TRAPANESE
Trapani-style Stuffed Mushrooms

Mushrooms come into Apulia in abundance from the neighboring region of Calabria, which is far more mountainous. They are often cooked in ancient wood ovens once used for baking bread. The ovens were built in the trulli, *Apulia's characteristic cone-shaped dwellings.*

18 medium-size *porcini* (boletus) mushrooms, or *shittake* mushrooms
1 onion, finely chopped
3 garlic cloves, finely chopped
6 anchovy fillets in oil, chopped
½ cup (4 fl oz/125 ml) extra virgin olive oil
salt and freshly ground pepper
1 egg, beaten
½ cup (1 oz/30 g) fresh breadcrumbs (crusts trimmed), soaked in milk and squeezed dry
½ cup (2 oz/60 g) freshly grated Parmesan cheese
¼ cup chopped parsley
⅓ (1½ oz/45 g) fine dry breadcrumbs
1 lemon

Wipe the mushrooms clean with a cloth but do not wash them. Cut off and chop the stalks. Combine the onion, garlic, anchovies and mushroom stalks in a skillet. Add half the oil and cook over medium-high heat, stirring, for 10 minutes. Remove from heat and season with salt and pepper.

Let the mixture cool, then add the egg, bread, Parmesan

and parsley and stir with a wooden spoon until well blended.

🍒 Fill the mushroom caps with this mixture and sprinkle with the breadcrumbs.

🍒 Preheat oven to 350°F (180°C). Brush a little oil on the bottom of a baking dish and arrange the mushrooms in it. Sprinkle with the remaining oil and bake until crumbs are golden, about 20 minutes. Squeeze a few drops of lemon juice over each and serve.

SERVES 6

Sardegna

CECI ALLO ZAFFERANO
Chickpeas with Saffron

In Sardinian cooking much use is made of dried legumes (pulses), and often they are flavored with saffron. Saffron is produced by drying the stamens of a certain type of crocus. There are only three in each flower, so one can understand why the spice is so expensive.

1 lb (500 g) chickpeas
3 tablespoons extra virgin olive oil
1 onion, chopped
3 ripe tomatoes, peeled and chopped
a pinch of hot red chili pepper or 1 fresh red chili pepper, chopped
salt and freshly ground pepper
¼ teaspoon saffron powder

🍒 Soak the chickpeas in cold water to cover for 12 hours. Drain and place in a saucepan, add plenty of salted water, and bring to a slow boil. Turn the heat down as low as possible and cook the chickpeas for 1½ hours. Drain them and reserve about ½ cup (4 fl oz/125 ml) of the cooking liquid.

🍒 Heat the oil in a skillet over medium-low heat. Add the onion and cook until translucent, but do not let it color. Add the chickpeas, then the tomatoes and chili pepper. Taste for salt, add pepper and pour in the reserved chickpea cooking liquid. Bring to boil, then simmer for 30 minutes.

🍒 Dissolve the saffron in a little water and add it to the pan. Mix well and simmer for 2 to 3 more minutes. Transfer to a bowl and serve.

SERVES 6

Lombardia

ZUCCHINE AL BURRO VERSATO
Zucchini with Black Butter Sauce

This is a very popular way of serving boiled vegetables; it is suitable also for fennel, celery, cardoons or asparagus. The sage may be replaced by parsley leaves which, like the sage, should be fried in the butter.

12 small zucchini (courgettes)
3 tablespoons (2 oz/60 g) butter
¼ cup fresh sage leaves
6 tablespoons freshly grated Parmesan cheese
salt and freshly ground pepper

Cook the zucchini whole in boiling salted water until tender but not mushy. Drain. Trim ends and cut the zucchini into pieces. Place them in a serving dish.

Meanwhile, heat the butter in a small saucepan with the sage until the butter is dark brown. Sprinkle the cheese over the zucchini. Add salt and pepper, pour the butter over and serve at once.

SERVES 6

Liguria

FRICASSEA DI FUNGHI
Mushrooms in Lemon Sauce

Mushrooms grow in abundance on the Ligurian mountains and inland hills. A fricassee is a sauce based on egg and lemon juice, which is also good with meat and fish. Fricasseed vegetables such as mushrooms, zucchini (courgettes) and green beans are a specialty of Genoa.

2 lb (1 kg) fresh *porcini* (boletus) mushrooms or
    champignons
3 tablespoons (2 oz/60 g) butter
1 tablespoon chopped parsley
2 tablespoons chopped borage
salt and freshly ground pepper
1 tablespoon all purpose (plain) flour
1 egg yolk
juice of 1 lemon

Wipe the mushrooms clean; do not wash. Trim and slice them. Sauté over high heat in 2 tablespoons butter for 5 minutes, stirring often. Scatter the parsley and borage over the mushrooms and season with salt and pepper.

Melt the remaining butter and stir in the flour, egg yolk and lemon juice. Pour this sauce over the mushrooms, off the heat. Stir well and place over low heat for a few minutes to thicken, but do not let sauce boil. Transfer to a serving dish and serve immediately.

SERVES 6

ZUCCHINI WITH BLACK BUTTER SAUCE (left)
AND MUSHROOMS IN LEMON SAUCE (right)

205

CARAMELIZED TURNIPS

Toscana

FIORI DI ZUCCA FRITTI
Fried Zucchini Flowers

The zucchini plant produces two kinds of flowers — the female, from which the fruit grows, and the male, which appear on the tip of an unproductive stalk. The latter are best for frying or using in other dishes.

1 cup (4 oz/125 g) all purpose (plain) flour
1 tablespoon extra virgin olive oil
½ cup (1 oz/30 g) firm, coarse-textured breadcrumbs
    (crusts trimmed), soaked in milk and squeezed dry
30 tightly closed zucchini (courgette) flowers
6 anchovy fillets in oil, mashed
1 tablespoon chopped parsley
oil for deep frying
salt and freshly ground pepper

Mix the flour with the olive oil and enough water to make a batter that is not too liquid. Cut some of the stalk off the zucchini flowers; remove the pistils. Mix the bread, anchovies and parsley and stuff the flowers with this mixture, pressing the flowers closed around the filling.

Preheat oil to 350°F (180°C), or just before smoking point. Dip the flowers into the batter and deep fry until golden on all sides. Season with salt and pepper. Drain on paper towels and serve at once.

SERVES 6

Trentino-Alto Adige

RAPE CARAMELLATE
Caramelized Turnips

Much use is made of spices — particularly cinnamon and cloves — in the vegetable cookery of this region, and vegetables are often cooked with sugar.

2 lb (1 kg) turnips, peeled and sliced
2 tablespoons butter
salt and freshly ground pepper
1 whole clove
2 tablespoons sugar

Place the turnips in a saucepan. Add the butter, salt and pepper to taste, the clove and a small amount of water. Cover the saucepan and cook the turnips over medium-low heat until tender, stirring from time to time and adding more water as necessary.

When all the cooking liquid has evaporated, add the sugar and cook over medium heat, stirring gently, for a further 2 minutes. Serve immediately.

SERVES 6

EGGPLANT AND BELL PEPPER STEW

Sicilia

CAPONATA DI MELANZANE
Eggplant and Bell Pepper Stew

This very tasty dish can be served not only as an accompaniment to meat or fish, but also as an entrée or as a sauce for pasta.

6 tablespoons extra virgin olive oil
1 onion, sliced
1 garlic clove, chopped
3 red and yellow bell peppers (capsicums), seeded and sliced
1 lb (500 g) eggplants (aubergines), cut into cubes
3 tomatoes, peeled and coarsely chopped
salt and freshly ground pepper
2 teaspoons dried oregano, crumbled
2 tablespoons drained capers
¼ cup (2 oz/60 g) black olives, pitted and coarsely chopped
3 anchovy fillets in oil, chopped

Heat the oil in a large saucepan, add the onion and garlic and sauté until translucent. Add the peppers and eggplant and cook over medium heat for 15 minutes. Add the tomatoes, season with salt, pepper and oregano, and cook until eggplant and peppers are tender but not mushy.
Add the capers, olives and anchovies. Remove from heat and let stand at room temperature for several hours before serving.

SERVES 6

Abruzzi and Molise

PATATE ALLE OLIVE
Potatoes with Olives and Anchovies

In the cooking of central and southern Italy, flavors are strong and distinct, oil takes the place of butter, and often vegetables are combined with anchovies, capers, olives or tomatoes.

2 lb (1 kg) baking potatoes, peeled
¼ cup (2 fl oz/60 ml) extra virgin olive oil
3 oz (90 g) black olives, pitted and chopped
1 tablespoon drained capers, chopped
6 anchovy fillets in oil, chopped
salt and freshly ground pepper
1 tablespoon chopped parsley

Cut the potatoes into wedges. Heat the oil in a cast iron skillet over medium-high heat. Add the potatoes; sprinkle with the olives, capers and anchovies. Season with salt and pepper.
Cover, reduce heat to medium and cook for 30 minutes, stirring gently from time to time but taking care not to break up the potatoes. Scatter the parsley over the potatoes and serve.

SERVES 6

Calabria

PATATE ALLA SALSICCIA
Potatoes with Spicy Italian Sausage

Calabria is a barren region where vegetables are scarce; the people eat mostly dried legumes (pulses) such as beans and chickpeas. Legumes and potatoes are often combined with sausages, which in this area are highly spiced.

7 oz (220 g) spicy Italian sausage
3 tablespoons extra virgin olive oil
1 onion, chopped
6 large baking potatoes, peeled and sliced
salt and freshly ground pepper

Remove the skin from the sausage and break up the meat. Heat the oil in a large cast iron skillet. Add the meat, onion and potatoes and cook, covered, over low heat for 30 minutes.
Uncover, increase the heat and sauté the potatoes until brown, stirring. Season with salt and pepper, and serve.

SERVES 6

Piemonte

PATATE AL GRATIN
Gratin of Potatoes

Potatoes cooked in this way can also be served as an elegant first course. They may be flavored with dried porcini mushrooms (or champignons) or with thinly sliced fontina or Gruyère cheese and chopped sautéed bacon or pancetta.

2 lb (1 kg) baking potatoes
1 tablespoon butter
2 cups (16 fl oz/500 ml) milk

POTATOES WITH OLIVES AND ANCHOVIES (top right), POTATOES WITH ITALIAN SAUSAGE (top left) AND GRATIN OF POTATOES (bottom)

1 cup (8 fl oz/250 ml) cream
2 cups (7 oz/220 g) freshly grated Parmesan cheese
grated nutmeg
salt and freshly ground pepper

Preheat oven to 350°F (180°C). Peel the potatoes and slice them thinly. Lay the slices slightly overlapping in a large baking dish greased with the butter.

Mix the milk, cream, half the Parmesan, the nutmeg, and salt and pepper. Pour this mixture over the potatoes and sprinkle with the remaining Parmesan. Bake until potatoes are tender, about 45 minutes, raising the oven temperature to 425°F (220°C) near end of baking time to brown the crust. Serve hot.

SERVES 6

STUFFED ZUCCHINI

Liguria

ZUCCHINE RIPIENE
Stuffed Zucchini

The zucchini for this dish should be firm and without seeds; this means they need to be small. They may also be filled with chopped cooked mushrooms, ham, leftover cooked meat or fish.

12 fairly small, round zucchini (courgettes)
½ cup (1 oz/30 g) fresh breadcrumbs (crusts trimmed),
    soaked in milk and squeezed dry
6 tablespoons freshly grated Parmesan cheese
1 egg, beaten
2 tablespoons chopped parsley
2 tablespoons chopped fresh marjoram

1 garlic clove, chopped
grated nutmeg
salt and freshly ground pepper
1 tablespoon olive oil

Cook the zucchini whole in boiling salted water until barely tender. Drain; trim ends. Cut a lengthwise slice from each and carefully scoop out a little of the flesh with a teaspoon.

Preheat oven to 350°F (180°C). Mix the bread, cheese, egg, herbs, garlic and nutmeg, and fill the zucchini cavities with this mixture. Season with salt and pepper and arrange in a baking dish brushed with the oil. Bake for 30 minutes or until top is browned. Serve hot.

SERVES 6

ASPARAGUS WITH PARMESAN CHEESE

Emilia-Romagna

ASPARAGI ALLA PARMIGIANA
Asparagus with Parmesan Cheese

The asparagus grown in Emilia-Romagna is a pale violet color. This method of preparing it is characteristic of the north of Italy, in contrast to the plainer oil-and-lemon dressing used in Tuscany. The dish is often served with eggs fried in butter.

4 lb (2 kg) asparagus
¾ cup (3 oz/90 g) freshly grated Parmesan cheese
salt and freshly ground pepper
3 oz (90 g) butter

⚜ In a tall, narrow saucepan, bring enough salted water to boil to reach just below the asparagus tips. Clean the asparagus, and tie it in bunches. Add to the saucepan and cook just until crisp-tender. Drain and transfer to a serving dish.
⚜ Untie the asparagus and sprinkle the green tips with Parmesan, salt and pepper. Keep hot.
⚜ Meanwhile, heat the butter in a small saucepan until light brown. Pour it over the asparagus and serve.

SERVES 6

Sicilia

SCAROLA CON I PISTACCHI
Escarole with Pistachio Nuts

Escarole is a slightly bitter lettuce which, in southern Italy, is often served as a cooked vegetable or gently fried and used as a pizza topping or as a sauce for pasta.

2 lb (1 kg) escarole or curly endive
¼ cup (2 fl oz/60 ml) extra virgin olive oil
3 garlic cloves, chopped
salt and freshly ground pepper
¼ cup shelled pistachio nuts

⚜ Trim the escarole, discarding tough stems and damaged or wilted leaves. Cut each bunch into quarters. Wash well and dry.
⚜ Heat the oil in a skillet, add the garlic and brown lightly over medium heat. Add the escarole, cover, reduce heat and cook for 5 minutes. Season with salt and pepper, scatter the pistachios on top and cook for another moment or two before serving.

SERVES 6

ESCAROLE WITH PISTACHIO NUTS

Campania

ZUCCHINE A SCAPECE
Marinated Zucchini

A scapece *is a method of preparing vegetables by first frying them and then marinating them in vinegar for a few days. They are usually served as an accompaniment to boiled meat or fish, or sometimes as an* antipasto. *Fish such as sardines and anchovies are also often prepared this way.*

2 lb (1 kg) zucchini (courgettes)
salt
oil for deep frying
½ cup (4 fl oz/125 ml) red wine vinegar
3 garlic cloves, chopped
a small piece of chili pepper
¼ cup fresh basil leaves

Trim ends of the zucchini and slice lengthwise. Sprinkle with salt and arrange the slices on a plate positioned at a slight angle so that the zucchini will lose some of its moisture. Let drain for a few hours, then dry in a kitchen towel.

Heat oil to 350°F (180°C). Fry zucchini slices in batches until golden. Drain on paper towels and sprinkle with salt to taste. Pour off all but 2 tablespoons of the oil. Add the vinegar, garlic and chili pepper to the pan and boil for 5 minutes.

Arrange the zucchini in a single layer in a bowl and pour the vinegar mixture over. Scatter the basil on top. Cover and marinate for at least 24 hours before serving.

SERVES 6

Lombardia

PATATE IN INSALATA
Potato Salad

In Italy, potato salad is usually simply dressed with oil and salt, sometimes with tarragon added. The oil dressing may be replaced by just-melted butter, a small amount of salt and some lemon juice.

6 baking potatoes
1 garlic clove, minced
2 tablespoons finely chopped parsley
salt and freshly ground pepper
6 tablespoons extra virgin olive oil

Cook the potatoes in their skins in boiling salted water until tender but not mushy. Peel them while still hot and let them cool to room temperature. Slice and arrange slightly overlapping on a serving plate.

Mix the garlic and parsley and sprinkle over the potatoes. Season with salt and pepper. Pour the oil over and let potatoes absorb the flavors for a few minutes before serving.

SERVES 6

MARINATED ZUCCHINI (top) AND POTATO SALAD (bottom)

PHOTO: GIAN LUIGI SCARFIOTTI

ARTICHOKES WITH CALAMINT

STEWED ARTICHOKES AND POTATOES

Toscana

CARCIOFI ALLA NEPITELLA
Artichokes with Calamint

Nepitella (satureia calamintha) is an herb that grows wild in Tuscany and many other areas of Italy during summer and autumn. It is used especially to add flavor to mushrooms and artichokes. The herb belongs to the mint family; if necessary, mint can be used as a substitute.

6 globe artichokes
juice of 1 lemon
3 tablespoons fresh calamint, catnip/catmint or mint
salt and freshly ground pepper
3 tablespoons extra virgin olive oil

Clean the artichokes and remove the tough outer leaves and spiky tips. Drop them into water acidulated with the lemon juice so they do not darken. Peel the artichoke stalks and chop them with the calamint. Season with salt and pepper.

Open up the leaves slightly and fill the spaces with the calamint mixture. Drizzle the artichokes with 2 table-spoons oil. Stand the artichokes upright in an oiled skillet. Pour a few tablespoons of water over them and cover the pan. Cook over low heat until artichokes are tender, about 20 minutes, basting from time to time with the pan juices.

SERVES 6

Puglia

CARCIOFI E PATATE IN UMIDO
Stewed Artichokes and Potatoes

There is a great wealth and variety of vegetables in this region, and they are cooked fairly simply in order to make the most of their flavor. In recent years, thanks to its climate and its vast plains, Apulia has become a center of vegetable production for the whole of Italy.

6 globe artichokes
juice of 1 lemon
¼ cup (2 fl oz/60 ml) extra virgin olive oil
½ onion, chopped
4 baking potatoes, peeled and cut into small wedges
salt and freshly ground pepper
1 tablespoon chopped fresh oregano

🍴 Clean the artichokes and cut off the stalks, tough leaves and spiky tips. Cut artichokes into wedges and drop into cold water acidulated with the lemon juice.

🍴 Heat the oil in a skillet over medium heat. Add the chopped onion, then the artichokes and potatoes and cook until tender, about 20 minutes, adding water as necessary to keep the bottom of the pan moist. Season with salt, pepper and oregano. Transfer to a dish and serve.

SERVES 8

FENNEL CUTLETS

Emilia-Romagna

FINOCCHI AL FORMAGGIO
Fennel in Cheese Sauce

In Emilia-Romagna vegetables are never served simply boiled or stewed, but are often made tastier by the addition of butter, milk or cheese.

Fennel is at its tenderest between September and March; the bulbs are white because they are continually covered with soil as they grow.

6 fennel bulbs
3 tablespoons (2 oz/60 g) butter
salt and freshly ground pepper
6 thin slices fontina or Gruyère cheese
grated nutmeg
¼ cup (2 fl oz/60 ml) milk

🍴 Trim the fennel bulbs and discard the tough outer layers. Cut bulbs into small wedges and cook in a small amount of boiling salted water until crisp-tender. Drain and place them in a baking dish greased with some of the butter.

🍴 Preheat oven to 425°F (220°C). Season fennel with salt and pepper; cover with the cheese slices. Sprinkle nutmeg over the top and pour on the milk. Dot with the remaining butter. Bake for 10 minutes. Serve hot.

SERVES 6

Piemonte

COSTOLETTE DI FINOCCHI
Fennel Cutlets

In Piedmontese cooking, vegetables are often coated in egg and breadcrumbs and fried in butter. Not only fennel, but also artichokes, pieces of celery and the white stalks of Swiss chard or silverbeet may be cooked in this way.

6 fennel bulbs
2 eggs
salt and freshly ground pepper
2 cups (8 oz/250 g) fine dry breadcrumbs
3 oz (90 g) butter

🍴 Clean the fennel bulbs and cut them into wedges. Cook in boiling salted water for 10 minutes; drain and pat dry. Beat the eggs with a pinch each of salt and pepper.

🍴 Dip the fennel wedges in the egg and coat with breadcrumbs, patting so that the crumbs adhere firmly to each piece. Melt the butter in a skillet and fry the fennel until crumbs are golden brown on all sides. Drain on paper towels and serve.

SERVES 6

FENNEL IN CHEESE SAUCE

213

Le Grandi Isole

PHOTO: LARRY GORDON/THE IMAGE BANK

Le Grandi Isole

The two largest islands off the coast of Italy, Sicily and Sardinia, have very distinct identities. For both, however, physical proximity to north Africa has meant that their cuisine, architecture and culture reveal definite Arab influences.

Sicily is a racial melting pot; over the centuries, Norman, Islamic, Greek, Spanish and German cultures have left their mark and been distilled into a unique way of life. Over Sicilian cuisine float the fragrant aromas of aniseed, cloves, mint and cinnamon. Sardinia, in contrast, is a geographically inhospitable island where piglets, kids or turkeys from the forests are cooked over open fires in the hills where bandits once roamed.

It has been said that Sicily is a continent, not an island, because there are elements in its geography and history that are unique and unrelated to the rest of Italy. Located strategically in the center of the Mediterranean, Sicily has seen a succession of great civilizations — the original pre-Hellenic society followed by the Greek, Carthaginian, Roman, Byzantine, Arab, Norman, French, Spanish and finally the post-unification Italian. Indeed, it has seen the civilizations accumulate one on top of the other, none of them actually disappearing. So the present economic, social and cultural structure of the island is simply the sum of all those that have preceded it over two thousand years.

Its cooking, simply another aspect of this age-old baroque construction, is also composed of successive strata. The first and oldest is occupied by pasta: this is the area where wheat was first cultivated and made into flour, and where it was first mixed into the dough from which macaroni

LUNCH-TIME PATRONS OF THIS SARDINIAN RESTAURANT WILL ENJOY A MEAL OF BOAR OR LOBSTER, OR PERHAPS A SOUP OF CRAB

PREVIOUS PAGES: THIS FISHING VILLAGE IN SICILY IS A DELIGHTFUL MIXTURE OF SARACEN, ROMAN AND SOME MORE MODERN ARCHITECTURAL STYLES

217

PHOTO: AUSTRALIAN PICTURE LIBRARY

is made. Pastrymaking, already known through-out the Mediterranean in Plato's time, was invented in Sicily. It was here at a later date that the seeds of orange and lemon trees, pistachio nuts, and dishes like couscous — tiny balls of semolina steamed with oil and then added to a rockfish broth — arrived from the Arab world. This is the birthplace of pasta with sardines, perhaps the most famous dish of the region. Recipes such as *caponata* from Spain and *stoccafisso* (salt cod) from Norway were collected and elaborated here. The list could go on.

In simple terms, the cuisine of Sicily can be divided into "dinners for the rich and food for the poor," as the historian of Sicilian folklore, Giuseppe Pitrè, wrote at the beginning of the century. From him we learn that the peasants lived mainly on bread: bread with onions, with broad beans, with olives, with cheese, and, when they could afford it, with soups containing pasta or vegetables. To this basic diet, of course, the fisherfolk added fish — mainly sardines, and tuna and swordfish for special occasions. And if worse came to worst, from August to December the entire island could count on the prickly pear. The nobility, on the other hand, dined in a luxury that left foreign visitors openmouthed: plates and cups of gold and silver, an extraordinary number of courses covering all the island's specialties, "fricassees, fricandeau, ragouts, etc." and for dessert "sorbets in the form of peaches, figs, oranges…."

The cooking typical of Sicily today is a combination of the eating traditions of the rich and the poor, with additional differences imposed by the changing seasons. Sowing, threshing, the grape harvest, Christmas, Lent, Easter and the festivals of patron saints are ritually accompanied by gastronomic customs that have been handed down from father to son, and proudly survive today despite the different values and meanings attached to the modern calendar. On Christmas Eve the women still make *caponata* (so-called because it was the traditional accompaniment for capon); on Sunday they still make pasta by hand; vintage time is still an occasion for eating roast peppers; and the return of the *paranze*, fishing boats, is still celebrated with the wonderful taste of freshly caught sardines cooked on a spit. Sicilians continue to eat *cannoli* made with flaky pastry at Carnival time, and meat pies at Easter; the saying "be frugal with salt, because it hardens the brain and the head" still goes; and — thank heavens — the aromas of garlic, bay leaves, aniseed, mint, cinnamon and cloves still dominate Sicilian cooking.

Porchetto (piglet), known as *porceddu* in the south and *porcheddu* in the north and center of the island, is the most famous specialty of Sardinian cuisine. It must be a free-range piglet from the mountains or the oak forests, and must be milk-fed right up to the time of slaughter. It is cooked on a wood fire in the open, 16 in (40 cm) from the fire and 12 in (30 cm) from the ground.

IN THE ROCKY WALL OF CAPE CACCIA IN SARDINIA, THE SEA HAS FORMED NEPTUNE'S GROTTO, A SPECTACULAR CAVE WITH DEEP STALACTITE-LINED CHAMBERS

PHOTO: MICHAEL SALAS/THE IMAGE BANK

COLLECTED BY DIVERS, SEA SPONGES ARE SOLD IN MANY SEASIDE MARKETS IN BOTH SICILY AND SARDINIA

In Sardinia today, both the piglet and the kid are destined to be victims of the sacrifice just as they were in antiquity. Whereas the priest with his ritual motions was attempting to gain favor with the gods, the modern cook is endeavoring to obtain the approval of his guests. Once cooked, the piglet is sliced and served either hot accompanied by celery and radishes, or cold after it has been left to rest for a day among the glossy, fragrant leaves of the myrtle. The same goes for *pastu mistu* — an enormous turkey that is stuffed with a duck, a chicken, a partridge and a lark or two and cooked in a pit lined with aromatic branches — and for the *griva*, a bird that is captured in nets and traps set in the woods, boiled over a high flame, salted, spiced and pressed between myrtle leaves.

The preparation of boar, lobster, turtle soup, *cassola* (a *brodetto* made with twelve different varieties of fish, plus crab and chili pepper) and of all the other specialties of Sardinian cooking remains a kind of ceremonial rite. This is evidence of how past and present, history and legend, the fabulous and the real coexist here on the best of terms, notwithstanding the passing of the centuries.

This natural state of permanent contrast is characteristic of Sardinia, beginning with nature: it has sea and inland rivers, mountains and plains;

and the local diet combines *fiore* cheese, manufactured on the plains from cow's milk, with mountain pecorino made from sheep's milk. Similarly, alongside the intensely urban coastal area lie the vast uninhabited spaces of the interior; a backward system of land allocation exists alongside an advanced industrial organization, and an ancestral mistrust of human justice survives in the area that six hundred years ago produced history's first female judge and legislator, Eleonora di Arborea. And there is further contrast between Sardinia's many different gastronomic traditions and the hundreds of ways of cooking the same food in different localities.

Sardinia is a small, closed world complete with its own logic. The writer Grazia Deledda, one of the island's most famous daughters, describes it in these terms: "Sardinians on the whole are without doubt a poetic people, and as such, they have a longing for the best, perhaps the unattainable.... The shepherd, the peasant, the woman confined to her house all dream in their long periods of solitude.... We have all, even the poorest and simplest among us, the certainty that in every slightly mysterious place, in the *nuraghes* [pre-Roman circular fortresses], the *domos de janas* [witches' homes] and the caves are hidden treasures, which we have only to seek in order to find."

I Dolci

A CERAMIC SIGN FOR A CAKE SHOP IN ERICE, SICILY,
ADVERTISING THE LOCAL SPECIALTIES

I Dolci

There is a saying that the dessert is the poetry of cooking, the lyrical point in any meal. Certainly it creates high expectations: "Is there dessert?" the guests wonder, as the end of a dinner party approaches. "If you're good, I'll give you a piece of cake" is a common promise made by mothers, grandmothers and aunts to small children. Sweet foods also generate considerable guilt feelings: "I swear this is the last cake I'll eat," and "desserts are just a concentration of calories." But they can also represent consolation, or a prize earned.

How is it that dessert has this function of pure gratification, while other foods have not? How is it that sweet foods manage to confer moments of such intense pleasure? Because sugar, their raw material and the source of the sweet taste, was until relatively recently a rare and precious substance. In the past, honey was used as a sweetener, while cane sugar, which came to Europe after the great discoveries of new lands, was, up to the eighteenth century, a luxury reserved for the tables of kings and princes. It was common to see knights and ladies carrying tiny, precious boxes in which their equally precious sugar tablets were jealously kept. Then in 1747 a German chemist succeeded in extracting sugar from beets, and during the nineteenth century it began to be commercially produced and to form part of everybody's diet.

And so, Italian cakes and desserts must be divided into two eras: the ancient and the modern. The oldest sweets were created as variations on or improvements to bread and bread dough, as can be clearly seen from their names: *Pane di Natale* (Liguria), *Pan Pepato* (Tuscany), *Pandoro* (Veneto), *Pan Meino* (Lombardy), *Pan di Spagna* (Tuscany), *Panettone* (Lombardy), *Panforte* (Tuscany) and so on. Or else they were variations beginning from the same basis as pasta, as in shortcrust pastry, Genoese pastry, almond pastry, marzipan, etc.

In more modern desserts and cakes the use of sugar is taken for granted, and the emergence of more elaborate and complex recipes marked the beginning of true pastrymaking and confectionery; consider the recipe for *gianduia* cake, for example, or *tiramisù*. There are a large number of traditional sweets and cakes, with an infinite number of local variations (recipes for sweet fritters, for example, are part of the tradition of every tiny community in Italy). The ingredients are few, and they are repeated from north to south — flour, milk, sugar, honey, almonds, chestnuts — all basic country ingredients which testify to a widespread agricultural economy and recall the cuisine of the ancient Romans, although adjustments have been made over the centuries.

The ingredients in today's cakes and desserts

PREVIOUS PAGES: LOOKING THROUGH ANY *PASTICHERIA*
WINDOW, LIKE THIS ONE IN ROME, IS A VISUAL DELIGHT
PHOTO: RAY JOYCE

are the same, with the addition of cocoa, liqueurs, and eggs in abundance. The principal difference is the introduction of highly sophisticated techniques, many of which were imported from nineteenth-century France, during the era of European "grand gastronomy" when pastry shops and coffeehouses abounded in the old capitals of the Belle Epoque.

But in Italian cooking the traditional home-made sweets and cakes continue to predominate. These are the classic family "plain but good" varieties (made by the women of the household rather than by great chefs), sweet dishes related to the farmer's calendar, local festivals and the work in the fields. *Castagnaccio*, a chestnut cake, *Pane dei Morti* ("bread of the dead") and *Pane di Miglio*, a millet cake, were always baked in November. There were cakes or desserts for Christmas, *Carnevale*, Easter and harvest time. The end of every season and every working cycle was an occasion for finishing a meal with a special sweet dish or having a particular cake midmorning.

Today's cakes and desserts, by contrast, nearly all originated with meetings of rulers or peace treaties or political events: a good example are the cakes and biscuits of Piedmont, most of which became famous in the years of the *Risorgimento* and the unification of Italy. Cake making requires, on the one hand, a certain amount of care and precision, and on the other a good deal of imagination — precision in quantities and cooking times, which must be strictly followed, and imagination in the addition of a particular flavor combination, some personal touch to make the creation unique.

If by chance you find the Italian proverb "not every doughnut comes out with a hole" to be true, do not lose heart. As Pellegrino Artusi wrote, "Cooking is a rogue; it often brings despair, but it also gives pleasure, because whenever one succeeds or overcomes some difficulty, there is a feeling of satisfaction and the joy of victory."

ICE CREAM AT A *GELATERIA* IN FLORENCE

PHOTO: JOHN SIMS

CHESTNUT CREAM MOUNTAIN

Piemonte

MONTEBIANCO
Chestnut Cream Mountain

Piedmontese cooks would only make this classic autumn dessert when fresh chestnuts are available. It resembles the peak of a mountain — Mont Blanc, in fact, the highest peak in Europe — underneath which there is a tunnel linking Italy with France.

2 lb (1 kg) fresh chestnuts or, if unavailable, 1 lb (500 g) canned chestnuts, drained well
2 cups (16 fl oz/500 ml) milk
½ teaspoon vanilla extract (essence)
1 cup (7 oz/220 g) superfine (caster) sugar
2 cups (16 fl oz/500 ml) cream
6 tablespoons powdered (icing) sugar

Make an incision in each chestnut. Boil the chestnuts in water to cover for 30 minutes, then drain and remove the shells and inner skins. Place in a saucepan, cover with milk, add vanilla and bring to boil. Cover and cook over low heat for 10 minutes or until chestnuts have absorbed the milk.

Force chestnuts through a sieve or puree in a food processor. Blend in sugar. Transfer the puree to a saucepan and cook over moderate heat, stirring constantly, until the mixture comes away easily from the sides of the pan. Remove from heat and let cool completely.

Press the chestnut puree through a food mill, letting it fall in a dome shape onto a plate, or puree in a food processor. Whip the cream with the powdered sugar to stiff peaks. Frost the dome with it, using a pastry bag fitted with a fluted tip. Serve cold.

SERVES 6

MIASCIA
Bread and Fruit Pudding

Miascia is a very light and tasty bread pudding, a specialty of Lake Como. The rosemary gives it a very special flavor. Sweet dishes in Italy are often given an added flavoring of herbs or flowers such as lavender, rosemary, roses or elderflowers.

¼ cup (1 oz/30 g) raisins
3 cups (6 oz/185 g) thin slices of stale, firm, coarse-textured bread (crusts trimmed)
⅔ cup (5 fl oz/150 ml) milk for soaking bread
3 eggs
½ cup (4 fl oz/125 ml) milk
pinch of salt
⅓ cup (3 oz/90 g) sugar
grated rind of 1 lemon
2 tablespoons all purpose (plain) flour
2 tablespoons cornmeal
2 apples, peeled, cored and sliced
1 pear, peeled, cored and sliced
½ cup red grapes, peeled
2 – 3 teaspoons chopped fresh rosemary
2 tablespoons sugar
1 tablespoon extra virgin olive oil

Soak the raisins in hot water to cover for 15 minutes; drain. Soak the bread in ⅔ cup milk for 2 minutes.

Preheat oven to 350°F (180°C). Combine the eggs, ½ cup milk, salt, sugar, lemon rind, flour and cornmeal and blend well.

Add the apples, pear, grapes and drained raisins. Generously butter a 10-in (25-cm) cake pan. Lay soaked bread in pan and pour batter over, arranging fruit evenly. Sprinkle with rosemary and 2 tablespoons sugar and drizzle with olive oil.

Bake for 1 hour or until a knife inserted in center comes out clean. Serve pudding lukewarm or lightly reheated.

SERVES 6-8

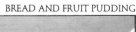

BREAD AND FRUIT PUDDING

Campania

PASTIERA

Easter Pie

Pastiera is the traditional Neapolitan Easter pastry. Each family has its own recipe and discusses it at length with friends and neighbors, everybody tasting each other's and commenting on them all. This pastry is offered to guests for at least a week around Easter time (and that is how long the pastiera *will keep).*

It is traditionally left in the pan in which it is baked, never turned out.

5 oz (155 g) whole wheat kernels (available in health food stores)
2 cups (8 oz/250 g) all purpose (plain) flour
4 oz (125 g) butter
⅓ cup (3 oz/90 g) sugar
4 egg yolks
1⅓ cups (11 fl oz/310 ml) milk
grated rind of ½ orange
⅓ cup (3 oz/90 g) superfine (caster) sugar
1 teaspoon vanilla extract (essence)
8 oz (250 g) ricotta
2 tablespoons orange flower water
1 tablespoon chopped candied citron (see page 247)
1 tablespoon chopped candied orange peel
1 tablespoon chopped candied pumpkin
pinch of ground cinnamon
2 egg whites

Soak the wheat in cold water overnight.

Combine the flour, butter, ⅓ cup sugar and 1 egg yolk to make a dough; form into a ball. Let rest while preparing filling.

Drain the wheat and combine with the milk, orange rind and 1 tablespoon sugar and cook over low heat until mixture is creamy and porridgelike. Remove from heat and stir in vanilla.

Combine the ricotta, 3 egg yolks, the remaining sugar, the wheat, orange flower water, candied fruit and cinnamon. Beat the egg whites until stiff and fold into the mixture.

Preheat oven to 350°F (180°C). Roll out ¾ of the pastry dough and use it to line a 9-in (23-cm) pie pan. Fill with the ricotta mixture. Roll out the remaining dough and cut it into ⅜-in (1-cm) strips using a fluted pastry wheel. Arrange the strips in a lattice over the filling and crimp the edges. Bake the *pastiera* for 1 hour or until the pastry is golden brown.

Let cool, then let the pie rest for a few hours before serving.

SERVES 6 – 8

Campania

CROSTATA DI RICOTTA

Ricotta Pie

Ricotta pie is a simplified version of pastiera. *It is also much richer because it contains chocolate. The pie may be finished off with toasted pine nuts or almonds, and a sprinkling of powdered (icing) sugar.*

2½ cups (10 oz/315 g) all purpose (plain) flour
3 egg yolks
⅓ cup (3 oz/90 g) superfine (caster) sugar
3 oz (90 g) butter
3 egg yolks
⅓ cup (3 oz/90 g) superfine (caster) sugar
2 tablespoons all purpose (plain) flour
1 cup (8 fl oz/250 ml) milk
3 oz (90 g) semisweet (plain) chocolate
¼ cup (2 fl oz/60 ml) maraschino liqueur
8 oz (250 g) ricotta
pinch of ground cinnamon
grated rind of 1 lemon
1 egg white, beaten

For the pastry, combine 2½ cups flour, 3 egg yolks, ⅓ cup sugar and the butter and mix into a dough. Form into a ball, cover with plastic and let rest in the refrigerator while preparing the filling.

For the filling, beat 3 egg yolks with ⅓ cup sugar until light. Add 2 tablespoons flour and the milk and cook the mixture in a double boiler over simmering water until thick. Melt the chocolate with the maraschino. Stir into the egg mixture and let cool completely.

Put the ricotta through a sieve. Gradually stir in the cooled custard, cinnamon and lemon rind. Mix well and set aside for 10 minutes.

Preheat oven to 350°F (180°C). Butter and flour a 10-in (25-cm) pie pan. Roll out ¾ of the pastry dough in a circle and line the pan with it. Pour in the prepared filling and roll out the remaining dough into a circle to cover the top. Crimp edges together. Brush the top of the pie with a little beaten egg white and bake for 40 minutes or until crust is golden brown. Let cool before serving.

SERVES 6-8 ·

RICOTTA PIE

ALMOND BISCUITS

golden, about 20 minutes. Cut the logs into 1-in (2.5-cm) slices while still warm. Separate them and cook for another 5 minutes. Cool on racks before serving. Store in an airtight container.

SERVES 6 – 8

Lombardia

PAN MEINO
Cornmeal and Elderflower Cake

This dessert is especially popular in spring, when the elders are in bloom. It is also possible to find dried elderflowers in grocery stores. The cornmeal gives the cake extra lightness. Sometimes pan meino *is baked in individual pans instead of a single large cake pan.*

2 egg yolks
6 tablespoons (3 oz/(90 g) superfine caster sugar
¾ cup (3 oz/90 g) all purpose (plain) flour
1¾ cups (7 oz/220 g) finely ground cornmeal
pinch of salt
2 teaspoons baking powder
1 teaspoon elderflowers, chopped
3½ oz (115 g) butter
½ cup (4 fl oz/125 ml) milk
1 cup (8 fl oz/250 ml) cream

Combine egg yolks with 4 tablespoons of the sugar and beat until light and lemon colored.

Set aside 1 tablespoon flour. Mix the remaining flour with the cornmeal, salt, baking powder and elderflowers. Melt 3 oz (90 g) butter in a small saucepan and blend into the yolk mixture. Add the flour mixture alternately with the milk, beating until well blended after each addition.

Preheat oven to 350°F (180°C). Grease a 9-in (23-cm) cake pan with the remaining butter and sprinkle it with a little of the reserved sugar mixed with the reserved flour. Spread the dough in the pan, making it slightly higher in the center. Scatter the remaining sugar over the surface. Bake until top is golden, about 40 minutes. Let cake cool. Serve cold with cream.

SERVES 6

Toscana

BISCOTTI DI PRATO
Almond Biscuits

These biscuits are also sometimes known as cantucci. *They are rather hard and keep very well in an airtight container. Traditionally they are dipped into a glass of* vin santo *as they are eaten.*

2¼ cups (9 oz/280 g) unbleached all purpose (plain) flour
¾ cup (6 oz/185 g) superfine (caster) sugar
1½ teaspoons baking powder
¼ teaspoon salt
2 eggs
1 egg yolk
⅔ cup (4 oz/125 g) unblanched almonds, chopped
1 egg yolk plus 1 tablespoon milk for glaze

Mix flour, sugar, baking powder, salt, whole eggs and the yolk and blend to form a smooth dough. Knead in the almonds.

Divide the dough into 4 parts and form each into a cigar-shaped log. Preheat oven to 450°F (230°C). Flour a baking sheet and place the logs on it, well apart. Bake until

CORNMEAL AND ELDERFLOWER CAKE

Veneto

CROSTATA DI MARMELLATA
Jam Tart

The Italian crostata with jam filling is particularly suited to afternoon tea (as the Italians have it) or for breakfast. The peaches may be replaced with other seasonal fruits, such as cherries, apricots, strawberries or raspberries.

2 cups (8 oz/250 g) all purpose (plain) flour
2 egg yolks
4 oz (125 g) butter
½ cup (4 oz/125 g) superfine (caster) sugar
pinch of salt
1½ lb (750 g) peaches, peeled, pitted and sliced
¾ cup (6 oz/185 g) sugar

❧ Combine flour, egg yolks, butter, ½ cup sugar and the salt and blend to form a smooth dough. Form into a ball. Flatten, wrap and chill for 30 minutes.
❧ Preheat oven to 350°F (180°C). Roll out ⅔ of dough on a floured surface; line a 9-in (23-cm) tart pan with the dough. Cover dough with parchment paper and dried beans or pie weights.
❧ Bake tart shell for 20 minutes. Remove beans and parchment. Roll out remaining dough and cut into strips; reserve.
❧ Combine peaches and sugar in a large saucepan and simmer until fruit is soft, about 10 minutes. Pass the peaches through a food mill, or puree, then return mixture to saucepan and simmer another 10 minutes, or until thick. Fill baked tart shell with the jam and top with lattice strips of dough. Bake until the pastry is golden, about 20 minutes. Serve cold.

SERVES 6

Toscana

CASTAGNACCIO
Chestnut Cake

This is an ancient and very popular cake recipe. Castagnaccio is often sold in the streets of Florence during autumn and early winter. It is best when freshly made, and should be served warm.

¼ cup (1 oz/30 g) raisins
3 cups (12 oz/375 g) chestnut flour
2½ cups (20 fl oz/600 ml) water
6 tablespoons extra virgin olive oil
pinch of salt
¼ cup (1½ oz/45 g) pine nuts
2 fresh rosemary sprigs, finely chopped

❧ Soak the raisins in water to cover for 1 hour.
❧ In a bowl, mix the flour, water, 2 tablespoons olive oil and the salt to form a creamy dough.
❧ Add 3 tablespoons pine nuts and the rosemary.
❧ Preheat oven to 450°F (230°C). Pour the remaining oil into an 11-in (27-cm) tart pan (do not use a pan with removable bottom) and add the dough. Do not pour off excess oil.
❧ Drain the raisins. Sprinkle the dough with the raisins and the remaining pine nuts. Bake for about 20 minutes or until the surface of the *castagnaccio* begins to crack.
❧ Pour off the excess olive oil. Remove *castagnaccio* from the pan and serve warm.

SERVES 6

CHESTNUT CAKE (left) AND JAM TART (right)

Toscana

TIRAMISÙ

Tuscan Trifle

Tiramisù ("pick me up") is a modern version of a dessert first created in Siena, where it was called zuppa del Duca *(the Duke's soup!). From there it migrated to Florence, where it became very popular in the nineteenth century among the many English people who came to live in the city at that time. And so it was called* zuppa inglese — *English soup. Only recently, the same dessert with some variation — chiefly the substitution of rich mascarpone cheese for the original custard — has come to be called tiramisù.*

3 egg yolks
3 tablespoons superfine (caster) sugar
1⅓ cups (11 fl oz/330 ml) *vin santo,* Marsala or brandy
¼ cup (2 fl oz/60 ml) very strong espresso coffee

8 oz (250 g) mascarpone cheese, room temperature
½ cup (4 fl oz/125 ml) cream
1 egg white
4 oz (125 g) *savoiardi* or ladyfingers (sponge fingers)

❧ Make a *zabaglione* by beating the egg yolks and sugar in the top of a double boiler until ivory colored. Add ⅓ cup (3 fl oz/80 ml) liquor and whisk over gently simmering water until the mixture begins to thicken. Let cool.
❧ Stir the coffee into the mascarpone. Whip the cream to soft peaks. Beat the egg white until stiff. Fold the egg white into the *zabaglione*. Dip the lady fingers into the remaining liquor and arrange in a single layer in the bottom of a 9-in (23-cm) bowl. Cover them with half the mascarpone, then half the *zabaglione* and half the cream. Repeat the layers, finishing with the cream. Refrigerate for several hours before serving.

SERVES 6

229

FIGS WITH ALMOND STUFFING

Calabria

FICHI MANDORLATI
Figs with Almond Stuffing

These baked figs are a real delicacy and will keep for a long time. Raisins may be prepared by the same method, using about a tablespoonful in each leaf.

½ cup (6 oz/185 g) honey
1 teaspoon ground cinnamon
18 grape (vine) leaves
18 large, fleshy fresh figs
18 blanched almonds
18 whole cloves

❧ Heat the honey gently until very liquid. Stir in the cinnamon. Blanch the grape leaves in boiling water for 1 minute; drain and spread on a towel to dry.
❧ Split the figs open down the center, leaving one side attached. Fill with the almonds and cloves. Press closed and dip in the honey. Place a fig on each leaf and wrap the leaf around it, tying it up with string.
❧ Preheat oven to 350°F (180°C). Arrange the bundles on a baking sheet and bake until the leaves dry out, about 30 minutes. Let cool completely before unwrapping.

SERVES 6

Emilia-Romagna

TORTA DI MELIGA
Cornmeal Cake

This very simple, crumbly cake is particularly suitable for serving with afternoon tea or at breakfast. It is delicious accompanied by a pitcher of fresh cream or dipped in a sweet dessert wine.

1 cup (6 oz/185 g) almonds
1 cup (4 oz/125 g) yellow cornmeal
¼ cup (1 oz/30 g) unbleached all purpose (plain) flour
½ cup (4 oz/120 g) sugar
pinch of salt
4½ oz (140 g) unsalted butter, softened
1 tablespoon powdered (icing) sugar

❧ Blanch the almonds for 1 minute. Pat dry and peel off the skins. Chop finely.
❧ Preheat oven to 400°F (200°C). In a food processor combine the chopped almonds, cornmeal, flour, sugar, salt and 4 oz (125 g) butter.
❧ With the remaining butter, grease a 9-in (23-cm) cake pan with removable base and spread dough in the pan.
❧ Bake for 30 minutes, or until light golden. Let cool slightly, then remove the bottom and transfer cake to a plate. Let cool completely, then sift powdered sugar over the top and serve.

SERVES 6

CORNMEAL CAKE

Emilia-Romagna

DOLCE DI TAGLIERINI
Noodle Cake

This is a classic dish that may be made with the fine egg noodles known as taglierini *or with the very thin spaghetti called* capelli d'angelo *("angel's hair") or vermicelli. The cake is particularly good served hot or lukewarm; if allowed to cool completely it becomes heavy.*

½ cup (2 oz/60 g) raisins
6 eggs, separated
1 cup (7 oz/220 g) superfine (caster) sugar
8 oz (250 g) dry *taglierini* (angel hair pasta or vermicelli)
8 oz (250 g) ricotta
1 teaspoon cinnamon
1 teaspoon ground cloves
pinch of salt
½ cup (2 oz/60 g) all purpose (plain) flour
½ cup (2 oz/60 g) fine dry breadcrumbs

1 cup (8 oz/250 g) orange marmalade
1 cup (12 oz/350 g) honey

Soak the raisins in lukewarm water to cover for 30 minutes; drain. Beat the egg yolks with the sugar until very light and lemon colored.

Bring a large saucepan of salted water to boil. Add the pasta and boil for 2 minutes. Drain, then rinse briefly under cold water.

Beat the ricotta with the egg yolk mixture, cinnamon, cloves and salt. Stir in the flour a little at a time. Add the drained raisins and *taglierini*.

Preheat oven to 400°F (200°C). Beat the egg whites to soft peaks and fold into ricotta mixture. Pour into a buttered 9-in (23-cm) cake pan lightly coated with breadcrumbs. Bake for 1 hour and 10 minutes. Puree the marmalade and honey in a food processor. Transfer to a saucepan and warm over low heat.

Unmold the cake onto a serving dish. While still warm, spread the surface with some of the marmalade sauce. Pour the remaining sauce into a pitcher and serve separately.

SERVES 6-8

NOODLE CAKE

SULTANA MOLD

Sicilia

SFORMATO DI ZIBIBBO

Sultana Mold

The sultana is an unusually sweet and now rare grape, grown mainly in Sicily and on the nearby small islands. Sicily is justly famous for the quality and flavor of its grapes.

1 cup (4 oz/125 g) sultanas or golden raisins
¼ cup blanched hazelnuts, toasted
¼ cup blanched almonds, toasted
1 qt (1 l) milk
pinch of salt
1 cup (5 oz/155 g) semolina
½ cup (4 oz/125 g) superfine (caster) sugar
4 eggs, separated
grated rind of ½ lemon
1 tablespoon almond oil, optional

Soak the sultanas in water to cover until needed. Chop the nuts finely. Pour the milk into a saucepan, add the salt and bring to boil. Briskly stir in the semolina and cook over low heat for 10 minutes, stirring frequently. Remove from heat and stir in the sugar. Cool completely.

Preheat oven to 350°F (180°C). Stir the egg yolks, chopped nuts, lemon rind and sultanas into the semolina mixture. Beat the egg whites until stiff and fold in.

Pour the mixture into an oiled 7-in (18-cm) ring mold and place the mold in a larger pan of boiling water. Bake for 1 hour, or until a knife inserted in the center comes out clean. Let cool slightly, then unmold onto a serving plate. Sprinkle with powdered (icing) sugar if desired and serve warm.

SERVES 8

Trentino-Alto Adige

STRUDEL DI MELE

Apple Strudel

Apple strudel is made with filo pastry, which is as thin as a veil, and rather difficult to roll out by hand. It is possible to use puff pastry instead, but then the strudel becomes extremely rich. It is important that the apples are the mealy kind.

2 cups (8 oz/250 g) all purpose (plain) flour
1 egg
1 tablespoon sugar
pinch of salt
3 tablespoons (2 oz/60 g) butter, melted
1 – 2 tablespoons butter, melted
2 lb (1 kg) baking (cooking) apples, peeled, cored and sliced
½ teaspoon ground cinnamon
¼ cup (1½ oz/45 g) blanched slivered almonds
¼ cup (1 oz/30 g) golden raisins (sultanas), soaked and drained
grated rind of 1 orange
½ cup (4 oz/125 g) apple jelly (jam)
3 tablespoons powdered (icing) sugar

To make the pastry, heap the flour on a board and make a well in the center. Mix in the egg, sugar and salt. Add the melted butter and enough water to form a smooth dough.

Cover with a heated bowl and let dough rest for 20 minutes. Then work it again, slapping it down on the board to make it more elastic. Gather dough up into a ball.

Roll dough out on a floured cloth with a floured rolling pin, making it as thin as possible. Brush the sheet with melted butter. Spread evenly with apples; scatter the cinnamon, almonds, raisins and orange rind on top. Spoon the jelly over and sprinkle with 2 tablespoons powdered sugar.

Preheat oven to 350°F (180°C). Carefully roll up the strudel, removing the cloth as you go, and flatten at each end so that the filling will not come out during baking. Butter a large baking sheet and slide the strudel onto it. Bake until golden brown, about 1 hour. Transfer the strudel to a plate, sift the remaining powdered sugar over it and serve.

SERVES 6

APPLE STRUDEL

MOLDED RICE PUDDING

Emilia-Romagna

BUDINO DI RISO
Molded Rice Pudding

This rice pudding may be enriched with soaked raisins and diced candied peel or citron.

1 cup (6 oz/185 g) Arborio rice
3 cups (24 fl oz/750 ml) milk
4 eggs, separated
6 oz (185 g) semisweet (plain) chocolate
3 oz (90 g) butter
½ cup (4 oz/125 g) plus 2 tablespoons superfine (caster) sugar
½ cup (4 oz/125 g) red currant jelly
¼ cup (2 fl oz/60 ml) *vin santo* or sweet white wine

Bring a saucepan of salted water to boil. Add rice and cook 5 minutes. Drain. Return rice to saucepan, add milk and cook over low heat until all liquid is absorbed.

Beat the egg yolks with ½ cup sugar until light. Melt the chocolate and butter together in a heatproof bowl set over simmering water. Beat the egg whites to stiff peaks, gradually adding 2 tablespoons sugar.

Preheat oven to 400°F (200°C). Combine rice, yolks, chocolate mixture and whites and fold gently to blend well. Turn into a buttered 9-in (23-cm) mold. Place mold in a larger pan; add boiling water to the pan to come halfway up sides of mold. Bake for 1 hour. Remove mold from water bath, reduce oven temperature to 325°F (160°C) and bake the pudding for 10 minutes longer.

Unmold onto a platter. Stir jelly and *vin santo* over very low heat until jelly dissolves. Drizzle over pudding and serve.

SERVES 6

Emilia-Romagna

CROSTATA DI CREMA
Lemon Cream Tart

The cream filling for this wonderfully light tart can also be flavored with cinnamon, vanilla or orange; substitute milk for the lemon juice.

2 lemons
2 eggs, separated
¼ cup (2 oz/60 g) superfine (caster) sugar
1½ cups (6 oz/185 g) all purpose (plain) flour
3 oz (90 g) butter
3 tablespoons superfine (caster) sugar
1 egg yolk
¼ cup (2 fl oz/60 ml) cream
rind of 1 orange

Grate the rind of the lemons and squeeze ¼ cup (2 fl oz/60 ml) juice. Beat together 2 egg yolks and ¼ cup sugar; add the lemon rind and juice.

Transfer mixture to the top of a double boiler and stir over gently simmering water until slightly thickened. Let cool.

Preheat oven to 350°F (180°C). Combine the flour, butter, 3 tablespoons sugar and 1 egg yolk and mix to form a pastry dough. Line an 11-in (28-cm) tart pan with the dough and cover the bottom with dried beans or pie weights. Bake for 20 minutes. Remove the beans and bake for another 20 minutes or until golden. Let cool.

Whip the egg whites and cream separately to soft peaks. Fold into the cooled lemon mixture. Cut the orange rind into fine julienne strips and boil for 10 minutes in water to cover. Drain and pat dry. Spread the filling in the tart shell and allow to chill in the refrigerator. Sprinkle with the orange peel and decorate with extra whipped cream if desired.

SERVES 6-8

Trentino-Alto Adige

KRAPFEN
Doughnuts

Krapfen are Austrian in origin but have become very popular not only in the Trentino region but all over Italy. In other parts of Italy they may be known by different names — such as bomboloni *in Tuscany. Sometimes they are filled with a small amount of custard cream or jam.*

1 oz (30 g) fresh yeast or 1 envelope dry yeast
¾ cup (6 fl oz/200 ml) warm milk
2½ cups (10 oz/315 g) sifted all purpose (plain) flour
2 eggs
4 tablespoons (2 oz/60 g) butter or lard, softened
¼ cup (2 oz/60 g) superfine (caster) sugar
¼ teaspoon salt
oil for deep frying
2 tablespoons powdered (icing) sugar

Sprinkle the yeast over the milk and let stand until dissolved, about 5 minutes. Mound the flour on a board and make a well in the center. Pour in the yeast mixture and mix to form a soft dough. Knead until smooth and elastic, using extra flour if needed. Cover with a kitchen towel and let rise in a warm place until doubled in volume. Break the eggs into the dough and add the butter, sugar and salt. Knead for 10 minutes, then form dough into a ball, using extra flour if needed.

Place on a baking sheet, cover with a damp cloth and let rise in a warm place for 5 to 6 hours.

Knead the dough on a floured board for 10 minutes. Form into a ball once more and place back on the baking sheet. Cover with a damp cloth and refrigerate for 5 to 6 hours. Cut the dough into pieces about the size of an apricot; shape into balls.

Heat the oil to 350°F (180°C) and fry the *krapfen* a few at a time until golden brown on all sides. Remove with a slotted spoon and drain on paper towels. Arrange on a serving plate, sift the powdered sugar over and serve.

SERVES 8

LEMON CREAM TART

RICE CAKES

Lazio

TORTINI DI RISO
Rice Cakes

These little cakes are often served in cafés with a cappuccino. To serve as dessert, spoon a fresh fruit puree over them.

¼ cup (1 oz/30 g) raisins
1 cup (6 oz/185 g) Arborio rice
2 cups (16 fl oz/500 ml) milk
½ cup (4 oz/125 g) sugar
grated rind of ½ lemon
pinch of ground cinnamon
4 oz (125 g) butter
4 egg yolks
1 egg white
powdered (icing) sugar

Soak the raisins in water to cover until needed. Boil the rice in 4 cups (1 qt/1 l) boiling water for 5 minutes; drain. Bring milk and sugar to a boil, add rice, lemon rind and cinnamon. Cook over low heat until rice has absorbed all the milk, stirring constantly. Stir in butter, drained raisins and egg yolks and let cool. Whip the egg white until stiff and fold into the rice.

Preheat oven to 350°F (180°C). Pour mixture into 6 buttered individual molds and bake for 45 minutes, or until a knife inserted in the center comes out clean.

Unmold puddings onto individual plates, sprinkle with sifted powdered sugar and serve.

SERVES 6

Piemonte

MERINGHE CON LA PANNA
Meringues and Cream with Chocolate Sauce

Meringues are sold in every Piedmontese bakery. Often cocoa is added to the mixture to produce chocolate meringues.

3 egg whites
3 cups (12 oz/375 g) powdered (icing) sugar
1 cup (8 fl oz/250 ml) cream
7 oz (200 g) semisweet (plain) chocolate
½ cup (4 fl oz/125 ml) milk

Preheat oven to 250°F (120°C). Whip the egg whites until very stiff and glossy, gradually adding the powdered sugar. Butter and flour a baking sheet. Spoon the meringue into a pastry bag fitted with a large plain tip and squeeze mounds of the mixture about 2 in (5 cm) in diameter, several inches apart on the sheet.

MERINGUES AND CREAM WITH CHOCOLATE SAUCE (right) AND MOLDED CHOCOLATE CREAM (left)

Bake meringues for 30 minutes or until hardened but still white. Loosen them from the sheet and let cool completely.

Whip the cream until it holds soft peaks. Join the cooled meringues in pairs with the cream; arrange on a serving dish. Melt the chocolate with the milk over moderate heat. Pour this sauce into a pitcher and serve separately.

SERVES 6

Piemonte

BONET
Molded Chocolate Cream

This is one of the best known of Piedmontese sweet dishes, along with the Montebianco on page 224. Turin, capital of Piedmont, and Naples, capital of the Campania region, are the two places in Italy where the best chocolate is made.

7 oz (220 g) semisweet (plain) chocolate, grated
3 cups (24 fl oz/750 ml) warm milk
6 egg yolks
2 egg whites
1 cup (8 oz/250 g) sugar
16 amaretti biscuits, powdered

Melt the chocolate in the milk. Beat the eggs with ¾ cup (6 oz/185 g) of the sugar. Beat in chocolate milk and amaretti crumbs.

Preheat oven to 350°F (180°C). Mix the remaining sugar with a little water and stir over moderate heat until it is a dark gold color. Pour it into a 7-in (18-cm) mold and turn the mold to coat the bottom and sides with the syrup. Pour in the chocolate mixture. Place the mold in a larger pan; add boiling water to the larger pan to come halfway up sides of mold. Bake 1 hour. Let the dessert rest for 10 minutes before unmolding onto a serving plate. Serve cold.

SERVES 8

CHOCOLATE SALAMI

SWEET POLENTA

Veneto

POLENTA DOLCE
Sweet Polenta

There are two kinds of cornmeal to be found in the Veneto — yellow and white. Generally speaking, coarse-ground yellow cornmeal is more often used in Lombardy, but in the Veneto cooks tend to use the fine-ground variety, whether yellow or white.

3 cups (24 fl oz/750 ml) milk
½ cup (4 oz/125 g) sugar
1 cup (5 oz/155 g) fine-ground white cornmeal
1 egg
4 egg yolks
4 tablespoons (2 oz/60 g) butter, softened
grated rind of 2 lemons
2 tablespoons fine dry breadcrumbs
powdered (icing) sugar, optional

🍀 Bring the milk and sugar to boil in a saucepan. Gradually pour in the cornmeal, stirring constantly. Simmer until very thick, about 30 minutes. Let cool to lukewarm. Stir in the whole egg and yolks, butter and lemon rind.
🍀 Preheat oven to 350°F (180°C). Butter a 9-in (23-cm) cake pan and sprinkle with the breadcrumbs. Spread the polenta in the pan and bake for 20 minutes. Turn out, sprinkle with powdered sugar and serve immediately.

SERVES 6

Emilia-Romagna

SALAME DI CIOCCOLATO
Chocolate Salami

A very rich dessert that is to be served cold, this cake may be decorated with whipped cream. When the slices are cut, they really do look like salami.

½ cup (3 oz/90 g) raisins
7 oz (220 g) semisweet (plain) chocolate
3 tablespoons (2 oz/60 g) butter
6 tablespoons sugar
3 oz (90 g) blanched almonds, finely chopped
7 oz (220 g) *petit beurre*-type biscuits (sweet plain), crushed
3 tablespoons mixed candied orange peel and citron
2 egg yolks

🍀 Soak the raisins in warm water to cover until needed.
🍀 Break up the chocolate and place in a saucepan or heatproof bowl with the butter. Place this over another saucepan of gently simmering water until melted (it must not touch the water). Add the sugar, almonds, biscuit crumbs, drained raisins and candied peel and mix well. Remove from heat. Stir in the egg yolks and let mixture cool completely.
🍀 Form mixture into a salami shape with your hands and place it on a sheet of waxed paper. Seal the paper around it and refrigerate for several hours. At serving time, remove the waxed paper, slice the "salami" and arrange the slices on a plate.

SERVES 6

Lombardia

FRITTELLE DI RISO
Rice Pancakes

These soft, crisp pancakes are very simple to make with Arborio rice, which contains sufficient starch to prevent them from falling apart as they cook. The starch and the egg together keep them in shape.

1 cup (6 oz/185 g) Arborio rice
2 cups (16 fl oz/500 ml) milk
2 tablespoons butter
pinch of salt
1 tablespoon superfine (caster) sugar
grated rind of 1 lemon
3 egg yolks
2 tablespoons rum
1 egg white
½ cup (2 oz/60 g) all purpose (plain) flour
oil for deep frying

Boil the rice in the milk until the liquid is completely absorbed. Mix in the butter, salt, sugar and lemon rind and let cool completely, then stir in the egg yolks and rum.

Beat the egg white until stiff and fold it gently into the rice mixture. Form into small balls; flatten into discs 2 in (5 cm) in diameter and ⅜ in (1 cm) thick. Dredge in the flour.

Heat the oil to 350°F (180°C). Fry the *fritelle* in batches on both sides until golden brown. Drain on paper towels. Arrange on a plate and serve hot.

SERVES 6

Sardegna

SEBADAS
Cheese Fritters with Honey

These are little pancakes of cheese and flour. They are generally dipped into honey as they are eaten, providing an interesting contrast between sweet and savory. This contrast is found in many foods in Sardinia, where pecorino cheese is an important component of almost every dish.

2½ cups (10 oz/310 g) semolina or unbleached all purpose (plain) flour
1 egg
5 oz (155 g) pecorino cheese, grated
pinch of salt
oil for deep frying
honey

Mound the flour on a board and make a well in the center. Mix in the egg, cheese, salt and enough water to make a soft, elastic dough.

Roll the dough into cylinders and cut them in small pieces. Roll between the palms of your hands to make 1-in (3-cm) balls.

With floured hands, flatten them into very thin circles. Heat the oil to 350°F (180°C). Fry the rounds until they turn pale golden. Drain on paper towels and serve with honey.

SERVES 6

CHEESE FRITTERS WITH HONEY (right) AND RICE PANCAKES (left)

PHOTO: GIAN LUIGI SCARFIOTTI

TUSCAN FRIED PASTRIES

Toscana

CENCI FRITTI
Tuscan Fried Pastries

These little "rags" (cenci) are mostly made at Carnival time. Carnevale is celebrated all over Italy with masks, decorated floats representing myths and allegories, and processions. The celebrations at Viareggio are famous: here the floats are decorated as send-ups of political situations, movie stars and other famous people.

2½ cups (10 oz/315 g) all purpose (plain) flour
2 eggs
3 tablespoons extra virgin olive oil
6 tablespoons (3 oz/90 g) sugar
1 teaspoon baking powder
oil for deep frying
2 tablespoons powdered (icing) sugar

Heap the flour in a mound on a board and make a well in the center. Add eggs, 3 tablespoons oil, sugar and yeast to the well. Mix with your hands, then knead until dough is smooth, soft and elastic.

Roll dough out into a very thin sheet. Using a fluted pastry wheel, cut it into 1¼ x 2½-in (3 x 6-cm) strips. Deep fry strips in hot oil a few at a time. Drain on paper towels. Arrange on a plate and sift the powdered sugar over them before serving.

SERVES 6-8

Umbria

ROCCIATE
Fruit and Nut Biscuits

Like many Italian cookies, these very traditional ones are made more often than not for times of celebration. They are perfect for offering to visitors with a glass of sweet wine.

½ cup dried prunes
½ cup raisins
½ cup dried figs, stemmed and sliced
2 apples, peeled, cored and sliced
¼ cup hazelnuts, coarsely chopped
¼ cup almonds, coarsely chopped
¼ cup walnuts, coarsely chopped
¼ cup pine nuts
¼ cup (2 fl oz/60 ml) Marsala
5 tablespoons extra virgin olive oil
5 oz (155 g) superfine (caster) sugar
1¾ cups (7 oz/220 g) all purpose (plain) flour
pinch of salt
powdered (icing) sugar

Soak the prunes and raisins in lukewarm water for 30 minutes; drain. Pit the prunes.

Mix the fruit and nuts in a bowl. Add the Marsala, 1 tablespoon oil and 3 oz (90 g) sugar. Sift the flour and salt together. Mix in the remaining oil and sugar, and enough water to make a soft dough. Form into a ball and let rest, covered, for 30 minutes.

Divide the dough into 12 parts. Roll out each piece into a very thin square. Spread some of the fruit mixture on each square of dough, dividing it evenly.

Preheat oven to 350°F (180°C). Roll the squares up into cylinders and place on a lightly greased baking sheet. Bake until golden, about 30 minutes. Sprinkle with sifted powdered sugar and serve.

SERVES 6

FRUIT AND NUT BISCUITS

PHOTO: GIAN LUIGI SCARFIOTTI

AMARETTI-STUFFED PEACHES

Piemonte

PESCHE RIPIENE AGLI AMARETTI

Amaretti-stuffed Peaches

The most flavorful peaches are generally those with white flesh. For this recipe, however, the yellow-fleshed freestone ones are used.

½ cup (4 fl oz/125 ml) white wine
½ cup (3 oz/90 g) sugar

6 ripe peaches, peeled, halved and pitted
12 amaretti biscuits, crushed
1 egg yolk, beaten
3 tablespoons cream, whipped

❧ Boil the wine and sugar for 5 minutes to form a syrup. Poach the peach halves in the syrup for 5 more minutes, then lift out with a slotted spoon and let cool.
❧ Fold the amaretti crumbs and egg yolk into the cream. Fill the peach halves with the cream mixture. Arrange on a serving plate and pour the remaining wine syrup around them.

SERVES 6

Sicilia

GELATO AL PISTACCHIO
Pistachio Ice Cream

Pistachio nuts are often used in Sicilian sweet dishes. This is probably a relic of the region's numerous Arab invasions; they are also widely used in Turkey and all over the Middle East.

1 tablespoon cornstarch (cornflour)
½ cup (4 oz/125 g) sugar
1 cup (8 fl oz/250 ml) milk
4 eggs, well beaten
1 cup (8 fl oz/250 ml) cream, whipped
1 cup (6 oz/185 g) blanched pistachio nuts*

❧ Mix the cornstarch and sugar in a saucepan. Stir in the milk gradually and bring to boil, stirring constantly. Stir this mixture into the eggs, then return mixture to the saucepan. Cook over moderate heat until mixture thickens (it must not be allowed to boil), then remove from heat and let cool.
❧ Chop the pistachios and fold into the custard with the cream. Pour mixture into an ice cream maker and churn until frozen. When the ice cream is ready, store in the freezer or serve.

SERVES 6

To blanch pistachio nuts, plunge the shelled nuts into boiling water for a moment, then remove their second skin.

Sicilia

CASSATA ALLA SICILIANA
Sicilian Cassata

These days cassata is made commercially with different kinds of ice cream, but according to the traditional recipe it should be made with ricotta.
*   For an even richer dessert, a layer of green almond paste may be added between the sponge layer and the ricotta.*

½ cup (4 oz/125 g) superfine (caster) sugar
1 tablespoon water
1 lb (500 g) ricotta
3 oz (90 g) semisweet (plain) chocolate, chopped
2 oz (60 g) candied citron (peel), chopped (see page 247)
2 oz (60 g) candied orange peel, chopped
2 oz (60 g) glace cherries
2 oz (60 g) blanched pistachio nuts
7 oz (220 g) sponge cake
1 cup (8 fl oz/250 ml) malmsey wine (from the Lipari islands) or sweet dessert wine

❧ Combine the sugar and water in a saucepan and place over moderate heat until sugar is dissolved. Put the ricotta through a sieve and mix it with the sugar syrup, chocolate, candied fruit and pistachios.
❧ Cut the sponge cake into slices ⅜ in (1 cm) thick, then cut the slices into strips. Moisten with the wine and line a 7-in (18-cm) mold with ⅔ of them. Fill the center with the ricotta mixture and top with a layer of sponge cake.
❧ Refrigerate for several hours. Unmold onto a platter and serve with whipped cream if desired.

SERVES 6

OPPOSITE PAGE: SICILIAN CASSATA
BELOW: PISTACHIO ICE CREAM

COFFEE ICE CREAM WITH AMARETTI BISCUITS

Piemonte

GELATO DI CAFFÈ CON GLI AMARETTI

Coffee Ice Cream with Amaretti Biscuits

Italian coffee is roasted much darker than the coffee in other countries and is also more highly concentrated; that is the secret of its excellence.

4 egg yolks
½ cup (4 oz/125 g) superfine (caster) sugar
1 cup (8 fl oz/250 ml) strong espresso coffee
1 cup (8 fl oz/250 ml) cream
2 egg whites
12 amaretti biscuits, crushed

Beat the egg yolks with the sugar in the top of a double boiler until thick and lemon colored. Add the coffee and, stirring constantly, cook gently in a double saucepan over simmering water until the mixture is thick. Let cool.

Whip the cream until it stands in soft peaks. Beat the egg whites until stiff but not dry. Fold half the amaretti crumbs, the cream and the beaten egg whites into the cooled custard. Churn in an ice cream maker until frozen. Divide the ice cream among 6 serving dishes, or freeze until serving time. Sprinkle with the remaining amaretti crumbs and serve.

SERVES 6

Sicilia

SORBETTO AL LIMONE

Lemon Sorbet

Lemon sorbet is usually served halfway through the meal because it is an excellent digestive.

Sicily is famous for its wonderfully fragrant lemons, certainly the best in the world. Lemon orchards are now replacing most of the orange orchards.

1 cup (8 fl oz/250 ml) water
1 cup (8 oz/250 g) sugar
3 cups (24 fl oz/750 ml) fresh lemon juice
1 egg white

Boil the water with the sugar for 5 minutes. Stir in the lemon juice and let cool, then place in the freezer until hard.

About a half hour before serving time, place sorbet in blender with the egg white and blend until it resembles snow. Return to the freezer for 30 minutes, then serve.

SERVES 6

Campania

GRANITA DI CAFFÈ

Coffee Water Ice

There isn't a coffee bar in Campania that does not offer granita di caffè in the summer months — sometimes with a dollop of whipped cream on top. In the more elegant bars the coffee is often flavored with a little cocoa.

4 oz (125 g) superfine (caster) sugar
2 tablespoons water
6 cups (1½ qt/1.5 l) very strong espresso coffee
2 teaspoons unsweetened cocoa powder

Combine the sugar and water in a saucepan and heat until sugar is dissolved, then boil the syrup for several minutes.

Pour the coffee into the syrup, dissolve the cocoa in it and remove from heat. Let cool completely. Pour the mixture into a bowl and freeze until solid, then transfer to a blender and blend for a few seconds until slushy. Spoon into 6 glasses and serve immediately.

SERVES 6

Toscana

RICOTTA AL CAFFÈ
Ricotta with Coffee

Ricotta is obtained from a second boiling of the ewes' milk after the making of pecorino cheese; it is thus very light and low in fat. In Italy, it can always be bought very fresh — sometimes still warm — and it is eaten as is or flavored with cocoa, sugar and cognac, or with coffee. It is also very good mixed with sugar and strawberries.

1¼ lb (625 g) fresh ricotta
3 tablespoons superfine (caster) sugar
2 tablespoons finely ground (not instant) espresso coffee

Make a dome of ricotta on a plate. Sprinkle it first with the sugar and then with the ground coffee, and serve.

SERVES 6

Lazio

BUDINO DI RICOTTA
Ricotta Pudding

Ricotta mixed with whipped cream and egg white makes a very light dessert that is simple to prepare. Cinnamon may be substituted for the coffee.

2 eggs, separated
8 tablespoons (4 oz/120 g) superfine (caster) sugar
¼ cup (2 fl oz/60 ml) very strong espresso coffee
2 tablespoons finely ground espresso coffee
2 lb (500 g) ricotta
½ cup (4 fl oz/125 ml) cream, whipped
1 tablespoon unsweetened cocoa powder or grated dark
    chocolate

Beat egg yolks with 5 tablespoons sugar and the coffees. Add ricotta and mix well.

Beat egg whites to soft peaks, gradually adding 3 tablespoons sugar. Fold cream into ricotta mixture, then fold in egg whites. Turn into a 7-in (18-cm) mold that has been moistened inside with water and refrigerate for several hours.

Place mold in warm water for a few seconds, being careful not to let any water run into pudding. Unmold pudding onto a plate. Sift cocoa powder or sprinkle grated chocolate over pudding and serve.

SERVES 6

Lombardia

PANETTONE RIPIENO DI GELATO
Panettone Stuffed with Ice Cream

Panettone is a typical Lombard sweet bread, which in the old days was made in the shape of a dome. Today it is more like a wide, inflated tower. The best-known commercially made panettoni *are the Motta and Alemagna brands. In Milan,* panettoni *are often stuffed with ice cream.*

4 egg yolks
½ cup (4 oz/125 g) sugar
grated rind of ½ orange
2 cups (16 fl oz/500 ml) cream
¼ cup (2 fl oz/60 ml) Grand Marnier
1 egg white
1 (1 lb/500 g) *panettone*

Beat the egg yolk, sugar and orange rind in the top of a double boiler until thick and lemon colored. Stir in the cream. Place over gently simmering water and cook until the mixture is thickened, stirring frequently.

Remove from heat and add the Grand Marnier. Beat the egg white until stiff and fold into the custard. Transfer to an ice cream maker and churn until frozen. (If you are not using the ice cream right away, store in the freezer until shortly before serving time.)

Cut a "cap" from the top of the *panettone* and scoop out most of the inside. Fill with the ice cream. Put the cap back on the top and serve at once.

SERVES 6

Sicilia

SCORZETTE CANDITE
Candied Peel

Many Sicilian desserts are based on candied fruit, in particular, orange, citron and lemon peel. Other candied fruits may be prepared by the same method, especially cherries and pumpkin.

rind of 2 oranges
rind of 2 citrons, limes or grapefruit
rind of 2 lemons
sugar
3 tablespoons water
1 tablespoon almond oil, optional

Boil each rind separately in water to cover generously for 2 minutes. Drain and let dry. Cut rinds into thin strips; weigh them, and weigh an equal amount of sugar.

Place the sugar in a copper saucepan with 3 tablespoons water and place over moderate heat, stirring constantly. When the syrup becomes foamy, remove from heat and add the rinds, mixing until all pieces are thoroughly coated.

Lightly oil a work surface, tip the rind and syrup onto it and separate the pieces with a fork. Let cool completely, then transfer to a jar for storage.

MAKES 1 CUP

PANETTONE STUFFED WITH ICE CREAM GARNISHED WITH CANDIED PEEL

TRICOLOR PARFAIT

PHOTO: GIAN LUIGI SCARFIOTTI

ZABAGLIONE WITH STRAWBERRIES

Veneto

ZABAIONE CON LE FRAGOLE
Zabaglione with Strawberries

Zabaglione is an old Venetian dessert which can be varied in infinite ways. The classic version is made with Marsala, but vin santo, white wine and other dessert wines are equally suitable.

6 egg yolks
6 half-eggshells of superfine (caster) sugar
6 half-eggshells of Marsala
1 egg white
10 oz (310 g) small strawberries

🥄 In the top of a double boiler, whisk the egg yolks with the sugar until frothy. Stir in the Marsala. Place over gently simmering water and whisk until mixture is very thick and double in volume. Remove from heat and, while beating, let cool completely. Beat the egg white until stiff and fold into the *zabaglione*.
🥄 Transfer the *zabaglione* to a serving dish, arrange the strawberries around it and serve warm.

SERVES 6

Liguria

PACIUGO
Tricolor Parfait

Paciugo is a specialty of the Bar Excelsior in Portofino. Many years ago, it was created by the proprietress, Signora Lina, and it became an immediate success. Raspberry syrup, most commonly used to flavor water or soda for a refreshing drink, is available in European markets and delicatessens.

1 cup (8 oz/250 g) vanilla ice cream
1 cup (8 oz/250 g) raspberry or strawberry ice cream
1 cup (8 oz/250 g) chocolate ice cream
½ cup (4 fl oz/125 ml) raspberry syrup
½ cup (4 fl oz/125 ml) cream, whipped

🥄 Alternate scoops of vanilla, raspberry and chocolate ice cream into 6 tall glasses. Drizzle the syrup over the top.
🥄 Spoon the whipped cream into a pastry bag and squeeze it over the top of the ice cream. Serve at once.

SERVES 6

Sicilia

CANNOLI
Sicilian Ricotta Fruit Pastries

To make cannoli *you need little metal cylinders called* cannelli, *which are about ¾ in (2 cm) in diameter and 4 in (10 cm) long. If they are not available, little wooden rods of the same size may be used.*

10 oz (315 g) ricotta
1 cup (8 oz/250 g) superfine (caster) sugar
3 oz (90 g) mixed candied fruit (citron, orange peel, cherries), chopped (see page 247)
2 tablespoons shelled pistachio nuts, halved
2½ cups (10 oz/315 g) all purpose (plain) flour
¼ cup (2 fl oz/60 ml) dry white wine
2 tablespoons honey
pinch of salt
1 egg
1 egg white
oil for deep frying
additional egg white
1 tablespoon powdered (icing) sugar

🥄 Mix the ricotta with half the sugar, the diced candied fruit and the pistachios. Refrigerate.
🥄 Mound the flour on a board, make a well in the center and pour in the wine. Add the honey, the remaining sugar, the salt, whole egg and egg white and knead until you have a fairly stiff dough. Shape into a ball, wrap in plastic and refrigerate for 2 hours.
🥄 Roll dough out thinly and cut into 4-in (10-cm) squares. Wrap around the cylinders and press closed, using a little egg white to make them adhere. Heat the oil to 350°F (180°C). Fry the tubes until golden brown on all sides. Drain on paper towels and cool completely. Slide the tubes of pastry off the cylinders before completely cold.
🥄 Spoon the ricotta mixture into a pastry bag fitted with a wide tip and fill the pastry tubes with it. Sprinkle with powdered sugar and serve.

SERVES 6

SICILIAN RICOTTA FRUIT PASTRIES (bottom) AND ALMOND AND CHOCOLATE CAKE (top)

Toscana

ZUCCOTTO
Almond and Chocolate Cake

When zuccotto *is turned out, its domed surface is decorated in brown and white wedges of cocoa and powdered (icing) sugar.*

The base of the zuccotto *is usually sponge cake, but* savoiardi *(crisp ladyfingers or sponge finger biscuits) may also be used.*

7 oz (220 g) semisweet (plain) chocolate
2 cups (16 fl oz/500 ml) cream
¾ cup (3 oz/90 g) plus 1 tablespoon powdered (icing) sugar
1 cup (3 oz/90 g) blanched toasted hazelnuts, chopped
1 cup (3 oz/(90 g) blanched toasted almonds, chopped
5 oz (155 g) sponge cake, cut into strips
¼ cup (2 fl oz/60 ml) maraschino liqueur
1 tablespoon unsweetened cocoa powder

❧ Chop half the chocolate. Melt the other half over simmering water in a double boiler; let cool, stirring occasionally.

❧ Whip the cream with the sugar. Fold half of it into the melted chocolate, adding the hazelnuts; fold the other half into the chopped chocolate, adding the almonds.

❧ Line a hemispherical 7-in (18-cm) bowl with waxed paper and then with the sponge cake. Brush the cake with the maraschino. Spread the almond mixture in an even layer over the cake, then fill the center with the hazelnut mixture. Smooth the surface and cover with waxed paper. Chill for several hours.

❧ Unmold the *zuccotto* onto a serving plate. Cut wedges from a circular piece of paper and hold over the cake; sift the remaining powdered sugar onto the cake to form white wedges. Cover the white wedges with the paper and sift the cocoa onto the alternate wedges. Serve at once.

SERVES 6

Glossario

Not all of the glossary entries appear in the recipes. Nonetheless, each offers an interesting piece of information about Italian food and cooking.

ABBACCHIO: The name given to lamb that is slaughtered before it is weaned. The method of killing the lambs used to be a blow on the head, and this is the origin of the term (*abbacchiare* — to beat down or knock down). Naturally, this spring lamb is wonderfully tender.

AGNOLOTTI: Filled egg pasta. Depending on region and shape, the same form of pasta can be known as *tortelli, tortellini* or *ravioli.*

AGRESTO: The juice of unripe grapes, used occasionally in some sauces instead of vinegar.

AL FUNGHETTO: A method of cooking vegetables quickly over high heat with some kind of herb, so called after the manner of cooking *porcini* (boletus) mushrooms (*fungo* – mushroom). The main vegetables cooked *al funghetto* are eggplants (aubergines) and zucchini.

ALLA PARMIGIANA: A description used for vegetables that are boiled and served with melted butter and grated Parmesan cheese. It is also used to describe veal scallops sautéed in butter and finished with Parmesan.

AMARETTI: Crisp macaroons made with bitter almonds (*amaro* means bitter), which will keep for long periods. The best known are the Lazzaroni di Saronno brand, packed in elegant red tins. There is also a sweet liqueur called *amaretto,* made from almonds.

ANCHOVIES: One of the so called "blue fish" (others are garfish and sardines) that are common in Italian seas all year round. Like Mediterranean sardines, anchovies are rather small. They are usually preserved whole in salt, and are thoroughly washed and boned and the heads removed before use. Fillets ready cleaned and preserved in oil are often used. In Liguria raw anchovies are used, "cooked" only in lemon juice.

ANTIPASTO: A course served before spaghetti or rice, or generally before any form of first course. Sometimes it is very rich, so that it has come to replace the first course.

ARBORIO RICE: A plump, oval-shaped grain, shorter and rounder than the American short grain rice. The best-quality Arborio rice grows in the Po Valley region of Piedmont. It is used in sweet and savory dishes and is at its finest when cooked in *risotto* (q.v.).

ARISTA: Chine or saddle of pork, mostly oven-roasted or cooked on a spit. It is usually seasoned with a mixture of garlic, pepper and rosemary.

BACCALÀ: The name given to cod preserved in salt. Dried, the same fish is called stockfish or *stoccafisso.* Both of these require lengthy softening under cold running water before cooking.

BAGNOMARIA: A method of cooking in which the container holding the food to be cooked is set into a larger pan of boiling water.

BATTUTO: Literally, "beaten"; in cooking terminology this refers to a mixture of finely chopped herbs, celery, onion and carrots.

BEET (beetroot): A much-used vegetable that requires lengthy cooking, generally in the oven. It can be bought precooked in almost any greengrocer's shop. Nowadays beets are cooked commercially and canned or sold in airtight packs.

BIGOLI: A larger form of spaghetti, homemade using only water, flour and a small amount of egg. They are a specialty of the Veneto and are served with a duck sauce.

BISCOTTI DI PRATO (also known as *cantucci* or *cantuccini*): Hard-textured sweet cookies with almond pieces, which keep for long periods and are now exported all over the world. They can be rather dry, and are often eaten dipped in *vin santo* (q.v.).

BOLLITO: Literally, "boiled"; a method of cooking widely used for meat. A *bollito* is generally made up of different kinds of meat such as beef, veal, tongue, chicken and the spiced pork sausage known as *cotechino.* It is served with a green parsley sauce. To make a good *bollito,* the meat must be put into water that is already boiling.

BOMBA DI RISO: A molded rice dish with a rich filling of ground meat cooked with various flavorings: herbs, mushrooms, diced cheese or ham, etc. The "rice bombe" is a specialty of the Parma area, and a similar dish made in Naples is called *sartù di riso.*

BRASATO: Literally, "braised"; a method of cooking over low heat with just a little liquid. At one time it was done in a pan with embers placed on the lid (charcoal or embers = *brace,* hence *brasare,* to braise). Today this kind of cooking is done in the oven. A *brasato* is also sometimes known as a *stufato.*

BRODETTO: The name given to the fish soup of the Adriatic area. In Livorno (Leghorn) it is called *caciucco,* in other regions simply *zuppa di pesce* (fish soup).

BRODO: Italian cooks make a broth or stock that is very light, using only chicken, beef, veal or fish without bones, and vegetables. They never use cooked bones as the French do. Sometimes uncooked bones are added if a jellied stock is desired, together with a trotter or snout.

BRUSCHETTA: Generally served before a meal, a very popular dish made with coarse-textured bread, toasted over coals and liberally dressed with extra virgin olive oil. In Tuscany it is called *fett'unta* or *fregolotta.*

BUTTER: In Italy, butter is never salted.

CACIOCAVALLO: A hard white cheese with a light rind, which keeps well. It is a bulk cheese with a rather strong taste, made from cow's milk.

CALAMARI: Squid (*calamaretti* if they are small); *seppie* are cuttlefish.

CANNELLONI: A type of pasta filled with meat or vegetables, shaped like a tube and about 1 in (2 cm) in diameter and 4 in (10 cm) long.

CARBONARA: *Spaghetti alla carbonara* is so named because in times gone by it was the usual fare for woodsmen to take as their lunch when they went to make charcoal. It is a complete dish on its own, containing *pancetta* (q.v.) and eggs.

CARPACCIO: A cold dish of raw meat that is sliced paper-thin and usually dressed with oil and lemon juice. Various seasonings may be added, such as flakes of Parmesan, chopped lemon rind or parsley. It was named after the famous Venetian painter by the proprietor of Harry's Bar in Venice, but its origin is definitely Piedmontese.

CECHE: Very tiny young eels, a specialty of Pisa, where they are fried with garlic and sage or mixed with eggs and flour and served as little pancakes. In Liguria, however, the name refers to *gianchetti* or *bianchetti,* tiny newborn fish.

CIBREO: An ancient Tuscan dish based on cocks' combs and sweetbreads, which used to be served with a molded vegetable timbale. In Piedmont *cibreo* is known as *finanziera*.

CIMA RIPIENA: A Genoese dish made of veal breast with a pocket cut into it, which is stuffed with one of various fillings.

CINGHIALE (boar): Wild pig, particularly abundant in Tuscany but also found in other regions. Its meat is very tasty and is usually served braised, or in a sweet and sour sauce of vinegar and chocolate.

CODA DI MANZO (oxtail): Especially popular in Latium, where it is served stewed and used in soups and *minestroni* (q.v.). It has excellent flavor but requires a long cooking time.

COOKING UTENSILS: In Italian a number of different terms are used to describe the same thing. More important than the terminology is the material: different types are suitable for different methods of cooking.

Tegame is the term used for the round wide shallow pan, usually of terracotta, which is used for cooking sauces, braising meats and stewing vegetables. Terracotta pans diffuse the heat particularly well.

Padella is a skillet, usually of cast iron, which is used above all for deep frying and for sautéing sliced meat or vegetables.

Teglia is a round, wide, shallow pan of copper, aluminum or stainless steel. It has two handles and is suitable for braising or roasting meat and vegetables.

Casseruola is a saucepan with higher sides. Italians cook in heavy aluminum when the object is for the food (usually meat) to stick to the bottom of the pan, so that browned bits can then be scraped up by stirring in stock or wine at the end of cooking to form a sauce or gravy. Stainless steel is used for *risotto*, soups, stocks, tomato sauce, and for boiling pasta, meat or fish.

A cast iron skillet is used for frying such dishes as *fritto misto*, fried potatoes (chips), etc.

Terracotta saucepans are used for tomato and meat sauces.

Tinned copper is the material used for cooking polenta and for baked dishes like lasagne and cannelloni.

Ceramic dishes are also used in the oven — not for meat because the juices are better retained in aluminum dishes, but for lasagne, cannelloni and gratinéd vegetables.

COSTOLETTE (cutlets): Rather thick slices of meat cut from the bony part, particularly the ribs (hence the name: *costolette*, from *costole*, ribs). The meat close to the bone is always tastier and tenderer. Cutlets are normally cooked in butter or oil after they have been dipped in egg and coated with breadcrumbs.

CRAUTI (sauerkraut): Served in Alto Adige, usually with smoked pork dishes. It is made from red or green cabbage, shredded very finely and left to ferment in casks for about three months. It is generally cooked in pork fat.

CREAM: There is only one kind of cream in Italy. It is not a thickened cream and is always used fresh.

CREMA DI VERDURA: Puree of vegetables, often with cream or milk added. Sometimes it is thickened with pureed potatoes or sieved cooked rice.

CRESCENZA: A very delicate, creamy cheese typical of Lombardy. It is also sometimes known as *robiola*, the best-known brand being Introbio. When aged, it takes on a very strong flavor and develops a crust.

CROSTINI: One of the most common types of *antipasto* (q.v.) in Italian cooking. Among the best known of the hundreds of varieties are the Tuscan *crostini di milza* (croutons with spleen).

DRIED MUSHROOMS: Always means dried *porcini* (boletus) mushrooms, which grow in chestnut or oak woods after the rains, while the weather is still warm.

DRIED PASTA: There is an infinity of varieties of dried pasta in Italy, known by an infinity of names according to region. Spaghetti is the most popular type, and it is cooked in a few minutes in a large amount of water with added salt, but no oil. It must be quite firm to the bite (*al dente*), and as soon as it is drained the prepared sauce should be mixed into it.

EGGPLANT (aubergine): Usually of elongated oval shape, not too large. The very large round ones now sold in Italy are imported and of inferior quality.

ERBETTE: Also called *bietoline*, a vegetable similar to spinach or beet greens. It has an elongated smallish leaf and a slim, tender green stalk. *Erbette* may be replaced by either of the other two greens.

FAGIANO: Pheasant, a game bird hunted in autumn and winter. It must be hung to ripen with the feathers still on and gut intact for at least five days so that the meat has the right degree of tenderness. True connoisseurs will hang the pheasant by its head and cook it only when the head comes off and the bird falls.

FENNEL: A sweet, aniseed tasting white bulb that is eaten raw in salads. The male plant, with its rounder bulb, is to be preferred for salads; the more elongated female bulb is usually cooked. For fennel to be white, it must be continually covered with earth as the plant grows.

FINOCCHIONA: A Tuscan salami that contains fennel seeds (*finocchio* = fennel). In contrast to most salamis, it must never be allowed to age.

FODERARE: To line, as in dressmaking (to line a coat or jacket); the term is used in cooking to indicate covering the sides of a mold with biscuits or sponge cake.

FONDUE: A Piedmontese dish based on melted fontina cheese, from which it gets its name — *Fonduta* (in Piedmontese *fondua*), meaning "melted." *Fonduta* is also used as a sauce for *risotto*, added at the end of cooking, and in a very elegant dish consisting of a large vol-au-vent filled with *agnolotti* (q.v.), over which the fondue is poured. When served with truffles it is usually presented in individual ramekins.

FONTANA (fountain): The instructions for making pasta in Italian usually begin with: "*Mettere la farina a fontana sulla tavola…*" (literally, put the flour in the shape of a fountain on the table). The tip of the "fountain" is then widened to form a well into which the eggs or liquid required to form the dough are placed.

FRIGGERE: Generally this means deep frying, or cooking in a pan full of very hot oil in which the food must float freely. Sometimes the word *friggere* is also used to mean sautéing in a smaller amount of fat.

FRITTATA: The most common form of *frittata* in Italy is the one resembling a flattened cake of eggs, possibly with other ingredients such as vegetables, cheese or fish. The rolled variety, more common in France, is called *omeletta*. Both the *frittata* and the *omeletta* are always cooked in a heavy cast iron or nonstick skillet, never in the oven. This type of mixture cooked in the oven becomes a *tortino*, which is drier in the center. A good Italian *frittata* must be *bavosa* — liquid in the center.

FRITTO MISTO: "Mixed fry," one of the most typical Italian dishes, which may be interpreted in many ways according to region. In Piedmont it is very rich, with little fruit fritters or semolina pancakes as well as different kinds of meat. In Tuscany it consists basically of white meats, in Latium of lamb and artichokes or brains; in the south it is based on fish such as young squid or rings of cuttlefish; and sometimes cubes of smoked mozzarella are included.

GAMBERETTI and SCAMPI: Both refer to shrimp (prawns).

GINESTRATA: A traditional light and very nutritious soup, which in the old days was seen as nourishing food for the elderly and for young children.

GNOCCHI: The name for small balls of potato, spinach or other ingredients. The name is also given to discs of semolina in Rome, and of polenta in the Veneto.

GORGONZOLA: A full-fat cheese with green mold veins, a specialty of a small town of the same name near Milan. Both mild and strong varieties are available.

GUANCIALE: Pig's cheek, a much sought after delicacy that is cured with salt and pepper in the same way as *pancetta* (q.v.). It is, however, rarer and more choice than *pancetta*.

HARD-COOKED (HARD-BOILED) EGGS: A very common summer *antipasto* (q.v.). There are many ways of stuffing them, and they are also used to accompany salad dishes or cold meats. A typical Italian *antipasto* consists of *prosciutto* (q.v.), salami, stuffed eggs and pickled vegetables.

IMPANATO (from *pane*, bread): The word used to describe meat, vegetables or fish that have first been dipped into beaten egg, then coated in breadcrumbs and cooked.

INSALATA VERDE: Green salad, usually meaning lettuce. Sometimes a green salad may also be made with curly endive or other varieties of lettuce known as *scarola* (escarole) and *valerianella* (lamb's lettuce). They are rarely mixed, only one type being served at a time. The salad is normally dressed only with extra virgin olive oil, salt and vinegar.

IN UMIDO: Another way of describing the braising or stewing method of cooking, where a small amount of liquid always remains on the bottom of the pan, as opposed to roasting, in which the meat is cooked in fat alone.

LASAGNE: Squares of fresh or dried pasta that are boiled in water, then drained and layered with various sauces. Among the most famous ways of serving *lasagne* are *alla bolognese*, with meat and mushroom sauce, and *al pesto*, with Ligurian basil sauce.

LEPRE: Hare, which is hung in its skin for several days before cooking. Wild rabbit, whose flesh has a slightly more delicate flavor, is prepared in the same way as hare.

MACCHERONI ALLA CHITARRA: The *chitarra* is a traditional kitchen utensil shaped like a guitar, with sharp cutting wires on which the sheets of pasta are laid so that when a rolling pin is passed over them, the pasta is cut into thin strips (see photograph page 66).

MALFATTI: *Gnocchi* (q.v.) of spinach and ricotta; a specialty of Tuscany, where they are also sometimes called *ravioli nudi* (naked ravioli) because they have no pasta covering.

MARROW: The internal part of the shank (shin) bone in beef or veal, used in cooking various dishes. The classic example is the Milanese *risotto*, which is cooked in equal parts of melted butter and marrow. The marrow gives the rice a special creamy consistency and it is also less fatty than butter. It is very easy to extract from the bone with finger pressure. Sometimes it is boiled before use. The marrow from the bones in *ossi buchi in gremolata* is particularly good.

MARSALA: A sweet dessert wine from the area around the city of Marsala in Sicily. It is widely used in Italian cooking for meat, vegetable and sweet dishes. The Venetian dessert *zabaglione al marsala* is famous; the wine was familiar to the Venetians from very early times, because they were able to travel the length of the country in their ships as far back as the era of the Crusades.

MELON: Italian melons are generally round, with a slightly lined skin and a pale orange color. They are very fragrant and are only to be found in late summer. Melon is often served with *prosciutto* (q.v.) as a first course, although *prosciutto* is equally tasty served with figs.

MESTICANZA: A mixture of small, tender salad greens that grow in spring and continue to produce as they are cut, until autumn.

MINESTRA: A thin soup with chopped vegetables, often with rice or the special small pasta made for soups. *Minestra* may also be chicken or vegetable broth in which these small pasta shapes (*pastina*) are cooked.

MINESTRONE: A vegetable soup with rice or pasta, in which the vegetables are cut into larger pieces than those for *minestra* (q.v.). The soup usually contains dried legumes such as white beans, lentils or chickpeas.

MOSTARDA DI CREMONA: Cremona mustard, a specialty of the city of Cremona, made from candied fruit preserved in a sweet syrup lightly spiced with mustard. It is an excellent accompaniment for boiled meat.

MOZZARELLA: A rindless white cheese made from buffalo milk, which is much sought after and becoming increasingly difficult to find. The only areas producing it are Salerno and Caserta. Mozzarella is now also commercially produced using cow's milk, but it has much less flavor.

MUSSELS: Known as *cozze* in many areas, and in others as *muscoli* or *pecei*. A similar mollusk is called *dattero di mare*, or date mussel. Highly prized and having an elongated light brown shell, it is found in the area around La Spezia.

OIL: In general, extra virgin olive oil is used. It contains less than 1% acidity, and it should be cold pressed. Not only does it have no cholesterol, it apparently actually helps to dissolve cholesterol.

OLIVES: The best are those in brine (a mixture of water and salt) or preserved in oil. Less delicate in taste are the olives preserved in vinegar. The black ones have the strongest flavor. In general, Italian olives are rather small.

ORECCHIETTE: "Little ears," a slightly concave pasta made by forming little balls of dough with the hands and pressing a hollow into the center of each. Today it may be bought in shops. It has quite a long cooking time and is often served with a lamb or other meat sauce, or simply with tomato sauce.

OVOLI: A highly prized mushroom which resembles an egg and has a bright orange cap. It is generally eaten raw as a salad.

PAGLIA E FIENO ("straw and hay"): *Taglierini* (q.v.) that are half green, made with spinach, and half white, using only egg. They are served simply with melted butter and Parmesan cheese, or sometimes with reduced cream and Parmesan.

PAN DI NATALE ("Christmas bread"): A term used to cover many traditional Christmas cakes of varying shapes and textures. The basis is generally a soft sweet yeast dough, to which candied fruit, raisins, pine nuts, etc. are added. One of the most classic versions is the Genoese *pan dolce*.

PAN PEPATO: A cake characteristic of Umbria. It is made with nuts, raisins, almonds, chocolate and hazelnuts and flavored with nutmeg and pepper.

PAN DI SPAGNA: A light-textured cake in which only eggs,

flour and a little butter are used. It serves as a base for many Italian desserts, generally being soaked in some kind of liqueur and combined with whipped cream and perhaps cooked fruit. It forms the basis of the dessert known as *zuppa inglese* (which is something like a trifle).

PANCETTA: Unsmoked bacon from the belly of the pig; it may be flat or rolled. It is cured with spices, salt and pepper.

PANDORO: A cake traditionally served at Christmastime in the city of Verona, but now also produced commercially year-round. It is very light in texture, like a sponge cake, and is shaped like an octagonal cone.

PANETTONE: The classic Milanese cake, now made commercially and sold all over the world. Usually shaped like a tall round loaf, it consists of a sweet yeast dough enriched with candied fruits and raisins. It is a difficult cake to make at home, tending to be rather heavy.

PANFORTE: Typical of the city of Siena, now also made commercially and exported throughout the world. It is a flat, very rich cake containing walnuts, almonds, hazelnuts, honey, candied fruits and lots of spices. It is said to have been carried by the Crusaders on their expeditions because of its energy-giving properties.

PANGRATTATO or PANE GRATTUGIATO ("grated bread"): Breadcrumbs produced by drying out stale bread in the oven and processing it in a food processor until it is like coarse sand. The name derives from the fact that the bread used to be grated to produce the crumbs. Breadcrumbs are now sold in transparent packs and also exported.

PANMEINO: Literally "millet bread," and it is very likely that at one time millet flour was used to make it. Today it is made with wheat flour and yellow cornmeal and flavored with elderflowers. The slices are dipped in a bowl of liquid cream as they are eaten.

PANZANELLA: Stale bread salad, typical of Tuscany. In times past, Tuscan bread was baked once a week, without salt (as it still is today), because salt was very costly and indeed was used as a means of exchange. It is worth noting that salt-free bread stays fresh longer. There are also well-known soups based on stale bread: *pappa al pomodoro*, again a Tuscan specialty; the Milanese *pancotto*; and the *acquacotta* of Grosseto, in which an egg is added to each serving.

PARMESAN: A hard cheese with a thick crust that is aged for at least two years. It is a specialty of Parma and Reggio-Emilia and the one with *parmigiano-reggiano* branded on the crust is the best. It is freshly grated over many dishes.

PECORINO: A cheese made from ewe's milk that is popular in various regions. In Tuscany it is fairly mild, and may be sold fresh or aged. In Sardinia it is usually saltier and stronger in flavor.

PEPPER: The type mostly used is freshly ground whole black pepper, which has the best flavor.

PESTO: A sauce obtained by pounding basil, garlic, oil and pine nuts in a mortar. It is a specialty of the city of Genoa.

PIADINA: A soft type of flat bread made in Emilia-Romagna, usually eaten with salami or *prosciutto* (q.v.). It may also be filled with sautéed spinach or with ricotta.

PINZIMONIO: A way of presenting raw vegetables that involves dipping them in bowls filled with extra virgin olive oil, salt and pepper. The Piedmontese version of *pinzimonio* is the *bagna cauda*, a cooked sauce made up of half butter and half olive oil, with a few fillets of anchovy and some chopped garlic blended in. This sauce is kept simmering in a terracotta saucepan in the center of the table, and the diners dip their *crudités* into it.

PIZZA: The same form as the *schiacciata* (q.v.) and made from the same dough. The difference is that the seasoning used on pizza is far richer and contains a number of different elements such as vegetables, mozzarella or other types of cheese, *prosciutto* (q.v.), etc. It is considered to be a first course, in contrast to the *schiacciata*, which is seen as bread enriched with added flavor.

PIZZAIOLA: A method of cooking that uses the basic ingredients of pizza topping: oil, tomato and oregano. Steak, leftover boiled meat, or fish may be served *alla pizzaiola*.

PIZZELLE: Deep-fried pizza dough, popular in many areas of Italy and used in different ways. It may be eaten plain, or with tomato sauce, sautéed vegetables or cheese.

POLENTA: A typical Venetian dish made from coarse-ground cornmeal that is sprinkled into boiling water and stirred as it cooks. It must be fairly firm when cooked, and is often served simply with fried sage leaves, melted butter and grated Parmesan. Or it may be sliced and seasoned in any number of ways — with meat or fish sauces, sausages, mushrooms, cheese, etc. Normally it is made with yellow cornmeal, but sometimes the Venetians use more finely ground white cornmeal.

POLPETTE: Small round or oval meatballs. They may be deep fried, sautéed in butter, or *impanate* — coated in egg and breadcrumbs. If deep fried they are sometimes called croquettes.

PROSCIUTTO: Ham from the pig's hind leg, one of the most common foods in the Italian diet. It may be raw (*crudo*) or cooked (*cotto*). Though usually unsmoked, in Alto Adige and Trentino it is also sold smoked.

PUNTARELLE: A special Roman salad green, served only in winter. The stalks, which are very long with a needle-like serrated leaf, curl when cut. This particular salad is served with a dressing consisting of oil, vinegar, salt, an anchovy fillet in oil, and crushed garlic.

RADICCHIO ROSSO: Red chicory; various types are available, the most sought after being the *radicchio di Treviso* which is whitened in the cellar under sand or compost before being sold. It has elongated leaves with long, soft white ribs and a dark red color just at the tips of the leaves. The most common *radicchi* are those from Castelfranco Veneto (small and round like a ball, with wrinkly leaves and a rather bitter taste) and Chioggia (very similar, but a lighter red in color).

RATAFIA: A sweet liqueur made by marinating black cherries in sugar.

RIBOLLITA: A famous Tuscan bean soup made with black cabbage, a very dark-colored vegetable with elongated leaves. Like all other types of cabbage, this one is at its best after the first night frosts, because it becomes softer and more flavorful.

RICCIARELLI: Sienese almond cookies (biscuits).

RICOTTA: A very light cheese made from milk that has been cooked twice (*ricotta* = recooked). Traditional ricotta is made from pure ewe's milk; it is still found in Tuscany, Latium and Sardinia. A far less tasty ricotta made from cow's milk is to be found in other Italian regions.

RISOTTO: Rice cooked in broth (stock) that is added gradually, so the rice remains just covered throughout cooking. The most suitable type of rice is Arborio (q.v.), with its large, oval-shaped grain. When cooked, *risotto* must be *al dente* (still firm to the bite) and have the consistency of porridge. It normally cooks in about 16 minutes. From the time the broth is added, a *risotto* must be stirred constantly, and it is not possible to stop the cooking and finish it off at a later time. See *risotto alla milanese*.

ROLLÈ: May be made from breast of turkey, thinly sliced and opened up like a book, or from veal or chicken breast. It is a popular dish and can be stuffed in many different ways. The stuffing usually contains bread that has been soaked in milk and squeezed dry, and *pancetta* (q.v.) or the fat of *prosciutto* (q.v.), which serve to keep the meat soft during cooking.

ROSOLIO: A very sweet traditional liqueur which at one time was only drunk by women because of its extremely delicate taste. It is now coming back into fashion, and an excellent one is produced by Gualtiero Marchesi, the only Italian restaurant with three Michelin stars.

SAFFRON: The stamens of the crocus, a flower that grows around l'Aquila in the Abruzzi region and is also cultivated there specifically for saffron. Kashmir is another major exporter of saffron. Crocuses need rather cold winters and hot summers for their development. The most expensive saffron is sold in the form of dried whole stamens; the less valuable powdered kind is more generally available.

SALSICCIA: Italian sausage goes by various names. In Lombardy and the Veneto, for example, it is called *luganega*. In northern and central Italy, as a general rule sausage is not spicy; ground pork is simply seasoned with salt and pepper and then put into the sausage skin. In the south, sausage is very hot. It may be thick or thin, long without links tied off, or fatter and divided up into short lengths. The sausages of Tuscany are famous, particularly those produced in the Chianti area. They are fried and presented on a bed of beans cooked with tomato, oil, garlic and abundant fresh sage.

SALTIMBOCCA: Literally "jump into the mouth," so tasty is this veal dish. Sometimes the slices of veal are rolled around the filling, and in this case they may go by various names — *messicani, rollatini, bauletti* (suitcases!), *involtini* — and have any number of fillings, from rich to very simple.

SAOR: A method of cooking food in a sweet and sour sauce containing vinegar. It is very common in several Italian regions, especially in the Veneto and the south. In Tuscany the *saor* is called *agrodolce* (sharp and sweet) or *dolceforte* (sweet and strong). The *dolceforte* method is more suited to cooking boar; it is made with melted bitter chocolate and raisins.

SBRISOLONA: A famous Mantuan cake, flat and crisp, made with a combination of white flour, cornmeal and chopped almonds. The Venetian version is called *fregolotta*.

SCAMORZA: A white cheese made with whole cow's milk, pear-shaped and with a smooth, thin rind.

SCHIACCIATA: The Tuscan name for a particular kind of bread, rolled out thinly like a pizza and seasoned only with oil and salt. Sometimes it is enriched with rosemary or sage. In Liguria the same bread is known as *focaccia*. Sometimes sliced onions or small pieces of olives are used instead of herbs.

SCOTTADITO ("burning finger"): Small cutlets on the bone, which are eaten with the fingers. They are eaten very hot, hence their name.

SOFFRITTO: A mixture of chopped vegetables (usually carrots, onions, celery and parsley — depending on the region) fried in oil or butter, used to flavor soups, sauces and meat dishes.

SOPA COADA: A famous soup from the Veneto which consists of layers of bread alternated with layers of boned roast pigeon. The name derives from the fact that it requires a very long cooking time (*sopa* is a regional word for soup; *coada* comes from *covare,* to hatch).

SPAGHETTI: Factory-produced dried pasta strings made with flour and water. There are various forms of dried pasta with many different names: *penne, penne rigate, bucatini, farfalle, fusilli, rigatoni,* etc. Dried pasta, found particularly in the south, takes oil-based sauces, often with tomato, vegetables or fish.

SPELT: A kind of hard wheat with the husk, which must be soaked in water before use. It was popular with the ancient Romans and is now widely used in Umbria and Latium and of course throughout the Middle East. It is used as the main ingredient for soups, both thick and thin.

STRACOTTO: Another word for *brasato* or *stufato,* in other words stewed or braised meat. *Stracotto* is the name used specifically for a Piedmontese meat dish cooked in this way, and it means literally "overcooked."

STRUTTÓ: Melted pork fat, which in some regions is known as *sugna* (lard). Foods fried in it are especially light and crisp.

SWISS CHARD: The white stalks of Swiss chard are served in many ways — with a sauce, with butter and cheese, boiled and dressed with oil, etc.

TAGLIATELLE: Handmade pasta cut just 3/8 in (1 cm) wide and a millimeter thick, a specialty of northern and central Italy. In some regions it is called *fettuccine* or *taglierini.* The Tuscan variety, *pappardelle,* is cut into strips more than double the width of *tagliatelle.* The pasta is made with flour and eggs and served with butter-based sauces.

TIMBALLO: Timbale; the name usually given to pasta that is cooked in a mold and filled with meat or vegetables. *Timballo di maccheroni* with a sweet crust is a specialty of the Campania region.

TORRONE: A sweet nougat based on honey and almonds, a specialty of the Cremona area. In other areas *torrone* may also contain figs or chocolate.

TROFIE: A kind of handmade pasta shaped like slightly elongated *gnocchi.* It is a specialty of the town of Camogli in Liguria, and is usually served with pesto sauce (q.v.).

TRUFFLES (tartufi): Found near the roots of oak or chestnut trees during October, November and December. They grow fairly deep below the surface and dogs are specially trained to identify their scent. Before a truffle is completely exposed, the dog is removed and man takes over so that there is no risk of damaging the truffle.

The most precious are the very light-colored truffles that grow in Alba, in the Piedmont region. Less tasty ones are also found in some parts of the Marches and Tuscany. Black truffles are common in Umbria, but they are less flavorful and not so precious. The truffles from Alba can be priced as high as 300,000 lire for 100 grams.

VIN SANTO: A Tuscan dessert wine made from grapes that have been dried away from direct sunlight for a couple of months before pressing. The wine is aged for four or five years, sealed in small oak casks kept under the rooftops so that it is exposed to temperature variations.

ZUCCHINI FLOWERS: Plentiful in Italy when zucchini begin to grow. Usually the male flower — not the female, which goes on to produce the vegetable — is used for cooking. It is recognized by its thinner stem. The zucchini flowers must be picked and eaten while they are still firmly closed.

ZUPPA: A soup, usually vegetable, meat or fish, that is poured over fried or oven-toasted bread.

Indice

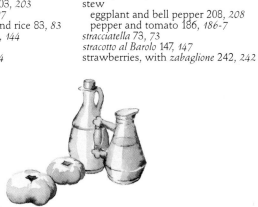